Kikuyu Women, the Mau Mau Rebellion, and Social Change in Kenya

Kikuyu Women, the Mau Mau Rebellion, and Social Change in Kenya

Cora Ann Presley

INPRINT EDITIONS
Baltimore

Kikuyu Women, the Mau Mau Rebellion, and Social Change in Kenya

Published 2013 by INPRINT EDITIONS
First published 1992

Library of Congress Number:

ISBN: 978-1-58073-047-1

Printed in the United States of America by
BCP Digital Printing,
An affiliate company of Black Classic Press, Inc.

To purchase or review Black Classic Press and INPRINT EDITIONS books, visit www.blackclassicbooks.com.

You may also obtain a list of titles by writing to:
Black Classic Press
c/o List
P.O. Box 13414
Baltimore, MD 21203

Preface to the Black Classic Press edition

October 2012 marked the sixtieth anniversary of the declaration of the State of Emergency in Kenya. During that month, the militant phase of the anti-colonial movement in Kenya attracted global attention. For the world of the colonial powers, this movement marked the first time that a colonial movement had to respond to African resistance in Sub-Saharan Africa with massive force since the end of the wars of conquest in the late 19th century and the early part of twentieth century. Suddenly, decades of self-appointed stewardship to lead African cultures and peoples into western ways of being, knowing and thinking were disrupted when Mau Mau freedom fighters chose to used armed resistance to the imposition of western culture. For the African and other colonial societies, the Mau Mau rebellion was an inspiration, a call to colonized peoples around the world heralding the possibility of conducting an armed resistance to western hegemonic forces. For those in the African Diaspora, such as the segregated black communities in the United States, Mau Mau became a call to militancy and a rejection of nonviolence as a means of forcing social change in the United States. In the 1950s and 1960s, leaders like Malcolm X, Medgar Evers and Kwame Ture (formerly Stokely Carmichael) referenced Mau Mau in their speeches and writings, holding them up as an example for their followers. For example,

Medgar Evers once suggested that a Mau Mau in Mississippi should be created.

Within months of the British declaration of war on the Mau Mau, the government authorized a study of the origins of the movement—to better understand it and defeat it. The Corfield Report marshaled government reports on African activities, and interviews with colonial officials, settlers, and missionaries were initiated, in addition to the clandestine surveillance of the Mau Mau organization which had begun as early as 1948. Over the next twenty five years, the Mau Mau rebellion was one of the most studied of the Sub-Saharan African independence movements, and it remains so today. However during that twenty-five year period, there were no studies of women's involvement in the movement. Scholars were not interested in telling the story of Mau Mau from the point of view of the women who participated in the movement or resisted it. The first edition of this book was the first study of women's involvement in the Mau Mau movement.

At the time the study was undertaken, the first generation of scholars who focused on the study of women in political systems in Africa were either young graduate students or professors in the early stages of their careers. At that time, we were asking rather basic questions: Was there participation by women in the various political movements? How did they contribute? How did that participation result in social change for women? I spent two years in the field doing the research for this book: seven months in London, immersed in the colonial archives, and five months in Nairobi, in the National Archives and the newspaper archives of the *Daily Nation*. Afterwards, this writer ventured into the rural districts to locate and to interview women leaders and rank and file members of the Mau Mau movement. All of that preparation did not reveal a much deeper connection that women in the movement made. Through their reflections, they revealed (1) that they viewed their participation as seamlessly and organically connected to their understanding of the need for cultural change in African societies; (2) that they believed African traditions which oppressed women needed to be reshaped; and (3) that they saw need changes in the economic roles they had inherited from the pre-colonial period---which had been reshaped by the colonial period and which were bound to change in the post-colonial world. Like other people in independence movements, they expected to be rewarded for their struggles, contributions and sacrifices in winning independence. They expected to be rewarded as individuals and ***as women***.

Since 1978 when this research was undertaken, Mau Mau studies have proliferated; so, too, have studies of women in African societies and women in the political struggle in Africa. However, starting in the 1980s, the generation of women engaged in Mau Mau began to die out. On August 30, 2011, Wambui Waiyaki Otieno Mbuga, the last internationally known Mau Mau woman leader, died. A new generation of women has emerged in Kenya and elsewhere. They were prominent participants in the pro-democracy movement in the 1990s, and, like Ellen Shirleaf, current head of state of Liberia, have stepped up to demand participatory democracy and an end to the ethnic conflicts that have plagued the continent. This book was a part of the beginnings of the discussions about the roles of women in politics in Kenya, and in Africa in general. The author took to heart the words of a Mau Mau leader who urged that the book be written for their daughters, who did not know what their mothers had done to fight for freedom. This book is a testament to the struggles, sacrifices and contributions of the courageous women who fought in African independence movements to effect political change.

Cora Ann Presley
August 2011

Contents

Tables and Maps

Tables

Maps

Preface

In this work I have tried to portray the importance of women's political involvement in Kenyan nationalism. My first acknowledgment must be to the Kikuyu women who allowed me to interview them. Wambui Wagarama, Nduta wa Kore, Phyllis Wambaki, and Mary Wanjiko were especially responsible for organizing women's resistance to colonialism and deserve special mention. They revealed their own involvement in nationalist protest and generously arranged for me to meet other women who were Mau Mau freedom fighters. Three other Kenyan women assisted me in collecting data. Mrs. A.B.M. Wandera, the community development officer for Kiambu district, graciously helped me by scheduling meetings with women's organizations in Kiambu. My research assistants, Rose Njoki and Patricia Weithera, diligently accompanied me on research trips and laboriously transcribed the texts of our interviews from Kikuyu to English. These Kenyan women made this study possible and urged me to complete it because of its importance in adding Kikuyu women to the nationalist history of their country.

The original suggestion for this study was made by Dr. Kennell Jackson, who suggested that I "do something on women" at a time in African historiography when encouraging a graduate student to explore a topic focusing on women was unusual. Dr. Jackson and Dr. Richard Roberts read numerous drafts of the work and pushed me back on track when I tended to stray. I owe them special thanks. Five other people gave me moral support at crucial times: My mother, Mrs. Lucy Wingfield, uncritically gave support when I despaired; Mrs. Lorraine Sinclair guided me through the administrative process at Stanford; Mrs. Sylvie Roder and Dr. Penn Handwerker read early drafts and offered advice that helped me to rethink its presentation; and Dr. Julian Wasserman read the final draft of the manuscript. Finally, I wish to thank Dotti Haller who generously gave up many of her evenings and weekends during the last three months to help me edit and prepare the text for publication.

The interviews of Kikuyu women were collected from June 1978 to June 1979, a sensitive time in Kenya's history. During that period, Uganda was invaded (several times during the war, Ugandans in Kenya were rounded up, questioned, and deported), President Idi Amin fell from power, and President Jomo Kenyatta died. With so many incidents of political upheaval, many of my respondents were reluctant to volunteer information about their past or present political activities. Others were reluctant to reveal their full names, which would include their lineage affiliations. I judged that this was less important than obtaining information that in five or ten years might be less politically sensitive; I have therefore made extensive use of interviews even when a respondent did not produce a full name. I have also respected requests for complete anonymity. For simplicity's sake, and to avoid confusion, I have used Kikuyu and Kikuyus in place of the more correct Mugikuyu and Agikuyu.

Cora Ann Presley
New Orleans, 1992

AFRICA

MAP A

TUNISIA
MOROCCO
ALGERIA
LIBYA
EGYPT
MAURITANIA
MALI
NIGER
CHAD
SUDAN
SENEGAL
GAMBIA
GUINEA-BISSAU
GUINEA
SIERRA LEONE
LIBERIA
IVORY COAST
UPPER VOLTA
GHANA
TOGO
BENIN
NIGERIA
DJIBOUTI
ETHIOPIA
CENTRAL AFRICAN REPUBLIC
CAMEROON
SOMALIA
RIO MUI
UGANDA
KENYA
GABON
CONGO
ATLANTIC OCEAN
RWANDA
LAKE VICTORIA
INDIAN OCEAN
ZAIRE
BURUNDI
LAKE ALBERT
TANZANIA
N
LAKE TANGANYIKA
ANGOLA
ZAMBIA
MALAWI
ZIMBABWE
MOZAMBIQUE
MADAGASCAR
0
1000
miles
NAMIBIA
BOTSWANA
SWAZILAND
SOUTH AFRICA
LESOTHO
TRANSKEI
© GAE 1991

PROVINCIAL AND DISTRICT BOUNDARIES OF KENYA

MAP B

CENTRAL PROVINCE OF KENYA

MAP C

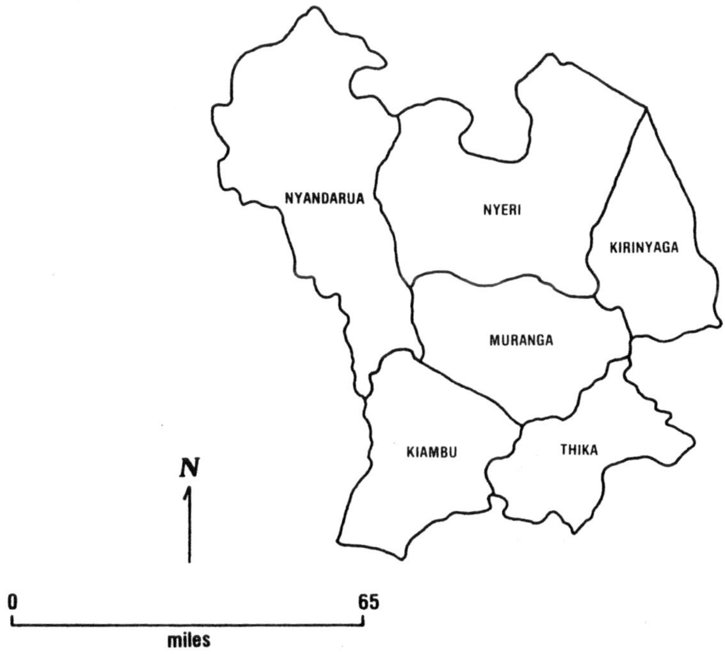

KIAMBU DISTRICT

MAP D

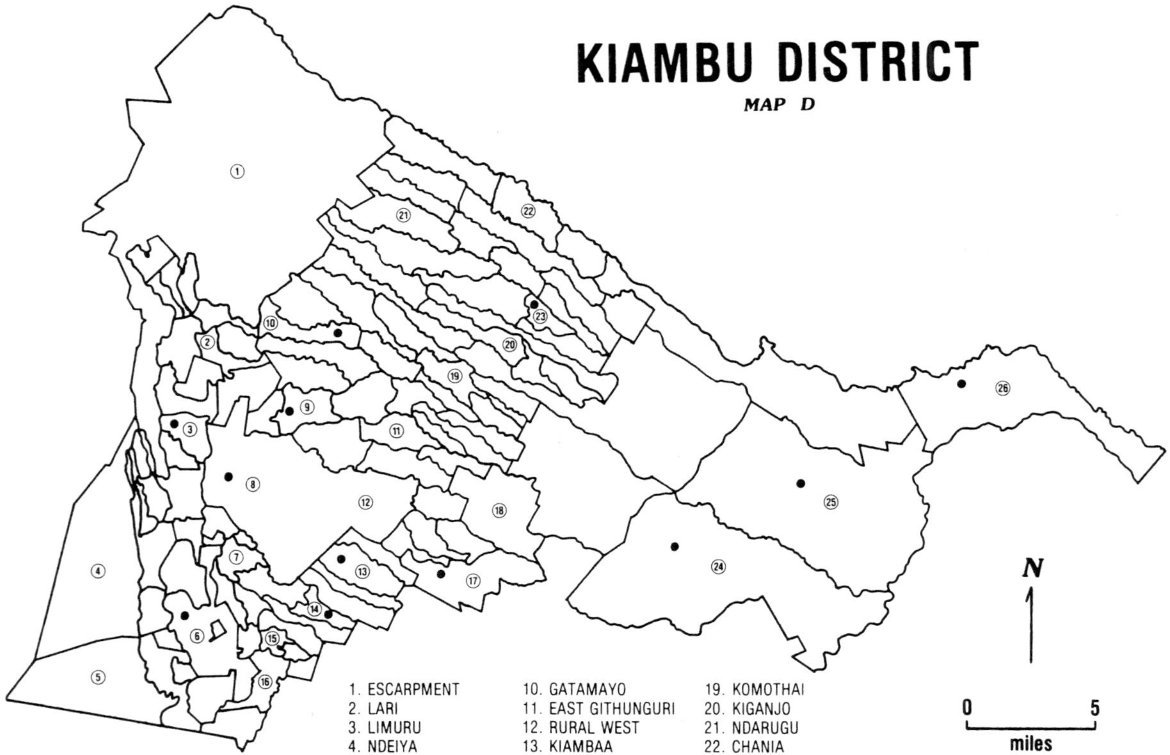

1. ESCARPMENT
2. LARI
3. LIMURU
4. NDEIYA
5. KARAI
6. KIKUYU
7. NGECHA
8. TIGONI
9. GITHUNGURI
10. GATAMAYO
11. EAST GITHUNGURI
12. RURAL WEST
13. KIAMBAA
14. KABETTE
15. MUGUGA
16. KINOO
17. KIAMBO TOWNSHIP
18. RURAL EAST
19. KOMOTHAI
20. KIGANJO
21. NDARUGU
22. CHANIA
23. NGENDA
24. RUIRU
25. JUJA
26. THIKA EAST

● Interview site

1

Introduction

Over the last 30 years, there has been a considerable growth in the literature written about African women. We have a better understanding of African women's roles in traditional society and the modern state. More recent studies explore the constraints placed upon women's mobility and their exclusion from the public arena. This work is intended to be a contribution to this growing literature on social change. I address the issue of women's interaction with the colonial state by looking at whether colonialism affected women differently than it did men and produced a different reaction.[1] Women's nationalism operated in tandem with men's nationalism since both protested labor exploitation, land alienation, and the erosion of culture. Frequently, however, women acted on their own when male associations failed to address women's concerns or to include them in their membership. Women's participation in these issues forced some fundamental changes in the societal perception of women, particularly when this came to be reified through defining women's legal and political status in the post-colonial state.

The major thesis of this work is that there was a basic transformation of women's roles from 1880 to 1962 because of Kikuyu women's significant involvement in the "politics of protest" from the 1920s through the Mau Mau period. This did not merely affect women's traditional status. The nationalist movement itself was enlarged because of female participation. The political conflict between Africans and Europeans lasted longer, included a larger portion of the population, challenged colonial social policy, and accelerated reform. The actual number of instances of protest increased when women staged their own demonstrations. The political conflict was broadened when issues primarily affecting women were added; this was done first by male nationalists and later by women acting independently. The parameters that had previously defined women's roles in traditional society broke apart.

This study of the changes in the sociopolitical status of women in colonial Kenya grew from my observation that, despite a large literature on nationalism and social change in the colonial period in Africa and in Kenya in particular, there was a gender gap. Rarely were women included in political studies. Most discussions of gender treated women as if they were apolitical. Since then, many Africanists have turned to the subject of women and the state and women as political activists.[2] Nonetheless, the treatment of women and nationalism is still largely confined to micro-level studies, a necessary stage before synthesis can occur. If the discourse on Mau Mau is typical of other nationalist historiographies, the gender gap is persistent. Women's history has not been incorporated into the general nationalist historiography. Even in the most recent studies of Kenya's colonial period, women's activism is presented as isolated incidents, if it is treated at all. Some political scientists and historians refer to women's roles in the nationalist movement.[3] However, excepting Tabitha Kanogo's recent work on squatters, none of the authors include oral testimony from men and women about women's participation in the war. Representative of this trend are Frank Furedi's recent *Mau Mau in Perspective* and David Throup's *The Social Origins of Mau Mau*. Without reference to gender, these studies are incomplete and fail to communicate the societal involvement in the nationalist struggle. The British introduced major changes in land ownership, labor patterns, and political control of Kikuyu society. Two Kenyanists, John Lonsdale and Bruce Berman, suggest that the analysis of the colonial state in Kenya and African reactions to it suffers from the tendency toward single issue analysis.[4] They argue that only by interweaving the issues can historians understand the complexities of shifts in authority and control in indigenous societies. Although in many ways theirs is a seminal work, Lonsdale and Berman ignore the presence of what may be an essential and separate area for analysis: the dynamic of colonialism for women in Kenya and the ways that dynamic may change the composite picture of protest and transformation in the nationalist era.

This study explores three major themes. First, it connects the issues of land, labor, and cultural nationalism to women's politicization. Second, it looks at the differences between women's actions and men's. Finally, it examines the differences between loyalist and nationalist women. These three themes are traced from the beginning of the colonial period up to the end of the Mau Mau rebellion. Because women did not begin to organize as political activists until the 1930s, it is only possible to explore the significance of their involvement and role transformation for three of the colonial decades. Moreover, women's articulation of their resistance to colonial penetration was not uniform, differing between groups and over decades. Within Kiambu district, where the bulk of the oral data was collected, males split into opposing loyalist and nationalist camps over the most effective strategies for lessening the impact of British colonial policy.[5] Women, too, split into factions of loyalists and nationalists. The main thrust of this study is chronicling the motives and actions of the most radical female nationalists: they eventually became the backbone of the Mau Mau movement in the district and recruited others, mostly women, into the rebellion.

Colonialism generally, as well as peculiar form it took in Kenya, was a crucial variable in the transformation of women's roles. When women became formal political actors, they changed the Kikuyu social contract. In traditional society, women did not participate in the formal political processes of their communities. Women's sphere was in domestic production: the care of the family, agricultural production, and trading.[6] Kikuyu women's involvement in nationalist politics changed this. After World War II they gained entry into formal politics. In the new order that emerged after independence, individual women had the same rights as men in many areas that had been closed to them before colonialism.

British colonialism created a new set of conditions that unintentionally provided opportunities for women to gain some economic independence and access to formal political processes. The British presence in Kenya came first in the form of the Imperial British East Africa Company (IBEAC) in 1885. The IBEAC arrived in Kiambu district in 1890. In 1895 the East African Protectorate was established and the British government formally assumed the responsibilities of the IBEAC. In the process, the British Crown assumed jurisdiction over governance, the legal system, taxation, choice of work, and location of work. The Kikuyu were concerned about European forays into matters that had been the purview of Kikuyu male elders—the adjudication of disputes over land ownership, the regulation of society, and the control of the political affairs of Kikuyu communities. At one time or another, the Kikuyu protested all of these issues. The most enduring issue was that of control over land since the Kikuyu mode of production was based on agriculture.

The land issue affected women directly, bringing them quite early into the ranks of radical young nationalists. The pre-colonial social contract vested land in men. However, women were the major cultivators. They controlled the disposition of food, determining what was to be consumed, stored, or traded. When the British expropriated and sold or gifted the most productive land to European males, African women were thrown into more intense competition for cultivation rights in the Reserves. Demographic changes for women seem to be directly related to artificially induced land scarcity. The number of polygamous marriages increased. Thousands of women migrated to urban areas where they worked as servants, traders, or prostitutes.[7]

Colonialism also produced change for women in non-household production. When the colonial government began its transfer of land to European settlers, large tracts of land were converted from peasant subsistence agriculture to large-scale farms producing cash crops. Under settler ownership, much of the land expropriated from the Kikuyu remained underutilized.[8] This forced a shift in the labor pattern for women in the Reserves. This new system reversed the Kikuyu traditional pattern. Where women once had been the primary farmers, now large numbers of Kikuyu men became farm workers. Women, however, had the double burden of cultivating the traditional subsistence crops and serving as wage laborers. Most women wage laborers were employed as coffee pickers on settler farms. The harvesting of coffee conflicted with the harvest season for traditional crops. Working for wages also reduced women's choices about where and for whom they would work. No longer did they work exclusively for their own families; now they were compelled to work for an alien employer who paid minimal wages. Until 1923 women were compelled, through the use of physical brutality or the threat of the use of force, to work on the coffee estates against their will and in opposition to indigenous traditions. Women's agricultural contributions to domestic production were a part of the economic "contract" developed by the Kikuyu; their work complemented men's herding contribution. Women had nearly full control over the disposal of food and the amount of time spent on cultivation each day. Wage labor undermined their autonomy in the labor process. Control over standards of work, the amount of time spent on cultivation, and the disposal of the "profits" from agricultural production were taken out of women's hands and placed in those of European settlers and government officials. Economic change for women was the result of their loss of control over the productive process and their organized struggle to regain it.

Changes in the Kikuyu political structure were induced even as the colonial government forced changes in land ownership and labor processes. As part of colonial rule, the British altered the process of decision-making in Kenya, placing a Governor at the apex of the structure. Traditional village elders' councils were changed in 1925 into British-appointed Local Native Councils, the lowest level in the structure. One of the outcomes of this shift was that women were able to force a wedge in a sphere which had previously been denied them. The course of the nationalist struggle was such that by the mid-1930s women had become active and important in protest politics. Their contribution to the nationalist movement became significant because the Kenya African Union (KAU) in the 1940s and Mau Mau in the 1950s depended on thousands of women who obtained and smuggled information, goods, and services. This female prominence created a legacy in independent Kenya. On the national level, elite women serve as high ranking political appointees. On the local level, women sit on local and district councils and serve as representatives of the national party. This was a radical change that was achieved through multifaceted protest politics. The primary issue was recovery of political control. The second issue was the return of alienated lands. Two other grievances were the loss of economic and cultural integrity under colonialism. All of these questions must be explored when female activism is discussed. Colonialism changed women's roles in important ways; their reactions to those changes show the degree of women's commitment to the liberation struggle.

Chapter 2 explores the gendered nature of domestic production, legal status, and political leadership from 1880 to 1910. Though many of the domestic duties and responsibilities of Kikuyu women remained unchanged from the pre-colonial period, what may be real structural change in women's positions in political, economic, and social relations is illuminated by comparing the pre-colonial, colonial, and independence periods.

A crucial area of change for gender roles was in labor relations. Thousands of women were forced into the new role of wage laborers, producing considerable resentment because of the element of force. This radicalized them and produced many dedicated political workers. Chapter 3 recounts women's conversion into wage labors. Chapter 4 introduces women's labor activism, work stoppages, and the linkages women labor activists made between labor protest and the political movement.

As a consequence of British colonization, social formations changed when European missionaries launched a frontal assault on cultural patterns. A missionary/government alliance attempted to eliminate some customs. Government cooperated by altering laws and devising new regulations that increased the power of the missionary societies. The most well-known of these assaults was the female circumcision dispute led by Dr. John Arthur in the late 1920s. Before the 1920s, Kikuyu males and the missionaries clashed over aspects of women's roles and status: marriage customs, female rites of passage, and religious beliefs. An important part of this was the contest between the elders and the missionaries for juridical control of marriage and widows. Frequently, missionaries represented themselves as African women's liberators. With the often unstated goal of changing Kikuyu traditions, they provided a refuge for women who were escaping the restraints of traditional life. The complex and changing relationship of the churches to women is the subject of Chapter 5.

The second part of the Chapter 5 examines mission education for females. The limited amount of western education available caused constant friction over the small number of schools and the restricted curriculum offered. The mission-run system gave priority to educating males. The curriculum for females was even more limited than that available to males. Kikuyu women added their special concerns about gender bias in the system to the dispute. This was partially resolved when the Kikuyu created Karing'a and Independent Schools during the circumcision controversy. The female circumcision controversy has been described by numerous scholars as an important root of political protest. However, women's views are rarely a part of that analysis. Chapter 5 includes data from women who sided with the missionaries as well as those who opposed them. Pro-circumcision women believed that clitoridectomy was a symbol of their womanhood and part of their cultural identity which became connected to their political dissent.

The final narrative chapters shift the discussion from cultural nationalism to women's participation in political organizations. Chapter 6 discusses the growth of political associations and women's relations with them. Chapters 7 and 8 examine women's participation in the Mau Mau rebellion and how that involvement created a real change in colonial social policy. Women were not politically passive from the 1920s through the 1950s. Their connection to the nationalist associations began in the 1922 riot which was sparked by Harry Thuku's arrest. Mary Nyanjiru, who was shot by the British during the riot, is the mother of female political protest. In the 1930s and 1940s, Kiambu women built on these traditions, organizing the Mumbi Central Association (MCA). The MCA was a radical revision of the traditional women's council (*kiama kia atumia*). MCA was used as a wedge for entry into the activities of the Kikuyu Central Association (1923-1940) which sprang to life after the colonial government banned Thuku's East African Association in 1922. The Mumbi Central Association's existence and activities pose new questions about the forms and duration of women's political activism and their later involvement in the Kenya African Union (1944-1952). The founders of MCA contend that this was a turning point in gender relations: the size and strength of the organization made it possible for women to join men's associations as rural politicians and as near equals. The MCA is also connected to Mau Mau. MCA members claim responsibility for promoting political consciousness among women. Through their efforts, thousands of women were recruited and mobilized for the guerrilla war.

Mau Mau has been studied exhaustively but never from a viewpoint which places at center stage the impact of the war on women and women's impact on the war. Much has been written about the complexities of the rebellion, although little evidence has been retrieved from women who were directly involved. Male participants have made limited references to the important roles of women. These included acting as spies, couriers, and serving as armed freedom fighters. Using oral histories collected in Kiambu district, Chapters 7 and 8 document the growth of women's political consciousness. Because of their activism, thousands of women were incarcerated as terrorists. Colonial social policy changed, largely in response to the overwhelming female participation in the revolt.

Methodology

The first four chapters of this book rely heavily on traditional sources: government reports and scholarship on the Kikuyu and Kenyan nationalism. The final chapters interweave official reports with oral histories from women activists which I collected in 1978 and 1979. The initial research was conducted in two phases. From November 1977 through September 1978, I researched the colonial archives held at the Rhodes House (Oxford, England), at the Public Records Office (Kew, England), and in Nairobi. I also read back issues of the *East African Standard* held at its Nairobi office. After I had read most of the colonial reports for Kiambu district, I began collecting oral interviews. With the help of three successive research assistants, I interviewed rural women who were located from three different sources. Group A were women who belonged to church organizations, primarily the Anglican Church, in Kiambu district. Some of the respondents in this category were obtained from associates at the National University of Nairobi who arranged interviews with their mothers and grandmothers. For Group B, I interviewed women who were members of rural women's self-help and cultural groups. The groups were identified by Mrs. A. B. M. Wandera, the Community Development Officer of Kiambu district. She generously provided introductions and occasionally sent one of her assistants with us. Group C women were known political activists. My research assistants were Kiambu locals and arranged interviews with women who were active in district politics. Local men and women identified other women who would reveal stories of how women fought for freedom.

The most plentiful and revealing interviews came from the third source. After three months of interviewing, I became known in the district, and word circulated about the purpose and possible danger of my study. I was greatly surprised to discover that even in 1978, women were fearful that, if the truth of their work for the Land and Freedom Army were to be revealed, there would be retaliation. I was often asked if I was spying for the Kenyan government or the CIA. For several months women responded to questions about Mau Mau with a stoic "I don't remember. " Trust between myself and the respondents was finally established when Mary Wanjiko, the local KANU representative, agreed to conduct me to the homes of former Mau Mau rebels. This was a turning point in the research. My research assistant and I had been allowed to interview members of a *kihingo* (economic self-help organization). Mary had heard about my visits and persistent questions; she came to inspect me. Unknown to me, she sat quietly in the corner until I had finished interviewing two elderly women about circumcision and employment on coffee estates. When I asked if there was anyone else in the group willing to be interviewed, she volunteered. I was sure I would meet with the usual evasive answers when I asked about politics. However, when I began asking questions about labor, conditions during colonialism, and whether she knew Mau Mau women, she volunteered a rich oral testimony. At the close of the interview, she directed other women to conduct me to the homes of former Mau Mau women. Her reason was that this story had to be told since the children did not know what their mothers had done in the fight for freedom. This one women's act of authority, trust, and legitimization made the collection of an abundance of information from Mau Mau ex-combatants possible. I am deeply indebted to her.

The Research Site

I selected Kiambu as the research site for several reasons: it was the first of the three Kikuyu districts to be contacted by European explorers and agents of the IBEAC; and it was the first of the Kikuyu districts to be conquered and effectively controlled by the British. I assumed that because of this early contact and land alienation the district would show the first changes for women agriculturalists. The next factor which led me to Kiambu district as the research site rather than Nyeri or Murang'a was the fact that many prominent Kikuyu politicians were Kiambu born. These included Waiyaki, an early collaborator, Kiyanjui, a prominent British-appointed chief, and later nationalists such as Harry Thuku, Peter Koinange, and Jomo Kenyatta. I reasoned that a district which had produced such visible and vocal male leadership—both moderate and radical—also would have produced a hidden contingent of female leadership. Kiambu is an important resource for research on the nationalist period because of its proximity to Nairobi, the capital city. Constant contact between rural Kiambu and Nairobi facilitated the spread of the political ideas of the urban based Kikuyu Central Association and the Kenya African Union. Members of these two organizations operated more freely in urban center than in the Reserve areas. In the countryside, a powerful settler/civil servant alliance, that shared assumptions and attitudes about Africans' relations with Europeans, influenced and suppressed dissent. It controlled government, land, and labor.

The Research Setting

Favorable conditions result in high agricultural productivity for Kiambu district, for its 2,448 square miles[9] contain some of the most productive agricultural land in Kenya. It has a mean annual rainfall of 30 inches to 70 inches[10] which falls in two rainy seasons (March–May and October–December). Maximum rainfall occurs in April and November.[11] The annual mean temperature is 22–26 degrees centigrade.[12] The typical terrain is a series of steep ridges with interlacing streams. Forest lands are an important resource; Kiambu ranks third in forested lands. Seventy-nine percent of the land is under agricultural production, the highest percentage in the nation.[13] Farming is the major source of income for the Kiambu population. Kiambu ranks second in production of coffee and sisal, two important cash crops. Other land is used to grow maize, pulses, wattle, potatoes, and fruit.[14] Even before the colonial period, Kiambu had a strong tradition of agricultural production with women as the main work force. Chapter 2 examines the social organization of labor in pre-colonial society and the relationship between women's agricultural labor and other kinds of labor.

Notes

1. For a discussion of the issues of women's interaction with pre-colonial, colonial and independent regimes in Africa see Jane Parpart and Kathleen Staudt, *Women and the State in Africa* (Boulder: Lynne Rienner, 1987); for a discussion of the colonial scenario, John Lonsdale and Bruce Berman, "Coping with the Contradictions: The Development of the Colonial State in Kenya, 1885-1914," *Journal of African History*, Vol. 20, 1979, pp. 487-505.

2. See Nancy Hafkin and Edna Bay, eds., *Women in Africa: Studies in Social and Economic Change* (Stanford: Stanford University Press, 1976); Denise Paulme, *Women of Tropical Africa* (London: Routledge and Paul, 1963); Stephanie Urdang, *Fighting Two Colonialisms: Women in Guinea Bissau* (New York: Monthly Review Press, 1979).

3. For nationalism, Carl Rosberg and John Nottingham, *The Myth of "Mau Mau": Nationalism in Kenya* (New York: Frederick A. Praeger, 1966; reprint edition, New York: Meridian Books, The World Publishing Company, 1970), and Donald Barnett and Njama Kariri, *Mau Mau From Within* (New York: Monthly Review Press, 1966); for wage labor, Adam Clayton and Donald Savage, *Government and Labor in Colonial Kenya 1895-1963* (London: Frank Cass, 1974); for colonial chiefs, John Lonsdale, "Some Origins of Nationalism in East Africa," *Journal of African History*, Vol. 9, 1968, pp. 520-536; for agriculture and land alienation, Roger van Zwannenberg, *Colonialism, Capitalism and Labor in Kenya, 1919-1939* (Nairobi: East African Literature Bureau, 1975); and for missionary activities, A.J. Temu, *British Protestant Missions* (London: Longman Group, 1972).

4. John Lonsdale and Bruce Berman, "Coping with the Contradictions: The Development of the Colonial State in Kenya, 1895-1914," *Journal of African History*, Vol. 20, 1979, pp. 487-505.

5. See Marshal Clough, "Chiefs and Politicians: Local Politics and Social Change in Kiambu, Kenya," (Ph.D. dissertation, Stanford University, 1978).

6. Jane Guyer, "Household and Community in African Studies," *African Studies Review*, Vol. XXIV, Nos. 2/3, June/September 1981, pp. 87-137; Jack Goody and Joan Buckley, "Inheritance and Women's Labour in Africa," *Africa*, Vol. XLII, No. 2, April 1973, pp. 108-110; Greet Kershaw, "The Changing Roles of Men and Women in the Kikuyu Family by Socioeconomic Strata," *Rural Africana*, No. 29, Winter 1975-76, pp. 173-194; Felicity Edholm, Olivia Harris and Kate Young, "Conceptualizing Women," *Critique of Anthropology*, Vol. 3, No. 9/10, 1977, pp. 104-105, 110-111, 116-117.

5. See Luise White, "Women's Domestic Labor in Colonial Kenya: Prostitution in Nairobi, 1909-1950," Working Paper No. 30, African Studies Center, Boston University, 1980.

7. Van Zwannenberg, *Colonialism, Capitalism and Labor*, pp. 1-80; and David Gordon, "Colonial Crises, Decolonization and the State: The Case of Kenya," (Ph.D. dissertation , University of Michigan, 1981), p. 299.

9. Kenya Government, *National Atlas of Kenya*, Third Edition (Nairobi: Government Printer, 1970), p. 53.

10. Ibid., p. 15.

11. Ibid.

12. Ibid., p. 21.

13. Ibid., p. 35.

14. Ibid., p. 21.

2

Women, Domestic Production, and Social Organization

Traditional Kikuyu social organization was highly gendered. This chapter discusses women's roles in agriculture and trading. Women's abilities to achieve economic independence through trading and agricultural production were constrained. Gender set limits on women's status in other areas. Because of their exclusion from political leadership, women's economic contributions were undervalued, and their legal status was degraded.

Women in Domestic Production

Women's labor was mostly consumed in crop production and family maintenance though in some areas men shared these responsibilities (see Tables 2.1, 2.2 and 2.3). Men's activities focused on intergroup maintenance and animal husbandry. Both genders performed agricultural labor. Cooperative work parties of men were responsible for heavy manual labor in erecting new homes or clearing new fields. Cooperative work details of women gathered the long grass used to thatch roofs and applied the mud covering to plaster the walls. Women also provided food and beer for these work parties (see Table 2.2).[1] The Kikuyu main base of subsistence was agriculture. However, some herd animals were maintained: sheep, goats, and cattle. Herding was a male concern except for the homestead milk cow which was cared for by women and children.

Travelogues, settler diaries, and the first generation of Europeans who spent time in Kenya have supplied eyewitness accounts of the apparent imbalance in the Kikuyu social division of labor. They wrote that the greatest burden of work, if not the entire burden of work, was placed squarely on women's backs.

TABLE 2.1 Gender Spheres of Work

Men	*Women*
ANIMAL HUSBANDRY (tending herds)	CROP PRODUCTION (planting, sowing, weeding, harvesting)
INTERGROUP MAINTENANCE (political and judicial system, defense, raiding)	FAMILY CARE (carrying wood and water, child care, cooking)

M.W. Dobbs, a member of the Ormsby-Gore commission that was sent to Kenya in 1924 to investigate the possibilities of coordinating policy, future economic development, and services in East Africa, reached the conclusion that women were the major producers :

> This commission spent two months in Kenya, collecting European and native views on various subjects. They came to the conclusion that among the natives, the women were expected to do most of the work. This was probably the case among the Kikuyu, for it was the women, with headbands strapped to their loads, who, bent almost double, carried the heavy weights.[2]

While travelling through Kikuyu country in 1913, C.I. Blackburne-Maze had observed women transporting heavy loads in this fashion and noted that women carried heavier loads than men or professional porters normally carried.[3]

These observations highlight a dramatic feature of women's work but ignore the complex gendered division of labor. Julius Carlebach's 1963 survey for the UN Economic Commission on Africa provides a clearer picture. The survey defined the traditional spheres of labor before colonialism changed production. Although conducted just after independence, this research can shed some light on the pre-colonial division of labor. Compared to the information in Table 2.1, the Carlebach data (see Table 2.2) gives a more complicated picture since it adds the categories of handicrafts, non-household construction, and seasonal occupations such as beermaking and honey processing.[4]

TABLE 2.2 Traditional Kikuyu Division of Labor

Men	*Women*
Heavy work in homestead building, e.g. cutting wood and framework; fences and granaries, cutting drains, making roads and bridges	Cutting and carrying grass for thatching houses with clay or dung
Night watchman	All housework: cooking, carrying water, washing, fetching firewood, carrying loads
Cultivation: clearing, cutting, and pruning big trees, breaking virgin soil, pruning bananas	Preparing ground for sowing, weeding, pruning
Harvesting: cutting and burning stalks, spreading ashes	Harvesting crops
Hunting	Grinding maize plants and millet
Tending cattle, sheep, goats	Tending hives, processing honey
Woodcarving, blacksmithing, beekeeping	Making pottery, weaving baskets
Preparing skins	Dressmaking
Slaughtering and distributing meat	Pounding sugar cane for beer
Warfare, legal and ritual duties	Overseeing women's social life

Source: United Nations, Economic Commission for Africa, *The Position of Women in Kenya*, by Julius Carlebach (E/CN.14/URB/9), 16 July 1963, p. 20.

On the surface, the data indicates an unequal gender based division of labor heavily weighted towards more work for men. Although men's work included a greater number of tasks, these were seasonal or periodic, whereas most of the tasks performed by women required a daily routine of uninterrupted work. Men's daily tasks consisted of night watch duty, tending cattle, sheep, and goats, weeding crops, and being constantly prepared for the defense of the community. By contrast, many of the tasks on the women's side of the roster were more demanding than men's.[5] Women's work included the daily domestic activities of washing, cooking, fetching water, grinding grains, and gathering firewood—which had to be carried in loads suspended down the back from the forehead by headstraps. Two other time-consuming activities were not included in Carlebach's survey: child care and trading. Women traded agricultural surplus with the Kamba, the Masai, and in local markets.

Work loads were unevenly distributed within genders with respect to age. Young males were responsible for hunting, tending cattle, warfare, stock raiding, and pursuing stock raiders. Older males monopolized governance, adjudication, and observance of ritual.[6] Age differentiation in women's work is less clear. Young girls assisted their mothers in domestic production: child care, agricultural work, carrying loads. Elderly women appear to have been responsible for these aspects of domestic production, though perhaps to a lesser degree if they had the assistance of their daughters-in-law and their children. Women's labor was more constant than men's since it was more labor intensive (more hours required for the completion of tasks) and since responsibility for domestic production covered a woman's life span. This pattern of women's constant labor and episodic and age-specific male labor is the scenario which caused many Europeans to believe that Kikuyu men were lazy and that women did all the work.[7]

Although the Kikuyu maintained herds of sheep, goats, and cattle, they were primarily an agricultural people. The Kikuyu agricultural calendar has two planting seasons which correspond to the "long rains" and the "short rains," so that some crop cultivation is done year round. Women were the major farmers; their work involved preparing the ground for sowing, planting, weeding, and harvesting. Some of these tasks were shared by men.[8] Crops were categorized according to whether they were "men's" or "women's" crops. There was, however, some flexibility in this division. Men assisted women in the heavy work requiring greater muscular strength such as clearing fallow ground, ground cutting trees, and tilling new fields. In an emergency, males could care for crops which were designated as "female" crops.[9]

Table 2.3 Gender Divisions in Crop Production

Crop	*Cultivation Time*	*Category*
Maize (Mwembe)	March to July	Women's crop, no male taboo
Bullrush millet (Mwere)	Oct. to Jan.	Women's crop, men prohibited
Sweet potato (Ngwaci)	March to July	Women's crop, no male taboo
Yam (Gikwa)	March to July	Men's crop
Lablab bean (Njahi)	March to July	Women's crop
Cowpea (Thoroko)	March to July	Women's crop
Kidney bean (Mboco)	March to July	Women's crop
Edible arum (Nduma)	Ten months after planting	Women and men, mainly women
Sugar cane (Kigwa)	In dry plots during rains; 18 months to maturity	Men's crop, women sometimes help
Banana (Irigu)	no data	Men's crop, women carry plants

Adapted from: L.S.B. Leakey, *The Southern Kikuyu Before 1903* (London: Academic Press, 1977), pp. 175-186.

Seven of the ten core staples were women's crops (see Table 2.3). The four that dominated the Kikuyu diet—maize (*Zea Mays*), the lablab bean (*Lablab Purpureus*), the kidney bean (*Phaseolus Uulgaris*), and edible arum (*Colocasia Esculenta*)—were almost exclusively women's crops. Males also cultivated the edible arum. Men's crops included tobacco, (*Nicotiana Tobaccum*) and sugar cane (*Saccharum Officinarum*). These were luxury crops. Sugar cane at least is a crop which was brought to Africa in recent times. Some men's crops were mainstay famine foods. Women, aided by girls and boys, produced the majority of crops in everyday use—the legumes and cereals.[10]

Cultivation was labor intensive. The amount of time expended in cultivation depended on the season and the needs of the household. The tool used in the *shamba* (Swahili: homestead farm) was a long digging stick (*munyago*) approximately six feet in length and two inches in diameter.[11] Despite the Kikuyus' extensive knowledge of blacksmithing, the digging stick was women's principle farming tool until the introduction of the metal panga in the 20th century. Daily activities of weeding and pruning were required to produce high yields. Plot size differed with the variations in the wealth of the family and the husband's lineage. Traditionally, a woman had exclusive cultivation rights in her own plot within the homestead plantation, although usufruct rights, assigned by the *mbari* (lineage) head, belonged to her husband or the male who had direct authority over her. When women married, they lost cultivation rights in their own lineage and received usufruct rights in their husband's lineage. A husband or landowner allotted land to his wife (wives) and female adult dependents, attempting to maximize the range of soil types for each woman and her access to water, thus allowing her to grow as wide a range of crops as possible.[12] Land assigned to women by the male head of household consisted of strips of different sizes, depending on the number of persons she had to feed (husband, herself, children, elderly male or female). A wife with a larger number of children received a larger portion of land.[13] After the harvest, her responsibility was to see to storage in her granary.[14]

The Kikuyu social contract included rituals, ceremonies, and cultural markers which governed human relationships and the relations of humans to the divine. In traditional society, males and females could become *thahu* (ritually unclean) for a variety of reasons, including unnatural death, circumcision, fighting, crossing forbidden social boundaries, adultery, rudeness to elders, and unusual conditions among herds.[15] Agriculture, so fundamental to group survival, had specific ritual observations associated with it. Various blood taboos connected to farming applied to women. If a man drew blood by beating a woman in a field, whether or not she was his spouse, the field had to be purified through a special ceremony. Other blood taboos specially applied to menstruating women engaged in field work. Although there was no specific prohibition against a menstruating woman working in her own field, she was not permitted to hang bananas or other foodstuff in the homestead courtyard. She was also not allowed to make gruel from millet or other grains, even though she had carried them from the fields. No taboos or conditions associated with ritual impurity were imposed on male farmers.[16]

Women farmers' labor was crucial to agricultural production, indeed they had the primary role in producing food. Vegetable products, which were mainly produced by women, comprised a larger portion of the diet. Meat, which men produced, was not consumed on a daily basis. Normally it was eaten only on special occasions; it was valued more for its status giving properties than for its nutritional value.[17]

Other aspects of domestic production came within women's purview: women were not merely the guardians of the food supply, they were also responsible for procuring the fuel and water supply each day. This was done by carrying heavy loads of water and fuel over what could be considerable distances from streams or forested areas. Children of both sexes came under women's authority: women fed them out of the store of food kept in their granaries and supplied all other aspects of child care. From the age of about seven, children's work became gendered. Boys gradually began to spend more time with men and were introduced to the complexities of caring for herds. Young girls began to assume responsibility for supervising younger children, assisting their mothers in cultivation, and carrying small loads of water and firewood.[18]

Good resource managers purposefully controlled the daily diet with the dual purpose of retaining a surplus of food as seed for future planting and for barter in the local market or with neighboring groups such as the Masai and Kamba who produced items which family labor could not supply.[19] In exchange for their produce, the Kikuyu traded for beads, cooper wire, medicines, cloth, war attire, and even food during times of famine or drought. Control over women's surplus became a joint affair when trading beyond the local market occurred. A husband had to be consulted about the disposal of any surplus, however, the actual decision of when to barter, how much to barter and how much to retain for family use was vested in the woman. She better than he knew the family's daily food needs and the requirements from harvest to harvest.[20]

Female Traders

Despite men's control over land and their ultimate control over the disposal of family resources outside the homestead, women's daily control of the food supply and commerce provided them with an opportunity to create some economic independence for themselves through trading. Armed with surplus from the *shamba,* Kikuyu women entered a trade network that connected their village to the wider world of East African trade and which ultimately reached across the Indian Ocean. Pre-colonial East African trade was multifaceted and structured in several complex overlapping layers. The most lucrative type of trade was the long distance trade whose purpose was to export rare goods from Africa and goods that had a high ratio of profit to cost of transport. From East Africa the primary exports were ivory, slaves, and certain "magic" items such as rhinoceros horns, believed in some Asian countries to have aphrodisiac qualities. Organizing this long-distance trade often profoundly changed traditional social organization. Pre-colonial organizations such as warrior guilds and kinship organizations sometimes adapted their structures to take advantage of new trade opportunities which became available in the later half of the nineteenth century. The Kamba and Nyamwezi were particularly successful at adapting and profiting from the new possibilities of expanded trade networks. Both became expert traders in ivory and were able to challenge Arab domination of the East African long-distance trade.[21]

A second type of trade was involved in the exchange of local goods (grains, vegetable products, craft items) in a more limited geographical range. The aim of this trade was to adjust to temporary deficiencies in supply.[22] The third type of trade and the one which is our major concern was the interregional trade of local produce and localized products between different ethnic groups who usually inhabited different climatic zones. This was to become an important trading sphere for Kikuyu women. Typically this was an irregular trade which became vital during famines or other ecological disasters. These traders received special consideration during wars. Women interregional traders were safe from attack even when they were travelling through hostile territory of wartime enemies.[23]

In the late 19th century, famine struck East Africa repeatedly. Interregional trade became all the more crucial for the survival of three of the major ethnic groups in Kenya. The Kamba and Masai probably depended more on this trade than the Kikuyu. Trade between them took an unusual form for East Africa. Caravans, composed exclusively of Kikuyu women, were organized under the direction of older women leaders and traveled from southern Kikuyu into Masai country. Caravan leaders were fluent in the Masai language and were familiar with the Masai territory. Such skills which were often possessed because the caravan leader had been a Masai child who was adopted by a Kikuyu mother during a trading expedition. *Hinga* (Kikuyu women who spoke Masai) were linguistic and cultural facilitators between the women traders and the Masai. Some *hinga* were Masai wives of Kikuyu men, others were Kikuyu women who had been captured during wars with the Masai and later redeemed.[24] A *hinga* informed other women of a planned expedition; on the agreed date, mature married women who wished to participate assembled. Unmarried girls were not allowed to journey to Masai country; women with young children rarely participated since their child care responsibilities could not be abandoned for the length of time required for the journey.[25] Each woman brought produce she intended to trade for herself and carry; a portion of which was set aside as the *hinga's* property as her fee for leading the caravan. Thus a *hinga* had a special method of acquiring wealth from trading because of a skill not common to Kikuyu women.

Sleeping out in the open where water and fuel were available and carrying food for the journey in addition to their trade goods, women traders travelled for the two to four weeks required for the round trip.[26] A male escort invited danger, since their presence during hostilities between the Kikuyu and Masai would result in an attack. Male escorts would be suspected of spying and immediately killed.[27] This form of female entrepreneurship continued well after the initial conquest of the Kikuyu by the British. While on safari in Kenya in 1913, C.I. Blackburne-Maze crossed trails with a women's trading expedition:

> Just as we got out of Nyeri, we passed a lot of women carrying bananas, sweet potatoes, and Indian corn; some of them were carrying enormous

> loads of about 100 lbs; they were going to Laikipia, which is in the Masai country, to barter the potatoes etc, for sheep.[28]

Once such a caravan reached an appropriate Masai village, the *hinga's* special talents were utilized. She negotiated for lodgings for herself and the members of the party and mediated the individual barter between the host Masai and the Kikuyu women. The trade also allowed Kikuyu families to adopt young children, usually girls, from the Masai or Kamba. During periods of famine, the Masai willingly offered children for adoption. This served two purposes: first the young child was guaranteed a home and survival as a member of an adopting household which was not threatened by starvation; second, the Masai family benefited by receiving foodstuffs which could insure the survival of the remaining members of the household.

This arrangement of Kikuyu households adopting Masai children resulted in the transmission of Masai culture to the Kikuyu. The adopted child was a conduit through whom cultural change occurred and, with marriage and procreation, a diversifier of the genetic pool. Later, of course, such a child could be the *hinga* leader for women's caravans. A special adoption ceremony was arranged while the caravan was in residence. Once this was completed, she belonged solely to the adopting Kikuyu mother. For the Kikuyu woman, adoption was an important way to enhance her status. Barrenness stigmatized women and was grounds for divorce. Adopting a child, Masai or not, could confer status on woman that was otherwise unobtainable, and since child labor was an important contribution to domestic production, the new mother also lightened her own domestic workload.

When the caravan returned to its home village, women's subordinate position in society was ritually reified. After trading and adoptions were completed, the return journey began. Having been informed of the estimated date of return before the journey started, male relatives were on the lookout for the caravan and met them at a prearranged spot a few miles from the village to welcome them back and help carry the trade goods the last leg of the journey.[29] On arrival, each woman symbolically handed over her goods to her husband (or eldest son if she was a widow). By doing so, she did not renounce ownership and use of the goods; rather, she acknowledged his authority over her. The items were her property and could not be used by the family or any other person without her consent.[30] The ritual handing over of the trade goods demonstrates Kikuyu women's subordinate position in society; female independence was constrained by male domination in land and property ownership and in formal participation in political processes.

Leadership and Gender Boundaries

The effect of gender on the development of African societies is of critical interest to development planners and the international scholastic community. In the 1980s, the issue became less academic. A debate which was sometimes bitterly divisive developed in several African nations between male and female constituencies. This question was thrust into various national dialogues partly because of the dissemination of western feminist ideas to western-educated elites in Africa, Asia, and Latin America and remains relevant in parts of contemporary African society. Kenya reflected these same tensions. Kenyan and Kikuyu society are highly gendered, which produces negative impacts on women's economic and political status. Before colonialism, women were were consulted when decisions about food production and the disposal of family resources were made.[31] A man dared not dispose of family property without consulting his wife.[32] However, consultation about resource management is not parity; it should not be mistaken for sharing formal political power with women. Older women's trading entrepreneurship should not be mistaken for independence. Confining women to domestic production freed male labor. Otherwise, men would have been compelled to divert their labor from political affairs—community governance and waging war—to food production.

Women's political status within the corporate body did not parallel the importance they achieved as farmers and traders. They did not have legal rights and duties as independent persons in the group with a status equal to men's; they were formally excluded from the male route to decision making which culminated in the elders' councils. Women were not warriors in the periodic raids into Kamba and Masai country.[33] Publicly, women were not consulted on corporate political decisions. Male domination in this aspect of society was rationalized on the basis of their roles as warriors and protectors. This system of a lesser political status for women developed out of the needs for internal governance and protection against groups competing for the same land.

Land was the major means of production. Access to land was a major concern of the Kikuyu from 1850 to 1900. Land hunger and population pressures on the older Kikuyu districts of Nyeri and Murang'a spun out columns of pioneering Kikuyu. Population densities had become acute enough to cause members of the more adventurous clans to migrate from their original homelands into Kiambu district. Competition for land influenced fluctuations in contractual relationships between individuals and moieties. These conflicts were between Kikuyu lineages and clans. There was also interethnic rivalry between the Kikuyu, Kamba, and Masai. Land and cattle ownership were the motif of domination. Dywer notes that law is an important element of the social control field which subordinates women and—when combined with socialization, religion, gossip, and scandal—is perhaps the most visible and concrete method of reinforcing a subordinate status.[34] She suggests that in analyzing the relationship of property control to a subordinate status it is necessary to distinguish between three relationships: ownership, occupation, and management.[35] Exclusion from landownership as prescribed by traditional Kikuyu law is the basis of women's subordination. The definition of *ene* (landownership) rights clearly illuminates women's unequal status. These rights were vested in males. Economic parity was impossible for women for neither law nor custom granted women the same legal rights to land as men enjoyed. In a limited sense, women farmers acted as land managers as they made decisions about its daily and seasonal use through planting, harvesting, and the disposal of the produce from the land. However, women could not manage land as owners with rights to sell, alienate or acquire it. Women could not inherit land, though they could act as regent (manager) for a minor until he reached adulthood.[36] Land passed from male to male.

There were only two other ways of gaining land: pioneering (which resulted in ownership) and becoming a client of a large landowner (the attainment of occupation rights). Gender constrained these routes; they were exclusive male routes to status enhancement and wealth accumulation. The two client relationships were *muhoi* (pl. *ahoi*) and *muthami* (pl. *athami*). *Ahoi* and *athami* entered into patron/client relationships with landowners to gain land. A *muhoi* received rights of cultivation on the land allotted to him but could not build a dwelling on the land. A *muthami* was given both cultivation and homesteading rights. Women could not aspire to either status. Though often the dependents of males who initiated these contracts, females were not allowed to seek such a patron/client arrangement.[37] However, they could be legally obligated by the arrangement. Daughters of land-rich Kikuyu lineages were sometimes required by the patron/client contract to marry the prospective client.[38] The *muhoi* gained access to land and was released from the obligation to pay bridewealth. Ownership rights in the land remained within the *mbari* (lineage) of the landowner. In theory, any Kikuyu girl could refuse a prospective bridegroom. In practice, daughters of wealthy families were often subject to strong social and parental pressures to marry to the advantage of their *mbari*.

More than landownership rights were controlled by the heads of the lineages. *Mbari* heads also controlled politics. Women were barred from becoming *mbari* heads. They were also excluded from membership on ruling councils (*kiama*) in villages, the district and ultimately in the entire Kikuyu territory. These councils exercised judicial authority. Men became members of the *kiama* by progressing through a series of graded steps which culminated in senior eldership. Eldership on the council meant having the privilege and duty of being responsible for the political and judicial regulation of society.[39] The *kiama* included the heads of different lineages represented in any village and contained junior and senior members. The process of attaining the most senior, prestigious and powerful positions on the councils was connected to the events in the male life cycle. Men were eligible to be junior members of the council (*kiama kia kamatimu*) after marriage. A man could enter the second level of the hierarchy (*kiama kia mathathi*) after the birth of his first child and payment of goats to senior council members. A man attained the third level (*kiama kia maturanguru*) when his first child was circumcised and the requisite fees in goats had been paid. Movement through the levels changed the council member's responsibilities. Junior members' lowly status meant that they performed the physical tasks connected with council membership and oversaw women's work in clearing land and preparing the council meeting place. This placed even the youngest adult males in authority over the most senior women in the society: a reaffirmation of sexual status transcending age status. Junior council members were also couriers and sergeants-at-arms during the meetings. Only the most senior members had access to knowledge which prepared them for deliberation on the more complex issues involved in governance.[40] All males in society including the landless *ahoi,* who merely possessed cultivation rights through contract, were eligible for *kiama* memberships. The only requirement was the payment of the requisite fees. However, such payments could so strain the resources of landless, impoverished Kikuyu men that they were unable to gain entrance to the more senior levels.[41]

Limited by wealth, males advanced from the status of junior warrior to senior elder through the age-set system. No such system existed for women. There were however, "generic" names for females at different stages of the life-cycle.[42] Women's, political authority did not increase as they passed from girlhood to old age. It would, of course, be misleading to argue that a young girl still under her mother's control had as much authority and respect as an adult woman with married sons. Such was not the case. Married women with mature sons received more respect from others. But this did not increase their power nor did it increase their legal status. The model of the Kikuyu as an equalitarian society cannot be sustained. Sons of wealthy men were in the best position to become men of senior status, authority, and power. Sons of landless men were hampered by their initial impoverishment. The standard description of Kikuyu society as "ascephalous" and "egalitarian" ignores the circulation of high status within the lineages of the land/goat rich to the exclusion of the landless. However, landless men did not form a permanent underclass in society. They had access to land through the *ahoi* or *athami* contracts and through pioneering. These options were closed to women. They were excluded from political leadership and landownership. Women could not become junior warriors and advance to the senior elders' council that settled land disputes, initiated warfare, heard cases about murder or witchcraft and decided if expansion into new territory should occur. These matters were solely the province of men.

The Women's Council

Excluded from the men's council, women did have their own assembly known as the *kiama kia atumia*. When so assembled, women corporately made decisions about "women's things" which included the scheduling of circumcision ceremonies for girls.[43] These councils had jurisdiction over matters which were outside the purview of the male sphere and included domestic or homestead affairs, farm matters, and the discipline and control of the social life of girls and women.[44] Women's councils also imposed sanctions against males who violated norms of social behavior. Kikuyu women respondents reported that the traditional women's council supplied the ceremonial food consumed when new members were admitted. The council regulated farm matters through arranging female cooperative work parties that completed labor intensive village projects such as cutting and transporting thatching for roof building (see Table 2.2).

The most cogent demonstration of the public subordination of women is to be found in the invisibility of the *kiama kia atumia* in corporate political affairs. They were not allowed to interface with the male *kiama* on matters of warfare, territorial expansion, or the maintenance and regulation of the judicial system. The exigencies and demands of the colonial state broke this dichotomy apart. In a significant transformation from its pre-colonial functions, the women's council of Kiambu district converted itself into a politically active body in 1930. They became advocates and organizers for more African control of their affairs and nationalist resistance to cultural imperialism.[45] The decisions to break with tradition and force a wedge for themselves as activists was not undertaken lightly. They evolved out of women's specific concerns over the issues of the erosion of Kikuyu landownership through land alienation, the missionary led attack on female circumcision, colonial labor policies, and the level of taxation the government imposed on the Kikuyu peasantry to force them into wage labor. Another situation which propelled women into the public arena as critics of the colonial state was the inability of the male nationalist organizations to change economic and political conditions. The process of *kiama kia atumia's* transformation into a women's political organization whose goals and activities were so markedly different form the council's socially sanctioned "charge" will be discussed in Chapter 6.

Before women initiated this limited change in the nature of their assembly, political interaction, and organization were based solely on the recruitment of males, especially those who were wealthy or who, through their lineage connections, had access to wealth. Patriarchy contradicts egalitarianism if one defines an egalitarian society as one where all adult members have equal access to status, power, wealth and control of public matters. Women clearly did not have access to formal judicial and political power. The gendered nature of the public sphere resulted in an asymmetrical society.[46]

Gender, Ritual, and Myth

There was ambiguity in women's social status. Though denied the right to exercise political power and defined as legal minors, older women were not totally deprived of status and some measures of authority within the homestead. Women played an important role on ceremonial occasions, acting as witnesses and participants in rituals of primary importance to the community. For example, when land south of the Chania River[47] was first acquired from the Wandorobo—the original forest dwelling owners—the ceremony of transfer was not complete without the presence and involvement of the Kikuyu participant's wives in the ritual that finalized the transfer of land.[48] A second example of women's inclusion in important rituals is purification ceremonies. When a property owner wished to cleanse his homestead after the infringement of a taboo which had rendered the homestead and its inhabitants ritually unclean the wife (wives) of the owner had to be present. In another case when the *kiama* elders wished to purify a village women's participation in the ceremony was required. Women's importance in some rituals was acknowledged. However, as in most African societies, women were also constrained by gender specific taboos and prohibitions which did not apply to males.[49] These were usually connected to menstruation and female sexuality. Women were also scapegoated; they were blamed for unfortunate happenings and accused of causing mis-fortunes by practicing witchcraft.

The ambiguity reflected in the necessity for women's presence at important ceremonial occasions and the scapegoating of them for ills which beset the society is crystallized in the "enabling" myths of society—those stories, legends and myths that explain the origin and basis of solidity and which define Kikuyu social identity. The origin of the Kikuyu clans is traditionally traced to the nine female progenitors who were the daughters of Gikuyu and Mumbi, the first couple god (*Ngai*) created.[50] The ethnic group bears the name Wakikuyu, the people of the legendary male progenitor Gikuyu. The clan names are the names of the nine female children born to Gikuyu and Mumbi. Yet another piece of folklore which complicates the question of the socially sanctioned status of women is one related by Jomo Kenyatta in his work on the Kikuyu. According to Kenyatta, women monopolized political power in the distant past. Men became disgruntled with the situation and plotted to overthrow them. Waiting until the women returned from war against their enemies, the men—by conspiracy—impregnated their powerful wives. With women thus rendered helpless while giving birth, men seized power and have since kept it.[51] This tale, self-exculpating as it is, shows a curious phenomenon in the Kikuyu concept of the right to rule. A close analysis of this particular story reveals the fact that the Kikuyu considered women capable of wielding power and ruling; however, they did not do so because men were more devious and outwitted them.

The contradictions between the prohibitions, myths, and ceremonial importance of women point to the ambiguity in this patriarchal society about the power women should rightly possess. Male economic dominance was threatened by its dependence on women because of their centrality in domestic production. The patriarchy was sustained by denying females access to formal political participation and access to landownership. Moreover, they were also reminded that they could not escape their subservience to men—even the measure of economic autonomy they had was only by male consent: thus the ritual of handing over goods they obtained from their trade expeditions. In the legal tradition, women's lives were not as valuable as men's.[52] This is illustrated by the punishment for murder. If the victim were male, the all male *kiama* levied a fine of 100 goats and sheep on the murderer and his/her relatives. If the victim were female, the fine was 30 goats and sheep. Society's protectors (warriors) and potential power holders (*kiama* members) were judged to be more important than females (non-warriors, agricultural producers, the bearers of children) who were politically dispossessed.

By the late 19th century, Kikuyu society was one where women were denied power and were frequently reminded of their inferior status. Power was gendered, women were proscribed from achieving political power and economic autonomy. Their participation in community decisions could only occur publicly through the women's council whose province was more social than political. Through trading women achieved one of their few possibilities for control. But this, too, was subject to potential male domination. Trading was a part-time occupation for Kikuyu women, a way of augmenting the resources available to the homestead, for women could do little with the goods obtained from the trade since they could not purchase land with the trade generated wealth. Possession of land was the only way of achieving true independence.

Kikuyu women were burdened with heavy economic responsibilities which were not translated into economic independence. Their most strenuous labor was the daily collection and transportation of water and firewood. This involved travelling considerable distances on foot with heavy bundles of wood loaded on their backs. The execution of this particular task often gave early European observers the exaggerated idea that the major burden of maintaining the economic well-being of society rested with women. Child care was another area which rested squarely on women's shoulders. According to custom and law which defined gender boundaries in pre-colonial society, the rightful sphere for women's activities was in domestic production which took place in the homestead and the field. Women could not be professional traders to the exclusion of domestic production and reproduction.

While much of the essential daily life of the community rested with women, men were not idle. Their duties lay in other realms. They were involved in agriculture to a lesser degree. They bore the brunt of the responsibility for care of livestock. Through herding, males could enhance their status and wealth. Such was not the case for crop production. Stock, not beans, could be exchanged for political office, land, and wives. The main responsibilities of men from youth to old age was the defense of the community and the administration of law and custom.

Governance of the community was a matter of consensus between male elders in consultation with young warriors. Women's participation in these concerns was not socially sanctioned: they were not consulted in adjudication, deciding on whether the society would go to war, what payments of bridewealth would be set, whether a lineage or family would migrate to new territory, or who had ownership rights in lineage land. That is to say, women's opinions were never formally sought by their husbands, fathers, and brothers. The pre-colonial, non-egalitarian Kikuyu proscribed a female public political role.

Notes

1. Jeanne Fisher, *The Anatomy of Kikuyu Domesticity and Husbandry* (London: Department of Technical Cooperation, 1964), p. 268.
2. M.W. Dobbs, "Recollections of Kenya 1906-1931" (Oxford: Rhodes House, 1964), p. 179.
3. C.I. Blackburne-Maze, *Journals of My African Travels* (Maidstone: W.E. Thorpe and Sons, 1913), p. 131. Women carried loads which were sometimes as heavy as 100 pounds. Forty pounds was the usual weight carried by African men employed as carriers in the porterage trade.
4. United Nations, Economic Commission for Africa, *The Position of Women in Kenya*, by Julius Carlebach (E/CN. 14/URB/9), 16 July 1963, p. 20; for a discussion of labor divisions see John Middleton and Greet Kershaw, *The Central Tribes of the North-Eastern Bantu: The Kikuyu including Embu, Meru, Mbere, Chuka, Mwimbi, Tharaka, and the Kamba of Kenya* (London: International African Institute, 1954), pp. 20-21.
5. Fisher, *The Anatomy of Kikuyu*, pp. 23-24.
6. Gavin Kitching, *Class and Economic Change in Kenya: The Making of an African Petite Bourgeoisie 1905-1970* (New Haven and London: Yale University Press, 1980), pp. 14-17.
7. L.S.B. Leakey, *The Southern Kikuyu Before 1903*, 3 volumes (London: Academic Press, 1977), pp. 9-10; Fr. Cagnolio, *The Akikuyu: Their Customs, Traditions and Folklore* (Nyeri: The Mission Printing School, 1933).
8. Jomo Kenyatta, *Facing Mount Kenya: The Tribal Life of the Gikuyu* (New York: Random House, 1965), pp. 53-55; Leakey, *The Southern Kikuyu*, pp. 175-186.
9. Greet Kershaw, "The Land Is the People: A Study of Kikuyu Social Organization in Historical Perspective," (Ph.D. dissertation, University of Chicago, 1972), p. 55; Leakey, *The Southern Kikuyu*, p. 178.
10. Kershaw, "The Land Is the People," p. 55.
11. Fisher, *The Anatomy of Kikuyu*, p. 268.
12. Leakey, *The Southern Kikuyu*, p. 93.
13. Leakey, *The Southern Kikuyu*, pp. 171-172; Fisher, *The Anatomy of Kikuyu*, pp. 213-214.

14. Penelope Ciancaneli, "Exchange, Reproduction and Sex Subordination Among the Kikuyu of East Africa, " *The Review of Radical Political Economics*, 12, Summer 1980, p. 26; W. Scoresby Routledge with Katherine Routledge, *With a Prehistoric People: The Akikuyu of British East Africa* (London: Frank Cass & Co. Ltd., 1910), p. 121; and Kenya National Archives (KNA): Provincial Commissioner (PC)/Central Province (CP), Political Record Book (PRB)1908-1919, p. 18.

15. C.W. Hobley, *Bantu Beliefs and Magic* (London: Frank Cass & Co. Ltd., 1967), pp. 103-153.

16. Leakey, *The Southern Kikuyu*, p. 205-206.

17. Middleton, *The Central Tribes*, p. 19; Leakey, *The Southern Kikuyu*, p. 255.

18. Godfrey Muriuki, *A History of the Kikuyu 1500 to 1900* (Nairobi: Oxford University Press, 1974), p. 9

19. Kershaw, "The Land Is the People," p. 55.

20. Kenyatta, *Facing Mount Kenya*, pp. 61-72.

21. See Edward Alpers, *Ivory and Slaves in East and Central Africa* (London: Heinemann, 1975); Richard Gray and David Birmingham, *Pre-colonial African Trade: Essays on Trade in Central and Eastern Africa Before 1900* (Oxford: Oxford University Press, 1970); and Kennell A. Jackson, "An Ethnohistorical Study of the Oral Traditions of the Akamba of Kenya," (Ph.D. dissertation, University of California, Los Angeles, 1972).

22. Gray, *Pre-colonial African Trade*, pp. 2-5.

23. Middleton, *The Central Tribes*, p. 20.

24. Leakey, *The Southern Kikuyu*, p. 480.

25. Ibid., p. 280.

26. Ibid., p. 482-483.

27. Ibid., p. 483.

28. Blackburne-Maze, *Journals*, p. 134.

29. Leakey, *The Southern Kikuyu*, p. 479.

30. Ibid., p. 485.

31. Fisher, *The Anatomy of Kikuyu*, p. 273; Leakey, *The Southern Kikuyu*, pp. 280-281.

32. Leakey, *The Southern Kikuyu* , p. 11.

33. Muriuki, *A History of the Kikuyu*, pp. 120-126.

34. Daisey Hilse Dwyer, "Outside the Courts: Extra-Legal Strategies for Subordinating Women," in Margaret Jean Hay and Marcia Wright (eds.), *African Women and the Law: Historical Perspectives*, Boston University Papers on Africa, VIII Boston, 1982, pp. 90- 91, 94.

35. Dwyer, "Outside the Courts," p. 93-94.

36. C.W. Hobley, *Ethnology of A-Kamba and Other East African Tribes* (Cambridge: Cambridge University Press, 1971), p. 137.

37. Fisher, *The Anatomy of Kikuyu*, pp. 222-225; verbal communication from Professor Greet Kershaw, May 21, 1988.

38. Kershaw, "The Land Is the People," pp. 61-62, 67, 80.

39. Muriuki, *A History of the Kikuyu*, pp. 128-129; Middleton, *The Central Tribes*, pp. 35-36, 43.

40. Kershaw, "The Land Is the People," pp. 86-87.

41. Ibid., pp. 84-86.

42. These names were: *kana*, baby girl; *karego*, small girl; *muhiki*, betrothed or married woman without a child; *wahai*, mother of young children; *mutumia* , mother of one or more initiated children; *theti* , old woman.

43. Kenyatta, *Facing Mount Kenya*, p. 108; Middleton, *The Central Tribes*, p. 36; and James Wellard, "Kikuyu" in *Man, Myth and Magic: Encyclopedia of the Supernatural*, p. 1563.

44. H.E. Lambert, *Kikuyu Social and Political Institutions* (London: Oxford Press for the International Institute, 1956), p. 100.

45. Interview with Nduta wa Kore, Kiambaa, April 21, 1979. Nduta wa Kore was the secretary of the council.

46. Until the last decade of Kenyan historiography, it was normative to describe the Kikuyu as an egalitarian and democratic society. Especially influential in promoting this idea were Muriuki, *A History of the Kikuyu* (p. 110) who describes the society as "patriarchal, uncentralized and highly egalitarian" and Kenyatta, *Facing Mount Kenya, inter alia*. This characterization of Kikuyu society as asymmetrical falls in line with literature on other traditional societies. See especially Leith Mullins, "Women and Economic Change in Africa," in *Women in Africa: Studies in Social and Economic Change*, Nancy Hafkin and Edna Bay (Stanford: Stanford University Press, 1976), pp. 239-264.

47. Later known as Kiambu district.

48. Kenyatta, *Facing Mount Kenya*, pp. 26-29; Leakey, *The Southern Kikuyu*, pp. 92-100.

49. According to the anthropological literature Kikuyu society was rife with taboos. When men became ritually unclean, it was because of a specific act. For women this state of *thahu* could be achieved not because of the commission of an act but simply because of her femaleness. See Routledge, *With a Prehistoric*, pp. 21, 49-50, 148, 170-172; Leakey, *The Southern Kikuyu*, pp. 165-167, 198, 248-250, 786-787, 810-812, 905.

50. The number of the clans is always given as nine. Anthropological and historical accounts of the clans always list them as being ten or "nine complete." The custom of stating that the number of clans is only nine derives from the Kikuyu precaution of not stating the unlucky number ten which was believed to cause pregnant women to miscarry.

51. Kenyatta, *Facing Mount Kenya*, pp. 3-7; Routledge, *With a Prehistoric*, p. 283.

52. Leakey, *The Southern Kikuyu*, pp. 1014-1016; KNA/Kiambu (KBU)/76, Dagoretti Political Record Book (DPRB) 1908-1912, pp. 111-112.

3

Women and the Colonial Economy

The Kikuyu system of governance changed dramatically after Europeans appeared in the interior and conquered them. One of the most important areas of potential change was in the gender roles. For the first twenty years of the British presence, the means of production and the relations of production were not disturbed. However, with the assumption of formal political rule (1895), the British government and its agents began to restructure the domestic economy and shift the monopolization of surplus accumulation from Kikuyu men to white settlers. This forced changes in the daily work life of thousands of Kikuyu women after the establishment of the settler operated coffee estates and the subsequent recruitment of women as seasonal wage laborers.

Women were not the primary targets of this capitalist penetration. Men—widely held by colonial theorists, economic planners, and the invading settler society to be surplus labor—were the first recruits into the new tax/wage labor equation. The equation was begun with the creation of an in-kind tax levied on male householders only. When cash—obtainable only from working for Europeans—became the only acceptable way of paying taxes, millions of males were forced into this new relationship. As a result, Kenyan societies were pushed from subsistence agriculture or herding to a cash based economy. Except for the shared burden of participating in communal work projects on roads or earthworks, women were rarely compelled to work for Europeans in the first thirty years of colonialism. However, the colonial regime specifically targeted women as desirable laborers in the World War I era. Strong arm tactics were used. After reforms were made in the recruitment system (1925) and after women were directly taxed (1934), compulsion was no longer permissible nor necessary. The wage labor dynamic conflicted with the traditional domestic production for women as well as men. Women's normal responsibilities remained constant so that they had a double burden of domestic agricultural production and farm labor for European settlers. The new function did not complement their role as food producers for the peak demand for women's wage labor conflicted with the traditional agricultural cycle. Until the latter part of the colonial period, Kikuyu women had little control over and few means to seek redress of the conditions of their employment, the nature of employment, or the remuneration they received for their labor. This chapter explores the impact of settler agriculture on women as wage laborers and the involvement of the colonial state in attempting to transform the female peasantry into a rural proletariat.

Famine, Warfare, and European Trade

The first European travellers who arrived in Kikuyu country as agents of British commerce were not particularly interested in siphoning off the fruits of women's labor. They were a part of the "scramble" for African trade. In the last quarter of the nineteenth century, European financiers and investors formed trading companies to try to get a share of Africa's vast natural resources. The company that monopolized the trade out of what was to become Kenya and Uganda was the Imperial British East Africa Company (IBEAC). Its agents' early relations with the Kikuyu, while not always trouble free, were less disturbing to the Kikuyu social contract than British/Kikuyu relations in the 20th century. The agents of the IBEAC were one of several groups of Europeans who journeyed to Kikuyu territory in these decades Some were travellers who were interested in mapping the interior of East Africa. Others were the forerunners of Christian missions dispatched to East Africa. Still others were adventurers and explorers who, through sometimes dishonest measures, sought to exploit Africa's resources. The final category of European travellers were those employed to build the railroad from Mombasa to the kingdom of Buganda.

A European presence was not the only agent of change for East African societies. They were beset by famine, plague, and interethnic warfare. Two factions of the Masai engaged in chronic warfare.[1] Kikuyu migration into the Chania River region aggravated these conditions and brought them into direct conflict and competition with the Masai for land. Recurrent famines in the 1880s and 1890s made hinterland peoples even more vulnerable to European pressures. Just before the IBEAC agents arrived, a particularly severe famine struck southern Kikuyu country. The famines began with a cattle epidemic and for the next ten years, plague and famine visited people and stock. A harsh famine occurred in 1899 because the rains had failed for two years. Epidemics of small pox, rinderpest, and pleuropneumonia swept through the area in 1898 and again in 1900.[2] Kikuyu, Kamba, and Masai herds were reduced from the rinderpest. The smallpox decimated the population and locust invasions wiped out much of the remaining crops.[3] These repeated disasters were so taxing that numerous homesteads and villages in southern Kikuyu were temporarily abandoned as families retreated to Nyeri to seek shelter and succor with relatives who had not joined in the migrations of the 18th century.[4]

Under these conditions, the appearance of Europeans interested in trade and later in colonies became even more fateful. While not a common sight, Europeans popped up fairly frequently in the region during the late nineteenth century; their advent created new trade opportunities for the Kikuyu, already established as traders in local and interregional networks. Kikuyu women quickly responded to the new opportunities for trade. The level of trade in general and women's long-distance trade in particular was at a low volume. The number of all female expeditions was probably reduced. The announcement of the arrival of a party of travellers was the signal for a high level of trade to begin. The parties usually included one or more Europeans and a contingent of African porters. In some measure, the caravan trade with the Europeans replaced the regional trade which famine, plague, drought, and out-migrations had curtailed.

European travellers and caravans depended on the produce from Kikuyu homesteads for the long trek to Buganda. Travellers and diarists like Sir Frederick Jackson (1889-1890), Count Samuel Teleki (1887-1888), and Frederick, later Lord, Lugard (1891-1892) frequently spoke of the Kiambu area as a garden district.[5] The first European travellers, such as Frederick Lugard, were part of the rush to open Buganda to trade. Kiambu was a convenient reprovisioning stop on the long journey from the coast to the Lake. The Kikuyu traded maize, beans, and green vegetables to the caravans.

When Sir Frederick Jackson passed through Kiambu in 1889 he reported that the Kikuyu eagerly offered their produce to the caravan porters:

> In lieu of *posho* the men received strings of beads and were able to vary their rations, and select what they liked best amongst the following: *mahindi* (maize), *mtama* (millet), *wimbi* (small grain like turnip seed), and other cereals, *biasi* (sweet potatoes, *bazi* (peas), *kundi* (beans), and *limbi* the tuberous root af a large-leafed plant, the leaves like an arum lily being a good substitute for spinach. Sugar-cane and bananas were also abundant.[6]

In this journal entry describing the substitution of beads for the daily allowance of food (*posho*) to porters, Jackson does not make clear that it was women who bartered food for trade beads. Kikuyu women produced the vegetable products described, and since women had disposal and trading rights on these items, it was they who initially moved into trading local vegetable produce with the numerous caravans and exploratory parties who entered the district. Sugar cane, which was a male crop (see Table 2.3), was an exception.

Another example of women's enterprise is seen in their relations with the porters. C.I. Blackburne-Maze reported that Kikuyu women were "subcontracting" from the porters. For wages, women carried the porters' loads part of the way through Kiambu district:

> On this trek, if the porters can, they get women to carry their loads. The women are very strong and carry very heavy loads. ... The porters pay them a few cents. ... We got off about 5.30. The porters had women to carry their loads for them, as it was very up and downhill again. The women can carry much heavier loads than the men. ... The porters give them about eight or ten cents for the trek, which is three halfpence or thereabouts. I think I'm correct in saying, that between Fort Hall and Nairobi would be the only place where women will carry men's loads while the men walk beside them.[7]

Blackburne-Maze seemed almost astonished by the physical strength of these Kiambu women who carried the heavy loads of the hardy and resourceful porters. What is of more import is that this passage documents an unexpected relationship with the caravans. We should not be surprised that local populations sought to extract wealth from the passing caravans. What is unusual is that women moved a feature of their domestic production—the carrying of loads of water or wood—into an income generating activity. Also of note is that, for the first time, women's labor was not performed for their own homestead or on communal projects but for non-kin who were aliens.

Lamentably, these good relationships and early eagerness for trade and income soon became strained. Europeans, like John Boyes, ranged freely over the country entering into local conflicts. Boyes became a petty warlord. Originally Boyes had formed a partnership with another European to supply provisions to railway workers. Already something of an adventurer, he quickly decided that more profit could be gained from trading with the Kikuyu. For several years he travelled through the three Kikuyu districts making treaties with locals and becoming so embroiled in village conflicts that he often used his firearms to attack the rivals of his Kikuyu allies. In 1903, he was summoned to Nairobi by the Protectorate government to answer charges of acting as a member of an armed band of robbers. Boyes had attacked Kikuyu villages in Fort Hall (later Murang'a) district and the northern Kikuyu district in 1901 and killed many since he believed that some of the residents were responsible for the death of a Swahili porter in his employ.[8] Boyes was convicted and deported.[9]

Boyes was one of the more notorious European adventurers who crossed trails with the Kikuyu. Other, more conventional, traders and travellers were Joseph Thompson (1883-1884), Bishop James Hannington (1885), and J.R.L. MacDonald (1891-1894).[10] They described Kikuyu society, the availability of food for trade, and the political relations they were able to establish with the Kikuyu.[11] Frederick Jackson, for example, observed that:

> The men are short, thickset, and strong, but their expression is spoiled by their hazel-red eyes, accentuated by inflamed lids due to wood smoke in their huts. The same applied to their even more sturdy little women, always cheerful and merry, and marvels at carrying loads on their backs with a supporting leather strap across their foreheads. Some of their loads of firewood were so heavy that the strap sank deep into the flesh below the level of the surrounding skin. To unload without assistance, they had to sit down and lean back; but they cannot get up without help when so loaded.[12]

Jackson also was astute enough to be able to see similarities in Masai and Kikuyu material culture. In all but weapons, a Kikuyu warrior seemed to be identical in appearance to a Masai warrior. The Kikuyu preferred weapon was the sword or bow and arrow.

Masai warriors used spears. Jackson thought that women's dress showed even closer cross-borrowings with the Masai:

> On the other hand, there was even more marked similarity in the dress of the women to that of the Masai with their dressed skins in place of small ornamental aprons, and also the brass 'catherine-wheel' ear ornaments of the married women, but there the similarity ends as the one was short, thickset and plump, the other tall and thin.[13]

When Jackson was recording his observations in 1890, attitudes of suspicion and hostility between the passing caravans and the local communities were normal.[14] Kikuyu accused the members of the caravans of committing acts of theft, crop destruction, abusing locals, and sexually abusing women. These incidents occurred regularly enough to engender antipathy towards the Europeans and the Arab or Swahili porters they employed. Kikuyu sensibilities had been so lacerated that the IBEAC agents were acutely aware of the problems. Nonetheless, IBEAC agents helped to perpetuate the negative attitudes. The company's agents carried out several military strikes against the Kikuyu. These acts of war continued until the company surrendered its charter and turned over its trading sphere to the British government when the Protectorate government was established on June 26, 1895.[15] The military strikes, referred to as "hammering the natives" by troops in the field, prejudiced the Kikuyu towards most Europeans. When IBEAC agents were choosing the location of their southern Kikuyu station, Frederick Lugard was reluctant to build on a site at Dagoretti because:

> It was in the heart of the villages and fields of the Kikuyu. This I knew would lead to constant trouble owing to passing caravans pilfering from the crops or interfering with the women. Finally a site above the Dagoretti stream was chosen under the guidance of the local chief Waiyaki.[16]

Despite contrary advice, the stockaded company fort was built. It was the seventh IBEAC trading and reprovisioning station. By October 1890, conditions were at a crisis stage. Caravans making use of the fort facilities:

> Owing to a want of discipline in the passing caravans whose men robbed the crops and otherwise made themselves troublesome, the people became estranged and presently murdered several porters.[17]

When the company tried to control the Kikuyu, they besieged the fort until the agent George Wilson was forced to abandon it in 1891 and move company operations to Fort Smith (later named Fort Hall) in Murang'a district. The Kikuyu set fire to the Dagoretti post and burned it to the ground. The company agent sent a retaliatory "hammering" expedition against the Dagoretti Kikuyu from Fort Smith resulting in many deaths and the destruction of crops and cattle.[18]

A second signal indicator of the poor relations is an incident between George Purkiss, the IBEAC agent, and Waiyaki, the supposed chief, who had assisted Lugard in deciding on the IBEAC Dagoretti site.[19] After provocation, and allegedly while drunk, Waiyaki attacked Purkiss who was also drunk. Company judgment on Waiyaki was that he should be deported. He died on the long march to the coast.[20]

These two incidents illustrate the general tenor of relations. The Kikuyu learned important lessons from both. From the first, they realized that the company agents freely used their superior military technology to "pacify" the Kikuyu and Kiambu district would be no exception. Other IBEAC forts were besieged by the Kikuyu in failed attempts to drive the Europeans out or at the least to punish them for acts of robbery and personal violence. Retaliatory expeditions were sent from Machakos district to bring the Kikuyu back into line.[21] The second incident taught the Kikuyu that even Kikuyu agents of the company such as Waiyaki were subject to IBEAC disciplinary actions as were those who were not allied with the company. The IBEAC—a trading company—acted as a government in all but name. It made war, adjudicated, disposed of prisoners, claimed territory, and levied assessments on local populations.

Seizing these powers did not save the company from ruin. By 1895, company resources were strained and it was nearly bankrupt. The officers in London dissolved the company on June 25th. The following day the British government assumed control of the defunct company's territory and the East African Protectorate was established. IBEAC agents in the field were put on the Colonial Office payroll to maintain continuity during the period of transition from trading sphere to colony. The Colonial Office kept the administrative and territorial structure the company had devised. A district officer was in charge of each district. Each one reported directly to the chief administrator at the coast.[22]

As the 19th century drew to a close, the British were on the brink of assuming formal political control in East Africa. The government inherited the former IBEAC territories, the problems of controlling local populations, and the right to exploit their resources. Throughout Africa in the decade after the "scramble for Africa," African populations tried to keep their political independence and economic autonomy in the face of British, French, Belgian, Portuguese, German, and Italian aggression. Anti-imperial wars affected every region. The Kikuyu population were no exception to this. The British sent several expeditions against the Kiambu Kikuyu. One of the earliest entries in the logbook kept by the district officials relates that repeated military strikes were made against the Kikuyu between 1896 and 1898. The Kiambu Kikuyu remained defiant even after a final strike was made against them in 1902.[23] The intent of these actions was to teach the Kikuyu lessons of obedience. By the beginning of the new century, the Kikuyu were enervated by twenty–five years of disaster: famine, epidemics, drought, and warfare with the Europeans. They had been "pacified." In the first decade of the 20th century, the Colonial Office, colonial officers in Nairobi, and district officers were able to turn their attention to transforming indigenous political, economic, and social structures so that other groups could be brought under colonial control.

Kikuyu women had eagerly grasped at the new market and trading opportunities. Perched on the edge of profound economic change, many women had willingly changed a portion of domestic production to serve a new need. The potential of this were profound. Women could have created a market garden industry to service the caravans and railroads. There was also a possibility of women initiating a vast business to export their products to Europe. Such a change did not occur. Before twenty years of colonial rule had passed, government officials and white settlers succeeded in pushing Kikuyu women and men into new economic patterns. Arbitrary taxation, land alienation, forced labor, and physical coercion were used to create a scenario which subordinated African economic interests to European ones.

Colonial Economic Policy

The policies that began this subordination were the Hut Tax Regulations (1901), the Crown Land Grants Act (1902), the Communal Labor Law (1908), and the Hut and Poll Tax Ordinance (1902). Direct taxation was imposed selectively. At first it applied to adult males only. Later it was expanded to include juvenile males and adult females. The alienation of land under the Crown Land Grants Act produced immediate impacts in all sectors of society. When the Protectorate was proclaimed in 1895, the British government began considering the question of how much legal right it had to assume control of land in the colony. The debate ended in 1899 when the British government accepted the argument that the declaration of the Protectorate gave Great Britain the right to assume sovereignty over all land as long as existing private ownership rights were not violated. This was interpreted to mean that the only land that could be declared Crown land was that which was not physically occupied by Africans in 1895.[24] The ultimate goal of the policy was to make land available for European settlement and ownership. Because of the enactment of the Crown Lands Act, African landowners lost great amounts of land. Moreover, the alienated lands were the most productive arable land with the best conditions for crop production and cattle raising. Most of the land was either sold or awarded as grant land to settlers. By 1904 220,000 acres of land had been redistributed.[25] Between 1904 and 1912, the Kiambu Kikuyu lost 60,000 acres. Land alienation had an important impact on women. The amount of arable land on which food for consumption could be cultivated was reduced. Loss of land meant that a large segment of the adult male population had to migrate to seek wages; therefore, women found themselves left on the homesteads to cope with the full responsibility for domestic production. Loss of land also meant that, over two or three generations, the size of homesteads were reduced. A result was that less land was allotted to Kikuyu brides from their husband's portion of the land. Even before land alienation, large numbers of Kikuyu were landless. Those who would have sought *ahoi* contracts with Kikuyu landowners were now left with the options of looking for squatter contracts with Europeans, wage labor in the cities and rural towns, casual labor on European homesteads, or joining the informal sector as hawkers, traders, or prostitutes.

Change in economic production was generated through the Communal Labor Law (1908) that was justified as necessary because of a lack of sufficient voluntary labor to build the physical infrastructure of roads, waterways, bridges, and railways.[26] Only Africans were required to give this labor which had its roots in the defunct traditions of corveé labor in pre-modern Europe. The British government's position was that such projects were for the public good. The government also persisted in the belief that offering wages for this work would be futile since Africans were unaccustomed to working for wages and could not be induced to work for them as their traditional economy supplied most of their needs.[27] Coercion, fines, and imprisonment were the punishments for failure to comply with the Communal Labor Law which required Africans to work for the state. In some cases, the law was used to force Africans to work for private individuals.

Coercion was a standard method used to insure obedience to labor and taxation requirements before 1910.[28] The Protectorate government involved Africans in local level government through the Native Authority laws (1910, 1912) which authorized government appointed headmen to compel Africans to perform corveé labor on government projects. Under these laws, entire village populations were forced to suspend their own work in domestic production on command of the European district officer as relayed through the headman and his hired retainers.[29] This uncompensated labor could be required of all able-bodied males and females for six days out of every three months. The penalty for noncompliance with the compulsory orders in the Roads Ordinance was a fine of thirty shillings or one month's imprisonment.[30] Women were regularly used in this communal labor; this was done legally before the revisions in the 1920s. Even after the reforms prohibited using African women for this kind of work, government representatives continued to force women to do hard labor in road-building.[31] During the World War I labor crisis, government officials forced women to work on coffee estates owned by European settlers. At the urging of the settlers, the Governor argued that this policy was necessary to make up for the loss of male laborers who had been conscripted to work as porters with the army.[32] Complaints about the use of coercion in Central Province were sent to the Colonial Office in London as late as 1935.

The Village Headman Ordinance (1902) authorized these government appointed officials to recruit labor for public work deemed to be in the interest of the village. This arrangement was subverted to serve the needs of settler agri-business for soon the settlers were using the authority of the headman to procure laborers for their estates and farms. European farmers paid chiefs and headmen to produce large numbers of village laborers.[33] The chiefs' tribal retainers also received monthly wages and bribes from European estate owners.[34] Local European officials cooperated with and sometimes assisted in this process.[35] Headmen came to view an ability to turn out labor as a measure of their capability. This was encouraged by the government policy of noting the amount of labor recruited by the chiefs in official district records. The District Commissioner (DC) arrested chiefs who did not produce adequate amounts of labor.[36] Under these arrangements where African and European officials were involved in producing African workers, arbitrary and forced recruitment practices often occurred. In Kiambu and Fort Hall districts, chiefs' agents terrorized the populations using tactics of expropriating property, beating men and women who resisted the forced labor, and sexually abusing women.[37]

Officially recognized full-time, non-government labor agents were authorized by the Senior Commissioner to recruit workers for public and private employees. These authorizations were good for one year and allowed the agent to work for a specific European employer. The labor agents notified the DC of their presence and activities when they visited the Reserves.[38] Incidents of recruiters operating without government permission occurred. Some recruiters represented themselves as having official authorization to force Africans to work even after that practice had been specifically prohibited by the Colonial Office in 1921.[39] In Kiambu, the district officer told chiefs to supply laborers for coffee estate owners before the practices were prohibited.[40] Recruiters also gave bribes to chiefs and headmen. When these and other abuses occurred, district officials protected the chiefs and agents by not reporting the incidents to the Provincial administration or the Colonial Office in London. Africans complained about the abuses with few results. Some missionaries such as Archdeacon Owen, medical missionary Marion Stevenson, Reverend L.J. Beecher, and Reverend H. Leakey publicized the labor exploitation and helped Africans who were trying to get the government to reform labor recruitment practices.

William McGregor Ross, who at one time worked as a government railway employee, also reported abuses in the labor system.[41]

The labor system was burdensome for African men and women even after reforms were made. They resisted it. The colonial government imposed taxes—the third linchpin after land alienation and forced labor—to overcome this resistance and transform independent African communities into a rural proletariat.[42] Arthur Hardinge, the first Commissioner for the Protectorate, created the first solutions to this problem. He proposed a scheme to tax Africans directly in 1899.[43] The Hut Tax (1901) served the dual purpose of creating revenue and converting African peasants into wage laborers.[44] The initial level of taxation was set at 2 rupees, but one year later, the rate was raised to 3 rupees. Three rupees was the amount of wages African laborers received for one month's labor. Taxes could be paid in cash, kind, or labor. At the discretion of the Commissioner, a tax of 3 rupees was levied on each adult in African households with more than one adult in residence.[45] In 1908, the Hut and Poll taxes were applied to the Kikuyu. The 1910 Hut and Poll Tax revisions eliminated the Commissioner's discretionary powers and all African areas were required to remit the taxes. The second major change stipulated that juveniles were required to pay the Poll Tax and a tax of 3 rupees was levied on all males over the age of sixteen. Over the next eight years, the tax was raised twice—to 5 rupees (1915) and 8 rupees (1920). Increased taxation was an early irritant and an important contributor to the Thuku riot in 1922 (see Chapter 6). After the riot, taxes were reduced to six rupees or 12 shillings.[46]

Hut and Poll taxes fulfilled Hardinge's initial purpose of raising revenue from Africans. Taxes collected in 1905-1906 totalled £44,451 British sterling. By 1910, the tax revenue collected from Africans had doubled to £105,000. Eleven years later, the amount had increased to £658,414 British sterling.[47] After 1934, chiefs were used as an instrument of tax collection.[48] They were involved in labor recruitment almost as soon as the polices were implemented. There was a thirty-three year lag in giving them a role in tax collection because the British believed that the poorly paid chiefs and retainers would steal the taxes. After the salaries were upgraded in 1934, chiefs and headmen were given tax collection responsibility. Thus, by the early 1930s, African chiefs were an important part of the local government and assisted in extracting two important commodities from Kikuyu households: labor and cash.

Women's Labor on the Coffee Estates

Males as head of households were responsible for the payment of the direct taxes. However, the effect of the taxation system was to redirect the entire family's labor to pay them. Up until 1937, the Native Affairs Department considered working for wages to obtain cash to pay taxes to be a family affair. Under the 1910 Hut Tax Ordinance, all adult males and females were counted in the tax assessment that a male head of householder had to pay. Failure to pay the taxes could result in a three month jail sentence unless one received a tax exemption because of infirmity or impoverishment.[49] In 1934 women were directly taxed for the first time under the Hut and Poll Tax Ordinance 40.[50] Old women and widows with little means to support their families could petition and obtain exemption from direct taxation.[51] Although the direct taxation of women came several decades after they were first used in wage labor on the coffee estates, the application of a tax liability to them coincided with an increase in the demand for females to work on coffee estates for there was an acute shortage of female laborers in the 1930s. Family cooperation and pooling of resources to pay taxes was declining by the mid-1930s, and women had to find the means to pay for themselves.[52] In Kiambu, their major source of cash was from seasonal labor on the coffee estates.

Coffee was first introduced into Kenya in the late 19th century. John Patterson is credited with making the first experiments when he obtained seed from the McKenzie Company and planted it at Kibwezi.[53] The McKenzie Company applied for a Crown Grant of land to plant coffee in 1895. By 1900, when Patterson left the Church of Scotland Mission station, the coffee trees had grown to a height of 20 feet and had sprouted into the multiple stem system.[54] European farmers in Central Province, where land had already been alienated, were growing the crop in 1902.[55] By 1912, coffee was produced in quantities large enough to be exported from the colony.[56] Coffee took a firm hold as Kenya's primary export crop. The value of the 1912 shipments was £68,798 British sterling. European exports constituted 5% of the total value of domestic exports from the colony in 1913 and coffee represented three-fifths of the total value. In 1932, European exports rose to 76% of the total value of exports; seventy-three percent of the European exports was the coffee crop.[57] Coffee proved itself to be one of the most important income producers for the settler population. The amount of land put under coffee production grew steadily in the first three decades of settler agriculture. In 1926, the amount of land that had been converted from indigenous production to settler coffee estates was 65,150 acres. The yield was 115,530 CWT of coffee.[58] In 1938, 94,000 acres of land was used for growing coffee.[59]

Settler enthrallment with producing coffee had taken firm root. The introduction and success of coffee production had far reaching consequences for Kikuyu women, changing in some part the nature of work and previous patterns of work. Once the crop was produced in large quantities, the settler community and local government officials struggled with the question of how to create a constant supply of seasonal labor for tending and picking the crop. Planters had partially solved the problem of an adequate labor supply for producing other commodities such as maize with the use of squatter labor. This solution was not workable for Kiambu as a coffee producing district because planters needed most workers on a seasonal basis only. To keep costs of production low, planters did not want to compensate these workers at even the most basic level on a full-time basis; part of the squatter contract allowed him and his family to be semi-permanent residents on European land with rights to graze stock and grow crops. Coffee plantations required nearly 70% of their yearly totals of workers between the months of September and December.[60] The very briefness of the labor contract made the work unattractive for most laborers in the colony. And since coffee pickers were paid the lowest adult wages in the colony, a voluntary flow of adult workers to the estates was difficult to sustain. As in other enterprises, most of the laborers for coffee were procured because of the administration's policies of increasing the labor pool for settlers and government by imposing taxes. Coffee planters, finding the available labor supply inadequate for their purposes, constantly lobbied for more assistance.

Settler pressure on the colonial government to solve the problem of attracting African labor bore fruit in the decade 1910-1920. In 1913, settlers proposed to the Native Land Commission that the government should choose from the alternatives of raising taxes, further reducing lands in the Reserves or using corporal punishment on Africans who refused to work for Europeans on the farms and estates.[61] The commission's solution was that government officials should be used to increase the number of Africans available for wage labor through what was termed "encouragement" of labor.[62] World War I forced a crisis in labor demand. The settler/government alliance was faced with a need for recruiting ever larger amounts of workers as the needs for labor conflicted. First, the pre-war expansion in the building of an infrastructure of roads, railways, and buildings continued. Second, cash crop production of coffee, tea, maize, and sisal expanded. And third, the war itself increased the demand for labor since thousands of African males were conscripted as porters for the British in the East African campaign. In 1916, the DC for Kiambu reported that the Reserve was so depleted of men that women and children were doing work which men had traditionally done.[63] The Dagoretti subdistrict report noted that:

> The two most important factors effecting the lives of the natives. . .have been the recruitment for the carrier corps and the levying of large fines under the Stock Produce Theft Ordinance. . . . The former has affected the life of the Wakikuyu considerably, removing as it has large numbers of young men from their traditional work. . . . These functions fall to the lot of the women and children more than in the past: one consequence being that women have less time to keep the *shambas* clean so that the food supply necessarily suffers to a certain extent.[64]

Severe food shortages resulted. Women and children had to prepare the new ground for sowing for the next rainy season (a male task). The increased work was so great that much of the crop of *mtama* was not harvested. It either rotted on the stalk or sprouted before it could be harvested.[65] The wartime conscriptions placed the added burden of doing "men's traditional work" on women, but the removal of the males also meant that Kikuyu women and children were viewed as a potential pool of wage laborers. The settlers began to use female and juvenile labor for coffee cultivation.[66]

This was a turning point in incorporating women and children into wage labor. Compulsory labor was officially endorsed by Governor Sir Henry Conway in 1917.[67] Under the leadership of his successor Governor Northey, the governor's office tried to fill the increasing settler demands for labor by raising Hut and Poll taxes. The amount of labor produced was not enough to meet state and settler needs. The Governor subsequently issued the Northey Circular (Labour Circular 1 of October 23, 1919), directing DCs, labor agents and African chiefs to procure female and juvenile labor for private and public projects. By 1920, they were heavily involved in "encouraging" women and children to work for settlers. A retiring DC for Kiambu noted in his handing over report:

> A very heavy coffee crop has been picked mostly by the women and children. . . . The whole situation has been somewhat altered by Labor Circular 1 in which we are instructed to obtain labor for private and public enterprises through chiefs and headmen.[68]

Local officials responded enthusiastically to the directive because it placed them in a favorable position with the often highly influential local planters. The response was also myopic for the officials often failed to note and appreciate African dissatisfaction with the system. Little control was exerted over recruiters or over the treatment African women and children received. In 1919, the newly appointed DC of Kiambu summarized the efforts in "encouraging" labor:

> The outstanding feature of the year has been the efforts of my predecessor to supplement the male labour with voluntary female help in coffee picking. I feel sure that this plan has been much appreciated and the former have cheerfully gone to pick, no cases of abuse of the scheme have, during my short tenure, been brought to my notice, but there is a tendency to use women for labour for other kinds of work which will undoubtedly cause discontent in the future and the whole scheme may have to be abandoned.[69]

Women were not cheerful about the scheme. According to Wambui Wagarama, a resident of Lower Kabete in Kiambu district and a veteran political activist, discontent and anger with the scheme was at a high level in the 1920s. Girls and their parents were deeply opposed to the practice of "obtaining" them for labor; they considered themselves to be working as slaves:

> We started asking for our freedom when we were young girls during the war of 1914. We started putting murram and tarmac along the road and were forced to push the leveller. We made the European feel angry. At that time one girl was killed on the road. She was beaten in the head and died, they were being led by Kiyanjui. Then Harry Thuku was jailed. And our parents said we shouldn't work on the roads but at that

> time we were caught again when there was a fight at Nairobi and the fight was because the women asked for the men's pants.
>
> We were brought to a coffee estate here. We were picking coffee and cultivating and after five weeks we were given thirty shillings and no food. There was a man who was looking after the women and if he saw that you left one part uncultivated he would beat you. A girl called Njeri was beaten and her leg was broken. After that we stopped doing the work of picking coffee and cultivating as well. When Harry Thuku was sent to Somaliland our parents refused to let us work. We were doing shaking and scratching (pretended illness) while working on the estates to annoy the Europeans. We did this so that Harry Thuku could be released.[70]

This recollection of conditions for women of Kiambu district describes how women and girls were used for road-building projects (pushing the heavy machines used to level the road and spread the tar) as well as for coffee picking. The road work was the "tendency to use women for other kinds of labor" referred to in the district commission report. The commissioner's mild concern, given early 20th century British notions of appropriate work for women of whatever class, underlines a colonial attitude of callousness towards African women which would not have been tolerated in Britain, even under wartime conditions. Kiyanjui was the local British appointed chief who was required, under the terms of the circular, to procure female and juvenile labor to build the road and work for settlers.

Road-building was not the only non-agricultural enterprise that used female laborers in this era. In the 1920s, the Forest Department sent uniformed African employees to recruit women to carry loads of planks from the forest. They were forced to transport the planks for "some twenty miles over one of the hardest pieces of country in the Protectorate."[71] Headman Mukui lodged a complaint about this with the DC who responded that Mukui should not recruit women to carry loads for the Forest Department.[72]

Physical coercion in the form of beatings was used to compel these women to participate in the unpopular work. The DC's misperception of cheerful attitudes may have come from the fact that women sang *muthirigos* (protest songs sung while shaking and patting the buttocks) as they worked. These songs were criticisms and complaints about the conditions. Women had used *muthirigos* as a way of criticizing pre-colonial male authority. When they were put on the estates, forced to build roads, or to carry planks for the

Forest Department, they turned this form of protest against government officials, local chiefs, and recruiters.

The labor system promoted violence against workers; women were not excluded from that circle of violence. Acting under the directive of Labour Circular 1, the agents of colonialism committed more acts of violence against women than they did in connection with any other colonial policy. The violence may have been systemic and deliberately used to intimidate women to turn out as laborers and to stifle their complaints to the district officers. Physical outrages and intimidation of women connected with coffee production reached a level which was only to be surpassed by violence perpetuated against them during the Mau Mau Emergency in the 1950s. If Kikuyu families were in a favorable enough financial position, they did not allow their women to work on the coffee plantations because they were exposed to sexual abuse.[73] On October 24, 1916, Kikuyu elders complained to the DC that a male escort was necessary for women who worked on the estates. Male laborers, especially on the Mbagathi farm, assaulted women laborers. The elders also told how women were being assaulted while they were cutting firewood in the forests. The DC's solution was to suggest that women go into the forest in groups to obtain firewood and the elders provide male escorts.[74] The problems became so acute that missionaries became concerned and began to petition the government and to solicit public support to stop the "encouragement" policy. In a memo written to the *East African Standard,* Protestant Bishops in East Africa revealed the defects of the system and their own reasons for objecting to employing women in non-domestic labor:

> The decision to "encourage" women and children to labour, bearing in mind the meaning that will inevitably be read into the word "encourage" seems to us a dangerous policy. The children below a certain age should be at home or at school. The women work at home: the plantations, the supply of the daily food, the cooking, the care of the children, and the home depend upon the mothers and the wives.
>
> To "encourage" as native headmen (with the fear of dismissal behind him) would "encourage" the women and girls to go out from their homes into neighbouring plantations, would be to court disaster, physical and moral. Whatever labour legislation is introduced the women and children should be left out of it.[75]

Disaster was indeed courted! By 1920 it was common practice for planters to give bribes to retainers for recruiting female laborers. Reports of the problem had made their way to the Governor's office. The Provincial Commissioner of Central Province recorded that:

> . . .tribal retainers who had escorted women to farms were in many cases being given monthly wages or gratuities and as it seemed likely that considerable abuse might arise the position was represented to His Excellency [the Governor] who has expressed his opinion that the arrangement is undesirable and should be stopped which has now been done.[76]

The DC tried to stop the bribes and abuse, but, one year later, was himself cautious about predicting how long the reform would last. He was very much aware that all the planters needed tremendous numbers of coffee pickers at the same time. He thought planters would continue to give bribes since it was "extremely likely that some will—to save their crops—offer inducements to the Retainers and Chiefs whereby much trouble may and probably will result in the forcing of women out to work by the Retainers."[77] The use of force on women to compel them to turn out was simple extortion. Planters, retainers, and chiefs needed to be watched to avert trouble and such was the advice recorded in the colonial record.[78]

Women Laborers, the East African Association , and Reform

By 1922, the abuses of the system of bribery and extortion were clear to residents of the district. Despite the DC's intervention, retainers were still bribed, and women were still forcibly recruited and subjected to assault. These conditions became a key issue in a confrontation between Africans and the colonial government at a meeting held at Dagoretti in Kiambu district. The champion of this and other issues, later identified with the nationalist movement, was a political association headed by Harry Thuku. Thuku was a Kiambu Kikuyu who received a mission education at the Gospel Mission Station, Kambui. Thuku worked for the settler newspaper, *The Leader*, from 1913 to 1917. In 1918, he was working for the Treasury Department. He was one of the founding members of the East African Association (EAA), the first African political association, in the 1920s. In the economic crisis which followed World

War I, colonial economic policy was changed to require African men to carry the *kipande*, a fingerprint and work history worn an a string around the neck. To cope with the crisis of production and falling revenue, the government doubled the Poll taxes and agreed to an across the board reduction of African wages by one-third. The EAA became an important articulator of African dissent. Thuku and the EAA held meetings in Nairobi and in rural areas to discuss and protest these policies. At a meeting held at Dagoretti in June of 1921 by a government commission investigating African complaints, the EAA brought up the questions of the *kipande*, the high level of taxation, and abuse of women resulting from the labor policies.[79] The EAA gave evidence on the labor abuses and, led by Thuku, maintained that women were frequently detained away from their homes by tribal retainers. According to their testimony, sixty women had recently been escorted by the retainers to a coffee estate and had not been allowed to return home. Also, a number of women had been sexually abused and impregnated. The EAA asked for reforms.[80]

Kikuyu women were aware and supportive of the activities of the association; they credited it and Harry Thuku with forcing the government to stop the abuses. When questioned on changes in government policy, respondents said that it was due to Harry Thuku that women were given more just treatment:

> Q: How were you treated as workers on the coffee estates?
>
> A: They treated us badly; we used to go to work from early morning until afternoon, we were beaten, and given hard work. They even refused to give us our wages.
>
> Q: Was there anyone to whom you could complain about your treatment?
>
> A: No, you couldn't complain. If you did you were punished again.[81]

Women perceived themselves to have no advocates and no power to sway the colonial representatives towards better treatment. They attributed the changes after 1922 to Thuku's efforts, even though many actors participated in the movement for reform. A considerable amount of criticism came from Commissioner Ainsworth, Archdeacon Owen, and missionaries from the Church of Scotland Mission. Owen, for example, sent a stream of correspondence to the Aborigines Protection Society in London which in turn applied pressure on the Colonial Office in London.[82]

Kikuyu women believed that "Harry Thuku is the one who

fought for us and stopped us from working like slaves."[83] Songs were sung in his praise. One popular song talked of his championship naming him "the leader of the women" and suggested that he became an political prisoner because he tried to help women:

> Philip should be frightened since he is the one
> Who caused the leader of the women to be deported.
> Therefore women are still in the coffee lands.[84]

In this song, Philip refers to Philipo Karanja who, along with Josiah Karanja and Chief Koinange, was a leader of the moderate Kikuyu Association (KA). This organization of chiefs opposed the East African Association and competed with it for Kikuyu loyalty. So fierce was the conflict that leaders of the KA helped the British secure evidence against Thuku. They cooperated with the government in his subsequent arrest leading to his trial and deportation in March 1922. The EAA was banned. Thuku's arrest caused a major riot in Nairobi. Another women's protest song describes women's use of the traditional method of protest—a physical gesture towards the buttocks:

> When Harry Thuku left that is the time I started
> Scratching my buttocks. When he came back
> The scratching stopped. Let the white man face that
> Because he is the one who forced Harry Thuku
> To go to Europe.[85]

The "scratching of the buttocks" refers to the method women used to criticize men when they had committed serious offenses against women. In this form of ritual cursing (*gutaramira ng'ania*) women of a village or ridge lined up in front of the offending male, turned their backs and lifted their skirts over their heads.[86] These *muthirigo* songs became a popular means of expressing criticism; they show how women adapted a traditional method of protest into a critique of colonial officials and their agents. This corporate action indicated that they no longer recognized the authority of the man who was cursed. Kikuyu women used these crude gestures and rude songs to speak for them since the usual method of lodging a complaint with the chiefs resulted in more punishment. Women also turned to this form of protest because the association which had spoken against their abuse was banned.

The malpractices were only slowly reformed and the effectiveness of the reforms was partial. In response to the complaints, the colonial government created the Native Women's Protection Act (1923). Three basic provisions were to govern labor conditions for females and juveniles. Estate owners were to provide proper accommodation for single women workers, women who were not living with a husband or father in residence on the estate were not allowed to remain on the grounds of the estates after dark, and women were not to work on estates which were further than three miles from their homes.[87] Official opinion held that the Act was successful. The Native Affairs Department noted in its 1928 report that:

> The women and children usually live in their own villages, or with squatters or relations on the estates. It is unusual to find a congregation of non-resident female or juvenile labourers, detached from their relations or friends, but separate huts are provided for any who require them. Conditions governing the employment of women are regulated by the Native Women's Protection Rules, 1923. So far no abuses have been reported. It is the choice of the women and children or that of husbands or parents, that they undertake this work. They appear to be quite contented with their conditions and their health is not adversely affected.[88]

Prices, Wages, and Work Requirements

The Labor Department kept careful records of the number and nature of violations of its own laws when the violators were African workers. To each report is appended an account of criminal acts and punishments given to Africans for those infringements. The colonial administrators were either unable or unwilling to record employer infringement of workers' rights whenever they were committed in the name of the government or as a result of the forced/voluntary labor on the coffee estates. In particular, the district officials did not give the same attention to labor abuses when the workers were seasonal and/or female. For this reason, it is difficult to estimate the magnitude of labor related abuses of women which were caused by the colonial labor laws. It is, however, possible to define some parameters which show the effect the work had on women's lives from oral interviews, district records, and labor reports issued by the Native Affairs Department.

Large numbers of Kikuyu women and children were involved in coffee production. In 1923, the Kiambu district officer estimated that on a monthly average, 3,098 women worked on the estates. The figure of 2,947 juvenile laborers appears for the same year.[89] Within two years, settler demand for this kind of labor had pushed the figures to a total of 11,721 women and children workers employed monthly. During the harvest season 27,994 women and children laborers were used.[90] The female and juvenile workers, counted as monthly workers on the coffee estates, represented a large proportion of African women and children who worked for settlers in agriculture and cattle raising.

TABLE 3.1 Women and Children Coffee Workers

Year	*Women CL**	*Children CL**	*Total W/C** Coffee Laborers*	*Total W/C** Farm Laborers*
1923	3,089	2,947	6,036	16,551
1926	5,477	11,315	16,792	20,000

Source: KNA. NAD Annual Report 1925, p. 64.; NAD Annual Report 1926, p. 79; EAS, 1 January 1926.
*Coffee Laborers
**Women and Children

In 1925, a total of 6,609 African women and 9,942 children were farm laborers. In 1926, out of 78,427 African workers, the average number of women workers per month was 5,477. Juvenile workers averaged 11,315.[91] In 1926, 16,792 of the 20,000 women and children who were employed for wage labor in the colony worked on the coffee estates.[92] Most of these workers lived in the Reserves and walked to the estates each day. Squatter labor was not the primary labor arrangement for women and children. Over the next thirty years in response to an expanding market for coffee, more acreage was expropriated and put under cultivation. As coffee became more profitable, the numbers of daily workers on the estates mushroomed.[93] By 1956 there were 27,000 women working on the estates in Kiambu district alone.[94]

The remuneration for women's work on the estates did not increase as coffee profits and labor needs spiraled upwards. International coffee prices rose twice during the colonial period. Between 1912 and 1919, the value of coffee exports from the colony rose from £68,797 to £244,468 British sterling.[95] Between 1926 and

1928, coffee production doubled rising from 115,530 to 246,292 CWT.[96] World prices for coffee declined in 1920 and despite increased production Kenyan settlers only earned £92,507 for their crop.[97] The Depression also pushed coffee earnings down. In 1926, coffee yielded £130 per ton. Prices in 1928 dropped to £120.[98] During the Depression years, the world market price fell to £65 per ton. There was an overall 39% decline in the value during the downward cycle.[99] As the international coffee prices fell, drastic wage reductions were instituted. African wages were reduced by 30% to 50% in every district.[100]

The second period of expansion occurred after 1940. World War II caused a boom in agricultural prices. Settlers were able to obtain government price supports and loans.[101] During the war export prices rose; the cost of goods in the colony also rose from 60% to 100%. For some African workers wages were increased. However, the only workers whose real wages kept pace with the rising cost of living were those employed by the government. Wages of non-government African male laborers lagged behind the cost of living increase since their wage increases ranged from 25% to 77%.[102]

TABLE 3.2 Minimum Wage Rates

Class	*Rate*	*Method of Payment*
Coffee Picker	15-20 cents*	Per 4 gallons w/food allowance
Farm Hands (squatter)	8-10 Shs.**	Per 30 days w/food
Dock Hands (Kisumu)	18 Shs.	Per 30 days w/food
Fuel Cutters	14-16 Shs.	Per 30 days w/food
General Laborers (Out districts)	14-16 Shs.	Per 30 days w/food
General Laborers (Towns)	18-20 Shs.	Per 30 days w/food
Railway Construction	16 Shs.	Per 30 days w/food
Juveniles (Generally)	6-8 Shs.	Per 30 days w/food
Women	10-12 Shs.	Per 30 days w/food
Railway Maintenance	14 Shs.	Per 30 days w/food
Plantation Hands (Sisal)	14-16 Shs.	Per 30 days w/food
Farm Hands (Generally)	12-14 Shs.	Per 30 days w/food

Source: KNA. NAD Annual Report 1925, p. 64; NAD Annual Report, 1925, p. 89; NAD Annual Report 1928, p. 110.

* Twenty five cents was equivalent to four British pence.

**Shillings

Women coffee estate workers experienced even greater decline in their real wages for they did not receive even these increases. Coffee pickers were among the lowest paid categories of workers. With the exception of child labor, women were the lowest paid workers in the colony. Table 3.2 displays official minimum wage rates for twelve categories of workers. Women permanent agricultural workers were paid 10 to 12 shillings per month with a food allotment. Juvenile farm laborers were paid 6 to 8 shillings per month with a food allotment.[103] In the 1920s, coffee pickers received ten cents to fifteen cents for each four gallons of coffee beans they picked and a food allotment of a pound of maize meal. In the 1940s the food allotment was discontinued.[104] Women received no wage rate increases for long periods, though some African males did receive small increases even before the substantial cost of living raises which came with the inflation cycle after World War II. For example, African Public Works Department employees received a wage increase of 2 shillings per month in 1926; in 1928 squatters were given an increase that placed their minimum wages between 6 and 12 shillings per month.

The peak period when workers were needed on the estates occurs from October to March. Tables 3.3–3.5 show the biannual distribution of labor, the average numbers of workers required for each 100 acres of coffee (units), the percentages of women and children that made up the labor force on coffee trees in the different stages of growth, and the numbers of men, women, and children employed on the estates in the three stages of production in Central Province.

TABLE 3.3 Coffee Trees at Three Years Old

April to September			*October to March*		
Units	%Men	%W/C**	Units	%Men	% W/C**
48	60	40	80	36	64
Total 22,110	Men 12,270	W/C** 8,840	Total 36,850	Men 13,266	W/C** 23,584

Source: KNA. NAD Annual Report 1926, p. 87.
**Women and Children

The comparison of the age of coffee trees and the percentages of male, female, and juvenile labor indicates that women and children were used mostly on coffee trees that were in the berry bearing stage (three years old). A smaller percentage of female and juvenile labor was used on trees less than three years old. Males were the only workers used in clearing and planting the trees which was considered to be heavy labor. Tables 3.3, 3.4, and 3.5 show that women and children were used twice as much as male workers to harvest coffee between October and March on the mature trees—they were 64% of the labor force. In the slack period (April to September) children and women were only 40% of the work force on mature trees. Women and children were 40% of the workers employed in weeding, hoeing, spraying, and pruning the plants.

TABLE 3.4 Laborers for Clearing and Planting

April to September			*October to March*		
Units	%Men	%W/C**	Units	%Men	%W/C**
39	100	0	39-77	100	0
Total	Men	W/C**	Total	Men	W/C**
1000	1000	0	1000	1000	0

Source: KNA. NAD Annual Report 1926, p. 87.
**Women and Children

TABLE 3.5 Coffee Trees One to Three Years Old

April to September			*October to March*		
Units	%Men	%W/C**	Units	%Men	%W/C**
25	60	40	25	60	40
Total	Men	W/C**	Total	Men	W/C**
5722	3442	2280	5722	3442	2280

Source: KNA. NAD Annual Report 1926, p. 87.
**Women and Children

The amount of work expected from each worker varied according to the assigned task. Table 3.6 shows the daily work requirements. The estimated requirements were more than the average adult female picker could manage. When questioned on their ability to meet the quotas, respondents stated that an average picker could manage five *debbes* per day. One *debbe* was equivalent to thirty pounds of coffee berries.[105] Since pickers were paid four pence per four gallons of beans picked if they met these numbers for a light crop, their wages would have been about eight pence each day. The expected amounts of beans could not be produced because picking coffee caused pain. At the end of a day of picking, a worker's arms were covered with smarting scratches from contact with the stiff branches. A beginning picker went home with stiff and swollen fingers from the constant contact with the trees.[106]

TABLE 3.6 Work Required of Coffee Laborers

Category	*Per day*
Picking (light crop)	6 gallons
Picking (heavy crop)	16 gallons
Pruning (heavy crop)	20 to 50 trees
Weeding and Cultivation	500 to 1000 square yards

Source: KNA: NAD Annual Report 1925, p. 87.

Physical pain was not the only disadvantage for women involved in this type of agricultural production. Working for wages, at such a low rate of remuneration, reduced the amount of time they were able to spend on household domestic production and cultivation of their traditional food crops. This was an important consideration in their decision to work on the estates after compulsion was reduced. The high demand for women's labor during the coffee harvest period coincided with the harvest of women's subsistence crops. As Table 2.3 (see Chapter 2) demonstrated, women produced the majority of food crops (six of the eleven food crops were their responsibility). One of these—millet—required women's intensive labor from October to January; five other crops (sweet potatoes, yams, lablab beans, cow peas, green gram, and kidney beans) needed large in-puts of labor from March to July. These high labor demand periods overlapped with the months when planters still needed thousands of women to turn out to pick coffee beans. The problem of conflict in interest of domestic production versus off-farm income generation was not taken into account by the local officials, planters, or recruiters who were delegated by the chiefs to recruit women. This overlap was the reason women were reluctant to go to the estates. Planters and officials voiced complaints about women laborers' willingness to work all through the colonial period. Seemingly, the settlers and officials could not understand that working for wages had a deleterious effect on the food supply. Poor treatment and conflicts in time management were not the only reason women resented the labor; like other workers in the colony, they wanted fair compensation for their labor or at least some leverage in determining what a fair wage should be. The dynamics of their struggle to obtain a fair wage parallels the workers' movement in Kenya. The following chapter places women's labor protest within the larger scenario of labor activism in the colony from the 1920s to the independence era.

Notes

1. Godfrey Muriuki, *A History of the Kikuyu 1500 to 1900* (Nairobi: Oxford University Press, 1974), p. 120.
2. See L.S.B. Leakey, *The Southern Kikuyu Before 1903*, 3 volumes (London: Academic Press, 1977), pp. 479-501; D.A. Low, "British East Africa: The Establishment of British Rule 1895-1912," in *A History of East Africa*, Vol. 2, eds. Vincent Harlow, E. M. Chilver and Alison Smith (Oxford: Oxford University Press, 1965), p. 4; Muriuki, *A History of the Kikuyu*, p. 173; and Kenya National Archives (KNA): Kiambu (KBU)/81, Political Record Book (PRB) 1890-1916, p. 32.
3. M.W. Dobbs, "Recollections of Kenya 1906-1931" (Unpublished manuscript, Rhodes House: Oxford, 1966) , p. 176.
4. George Bennett, *Kenya, a Political History: The Colonial Period* (London: Oxford University Press, 1963), p. 5; Dobbs, "Recollections," p. 177; C.C. Wrigley, "Patterns of Economic Life 1902-1945," in Harlow, *A History of East Africa*, pp. 212-213.
5. Dobbs, "Recollections," p. 176.
6. Frederick Jackson, *Early Days in East Africa* (London: Dawsons of Pall Mall, 1969), pp. 170-171.
7. C.I. Blackburne-Maze, *Journals of My African Travels* (Maidstone: W.E. Thorpe and Sons, 1913), pp. 130-131.
8. Thomas Toulson, "Europeans and the Kikuyu to 1910: A Study of Resistance, Collaboration and Conquest," (M.A. Thesis, University of British Columbia, 1976), pp. 139-140.
9. See John Boyes, *King of the Wakikuyu* (London: Metheun and Co., 1911), for Boyes' adventure in Kenya.
10. Kenya Government, *National Atlas of Kenya, 1970*, Third Edition, (Nairobi: Government Printer, 1970), p. 83.
11. For a full account of the expeditions into the East African interior see Charles Richards and James Place, *East African Explorers* (Nairobi: Oxford

University Press, 1967); and Reginald Coupland, *The Exploitation of East Africa, 1856-1890: The Slave Trade and the Scramble* (Evanston: Northwestern University Press, 1967).

12. Jackson, *Early Days in East Africa*, p. 171.

13. Jackson, *Early Days in East Africa*, pp. 171-172; for a full description of Kikuyu dress, decorations and weaponry see W. Scoresby Routledge with Katherine Routledge, *With a Prehistoric People: The Akikuyu of British East Africa* (London: Frank Cass & Co. Ltd., 1910), pp. 26-37.

14. Toulson, "Europeans and the Kikuyu," pp. 104-105, 125-126.

15. KNA. KBU/81, PRB 1890-1916, p. 31.

16. Ibid., p. 30.

17. Ibid.

18. F.D. Lugard, *The Rise of Our East African Empire*, 2 vols., (Edinburgh: W. Blackwood, 1893), pp. 326, 535.

19. The Kikuyu had no chiefs. Kikuyu oral tradition maintains that Waiyaki was an ambitious young man from a poor lineage who believed he could become a man of status, wealth and authority by working with the Europeans.

20. KNA. KBU/81, PRB 1890-1916, p. 30. Ironically enough, Purkiss later died making this same journey to the coast. While en route to Kibwezi after his retirement in 1893, he contracted Blackwater fever and died.

21. KNA. KBU/81, PRB 1890-1916, p. 30.

22. Ibid., p. 31.

23. Ibid.

24. Malcolm Hailey (Lord), *An African Survey: A Study of Problems Arising in Africa South of the Sahara* (London: Oxford University Press, 1938), pp. 742, 744-745.

25. Martin Kilson, "Land and the Kikuyu: A Study of the Relationship Between Land and Kikuyu Political Movements," *Journal of Negro History*, 40, April 1955, p. 112.

26. The Communal Labor Law was revised as the Roads in Native Reserves Ordinance in 1910, 1912, 1922 and 1927.

27. Granville St. John Orde-Brown, *The African Laborer* (London: Frank Cass, 1967), p. 29; Richard Sandbrook, *The Development of an African Working Class: Studies in Class Formation and Action* (Toronto: University of Toronto Press, 1975), p. 13.

28. Orde-Brown, *The African Laborer*, p. 37.

29. Adam Clayton and Donald Savage, *Government and Labor in Kenya, 1895-1963* (London: Frank Cass, 1974), p. 44; Roger van Zwanenberg, *Colonial Capitalism and Labor in Kenya, 1919-1938* (Nairobi: East African Literature Bureau, 1973), pp. 125-126, 143-144, 148.

30. Orde-Brown, *The African Laborer*, pp. 150-151.

31. Van Zwanenberg, *Colonial Capitalism*, pp. 125-126, 143-144.

32. KNA. AR/273/KBU/9, Annual Report 1915-1916; KNA. AR/275/KBU/10, Annual Report 1916-1917, p. 1.

33. Van Zwanenberg, *Colonial Capitalism*, pp. 115-116.

34. KNA. AR/279/KBU/14, Annual Report 1920-1921, p. 44.

35. Clayton, *Government and Labor*, p. 29.

36. Van Zwanenberg, *Colonial Capitalism*, pp. 125-126.

37. Robert Tignor, *The Colonial Transformation of Kenya: The Kamba, Kikuyu and Maasai from 1900-1939* (Princeton: Princeton University Press, 1976), pp. 48, 167.

38. Orde-Brown, *The African Laborer*, p. 148.

39. Van Zwanenberg, *Colonial Capitalism*, p. 130.

40. Tignor, *The Colonial Transformation*, p. 104; KNA. KBU 13/ HOR, 1918-1920, p. 4; Kilson, " Land and the Kikuyu," p. 131.

41. Van Zwanenberg, *Colonial Capitalism*, pp. 123-124.

42. Norman Leys, *Kenya* (London: Hogarth Press, 1924), pp. 185, 187.

43. Gordon H. Mungeam, *British Rule in Kenya, 1895-1912* (Oxford: Clarendon Press, 1966), p. 55.

44. Wrigley, "Patterns of Economic Life," pp. 230-231.

45. Hailey , *An African Survey*, pp. 570-571.

46. The shilling currency replaced the rupee in 1922. Twelve shillings was still the equivalent of one month's labor for most African workers.

47. David Frank Gordon, "The Colonial Crisis, Decolonization and the State: The Case of Kenya," (Ph.D. dissertation, University of Michigan, 1981), pp. 151-152.

48. Hailey, *An African Survey*, 572; KNA. Provincial Commissioner (PC)/Central Province (CP)/1/1/1, PRB 1901-1926, p. 22.

49. Van Zwanenberg, *Colonial Capitalism*, pp. 76-77.

50. Hailey , *An African Survey*, p. 573.

51. KNA. Native Affairs Department (NAD), Annual Report 1937, p. 3.

52. Ibid.

53. J.S. Kieran, "The Origins of Commercial Arabica Coffee Production in East Africa," *African Historical Studies*, 2, 1969, p. 55; M.E. Hill, *Planters Progress: The Story of Coffee in Kenya* (Nairobi: Coffee Board of Kenya, 1956), p. 6.

54. Hill, *Planters Progress*, p. 6.

55. Kenya, *National Atlas*, p. 38.

56. M.P.K. Sorrenson, *The Origins of European Settlement in Kenya* (Nairobi: East African Literature Bureau, 1968), p. 120. Sisal was also an export crop.

57. Nicola Swainson, *The Development of Corporate Capitalism in Kenya, 1918-1977* (London: Heinemann, 1980), p. 34. Sisal and sodium were the next largest in value totaling 8% each.

58. *East African Standard*, 2 January 1926.

59. E.A. Brett, *Colonialism and Underdevelopment in East Africa* (London: Heinemann, 1973), p. 175.

60. Sorrenson, *The Origins of European Settlement*, p. 156.

61. Jeremy Murray-Brown, *Kenyatta* (London: Allen and Unwin, 1972), p. 63.

62. Tignor, *The Colonial Transformation*, p. 164.

63. KNA. AR/273/KBU/9, Annual Report 1915-1916, p.1.

64. KNA. AR/275/KBU/10, Dagoretti Subdistrict Annual Report 1916-1917, p.1.

65. KNA. AR/273/KBU/9, Annual Report 1915-1916, p.1.

66. Granville St. John Orde-Brown, *Labour Conditions in East Africa*, Colonial Paper No. 193 (London: HRMSO, 1946), p. 72.

67. Kilson, " Land and the Kikuyu," p. 129.

68. KNA. KBU/13/HOR 1918-1920, p. 4.

69. KNA. AR/278/KBU/13, Annual Report 1919-1920, p. 32.

70. Interview with Wambui Wagarama, Kabete, April 29, 1979. The respondent is in error in stating that Thuku was sent to Somaliland. He was actually sent to Kismayu. KNA. AR/289/KBU/15, Annual Report 1922, p. 4.

71. KNA. KBU/114, PRB 1911-1927, p. 49.

72. Ibid.

73. Interview with Cecelia Wanga, Rabai, December 12, 1978.

74. KNA. KBU/77, Dagoretti II PRB 1913-1919, pp. 84-85.

75. KNA. PRB/220/PC/CP/1/1, Central Province PRB 1901-1926, p. 269.

76. KNA. AR/279/KBU/14, Annual Report 1920-1921, p. 44.

77. Ibid., p. 28.

78. Ibid.

79. Also present at the meeting were European missionaries and delegates from the chiefs association.

80. W. McGregor Ross, *Kenya From Within: A Short Political History* (London: Allen and Unwin, 1927; reprint edition, 1968), pp. 225-226.

81. Interview with Tabitha Wambui, Kiambu Town, October 3, 1978.

82. Van Zwanenberg, *Colonial Capitalism*, pp. 122-126, 143-145.

83. Interview 1 (informant preferred to remain anonymous), Rabai, October 1, 1978.

84. Clayton, *Government and Labor*, p. 121. Original Kikuyu version: Filipu aramakugwo/no matwarithirie munene wa Nyaching'a/ Nyacing'a ituiru kahawaini.

85. Interview with Wambui Wagarama, Kabete, April 29, 1879. Original Kikuyu version: Kinya Harry Thuku athii/ No ugo ndagwa thikiae/ Ni muithuwa wa ithina/ Harry Thuku agicoka/ Muithuwa ucio wathira/ Wa wathira wa itina/ Muthungu anaface uguo/ Harry Thuku Europe.

86. James Wellard, "Kikuyu" in *Man, Myth and Magic: Encyclopedia of the Supernatural*, pp. 1561-1565; H.E. Lambert, *Kikuyu Social and Political Institutions* (London: Oxford Press for the International Institute, 1956), p. 99.

87. Clayton, *Government and Labor*, p. 119.

88. KNA. NAD Annual Report 1928, p. 100.

89. KNA. AR/290/KBU/16, Annual Report 1923, p. 19.

90. KNA. NAD Annual Report 1925, p. 64.

91. Ibid.

92. KNA. NAD Annual Report 1926, p. 79.

93. In 1957 the value of coffee exported from Kenya was thirty-one million dollars. Coffee exports were 6% of Kenya's GNP. See United Nations, *The World Coffee Economy* (FAO: Rome 1961), p. 3.

94. KNA. NAD Annual Report 1956, p. 40.

95. Tignor, *The Colonial Transformation*, p. 100.

96. Ian Spencer, "Economic Development of Kenya, 1895-1929: A Reconstruction," Staff Seminar Paper, No. 6 1978/1979, University of Nairobi, November 1978, p. 3.

97. Tignor, *The Colonial Transformation*, p. 145.

98. KNA. KBU/114, PRB 1924, p. 2.

99. Clayton, *Government and Labor*, p. 173.

100. Van Zwanenberg, *Colonial Capitalism*, p.53; Clayton, *Government and Labor*, p. 175.

101. Ian Spencer, "Settler Dominance, Agricultural Production and the Second World War in Kenya," *Journal of African History*, 21, 1980, pp. 487-504.

102. Clayton, *Government and Labor*, p. 274.

103. KNA. NAD Annual Report 1925, p. 64.

104. KNA. AR/313/KBU/32, Annual Report 1947, p. 7.

105. J.K. Makohkah Bunyasi, "Labour in the Kenya Coffee Industry" (M.A. Thesis, University of Nairobi, 1973), p. 19.

106. Interview with Virginia Gachiku, Kiambu Town, November 12, 1978.

4

Kiambu Women's Labor Protest, 1912-1960

The Kenya Trade Union Movement

The study of women's labor organization is connected to the general history of labor resistance, protest, and organization in Kenya. Women's labor actions reached a peak at the same time as African trade unionism was at its height. The trade unionism movement was particularly strong from 1947 to 1952, and it was mostly urban-based.[1] This movement was, according to Sharon Stichter, the militant phase of worker organization and class formation. African labor resistance occurred in three stages.[2] In the first stage of labor action, Africans resisted their transformation into wage laborers. The colonial government used forced labor, taxation, and imprisonment to effect this change. African resistance to these policies—a protest against wage and communal labor itself—was individual rather than communal and situational rather than organized. This period of protest began when the Communal Labor Law was applied in 1908 and continued up to World War I. The second stage of labor protest began after World War I and lasted until 1947. In this period, Africans tried to change the conditions of labor. As individual as well as ethnic and political associations, protestors tried to improve wage levels and get more generous amenities of food allotments which were a part of their pay. An important focus of their protest was directed at the *kipande* (Swahili: work registration which all African adult males had to carry on their persons). The anti-*kipande* protest was well articulated by the East African Association in the 1920s. The final stage of labor protest occurred in the post World War II era when labor organization reached maturity and became effective. Under the direction of labor leaders like Chege Kibachia of the African Workers Federation (1947) and Fred Kubai, of the East African Trade Union Congress (1949), labor protest became widespread and achieved success in improving wage rates for several categories of workers.

The protest took the form of large scale strikes and stoppages. One of its chief purposes was to eliminate the use of race to set different wage scales for Africans, Asians, and Europeans who were performing the same jobs. Another object of the organized protest was to improve African wage rates and to have them keep pace with the rises in the cost of living.[3]

In all three periods, government reaction was repressive. Up to World War I, the government punished individuals and entire communities for labor resistance with fines, imprisonments, and confiscations of property. The government response to protest in the second period of protest was to receive the petitions, initiate inquiries but ultimately to restrict protest by arresting the leadership and banning the protesting organizations or associations. This was the fate of the East African Association when it protested the abuse of women laborers and the *kipande* in 1922. However, the colonial government began to accept the idea of African unions in 1937. Even then, government policy was directed at insuring that unions were not political. To achieve this, unions were required to register with the government before they could operate as legitimate trade unions. Registration could be refused upon the recommendation of the Labor Department and the registrar.[4] The government response to assertive labor organizations was imprisonment. The leaders were jailed. The organizations were declared illegal and disbanded. This was done to Chege Kibachi and the African Worker's Federation in 1947. These same tactics were used against the East African Trade Union Congress in 1950.[5]

Women's Labor Protest

Kikuyu women's labor protest occurred in two phases and their protest evoked similar official reactions. The first phase covers the years 1895 to 1919. Women resisted entering into the new labor relations of wage and corveé labor. Nonetheless, the government forced women and men into unpaid work on road projects; men and women were drawn into wage labor for settlers through the application of taxes and communal punishments. The second period of Kiambu women's protest began with the official policy of converting women into seasonal wage laborers for the coffee agribusiness. Up to 1930, women's protest against this was characterized by individual rather than collective resistance. However, beginning in the 1930s, women's labor action became collective and highly organized. They protested labor conditions by arranging work stoppages. Although it was very well coordinated on the local level with an efficient method of communicating grievances, women's labor protest never became formally linked to the vigorous trade union movement in Kenya. This may have been caused by the fact that most labor protest in Kenya was urban-based. The second factor is that the urban trade unions were themselves unable to survive the perennial government repression. The third contributing factor to the lack of linkage between women's labor organization and men's was that women were seasonally employed on the estates. The labor unions may have been uninterested in these women, who were extremely poorly paid, because they formed such a small proportion of the total African labor force in the colony. Despite the lack of linkage to the male organizations, women's protest reveals the beginning a rural female proletariat collective consciousness. They did more than recognize the commonality of their work conditions; they planned demonstrations aimed at improving their rate of pay. And importantly, they did so without the formal aid of male dominated political associations and trade unions.

Tensions between the Kikuyu and the planter/government alliance over women's wage labor primarily focused on coercion used to procure women from 1912 to 1923. The first mention of this occurs in the colonial records on May 31, 1912. A complaint was lodged with the District Commissioner's office about a refusal to allow women to be taken to work on a coffee estate. A man called Wahotho prevented his wives from going to work for a Mr. Lushington. Lushington employed an African, Kiwangika, to recruit women to work for him. Lushington told Kiwangika that he was "of the government" and that the DC had said Kiwangika should recruit for him. When Kiwangika ordered women to work, Wahoto refused on the grounds that his wives were helping to build his homestead.[6] This type of confrontation was not a typical pattern of women's refusal to work for Europeans. In this case, a male intervened in the process and claimed that his wives' traditional responsibilities superseded the new labor conditions. From the late 1920s up to the end of the colonial era in 1963, women protested labor conditions on their own and attempted to change their conditions of work. As the coffee agri-business expanded and gross exploitation of the workers was reformed, the focus of women's protest shifted to the amount of their wages and food allotments. This question was a continuing irritant for the settlers and the DCs. There was a tendency to categorize women's labor protest as politically subversive.

Planters were always concerned about subversion, the constancy of the labor supply, and the dependability of the labor force. Major F. LeBreton, a planter, stated the problem as planters saw it in a letter to the *East African Standard:*

> The East African Labour Problem is the reverse of that of most of the rest of the world. It is not a question of finding work for the unemployed, but of finding native labourers to do the work on offer.[7]

Major LeBreton might well have added to his statement, *at the price we are willing to pay*. But planters did not offer higher wages to attract African workers. Major LeBreton offered three solutions to the problem of increasing the labor supply: finding new sources, increased attractions for available labor, and increased efficiency from workers. Increasing wages was, in his estimation, an impracticable solution:

> To our second alternative—increased attractions, increased pay is only practicable to a very limited extent. Farming is an economic proposition in which the margin of profit is not large, and the limit of increased wages if not accompanied by increased efficiency is soon reached.[8]

Major LeBreton concluded by suggesting that increased amenities such as the distribution of medicine to sick workers could be used to induce and keep an industrious labor force.

Another planter took a different view of the situation, insisting that the African labor force could indeed be attracted by increased wages, as he himself had no problems since he gave a "square deal":

> I am always being pestered by natives looking for work and have asked a few why they do not go to the coffee *shambas* as there is demand there. The answer is always the same—'We will only be paid from six to nine shillings per month which means that we have to work two months to

> pay our *kodi* (Swahili: taxes) and where are our clothes etc, coming from?' I have asked them if they would go for 12 shillings per month and the reply is "yes" immediately.[9]

He concluded, generously for the times:

> There are lazy natives certainly but piece work cures this, and I would add that I have a crew of natives who will work alongside any Europeans in Kenya and have always found that the native if treated decently is not a bad fellow.[10]

Other planters were less generous, as this letter one day later expressed:

> It is certainly a scandal to think that all these unemployed boys are allowed to roam the town, while firms giving employment to sound natives are called upon to stop production so that government can collect their taxes. Coffee and sisal estates are crying out for labour, and I personally could do with one hundred or so in my quarries. It simply goes to show that the native is too well-off to work.[11]

Despite a European perception that surplus labor existed, the majority of planters had serious problems when they sought coffee pickers. Kiambu planters experienced difficulty in obtaining women to pick coffee in most years. The shortage was particularly acute in the years 1924, 1925, 1934, 1937, 1941, and 1947. At a coffee conference held in 1937, the planters urged the government to conduct an inquiry into the shortage of labor. According to a newspaper report, the shortage had reached such proportions that the ripe crop could not be picked; laborers had to be diverted from maintenance activities on the estates in order to make up the shortfall. Because men did not want to work on the estates, either as permanent workers or as seasonal pickers, planters relied increasingly on women and children. Men preferred not to work on the estates because first, the work was largely seasonal and second, as Table 3.1 (see Chapter 3) displays, coffee laborers were the worst paid adult workers in the colony. Using women workers, however, did not fully resolve the planters' labor problems. When labor was in short supply, women tried to push up the pay rate. In 1937 the *East African Standard* observed that, "Pressure is being applied by African women for an increase in their pay packets for picking, which...averages about ten cents per tin."[12] Ten years later planters were still complaining about a shortage of labor. The question of the constancy and availability of labor had not abated despite resolutions by coffee boards and government inquiries into the matter. During the picking season of 1947, planters had what one correspondent to the *Standard* called "a few bad moments" in their attempts to find pickers.[13]

Women used work stoppages to voice their complaints about wages and working conditions and tried, without success, to force up the wage rate. These labor actions involved staying away from work and sometimes forming picket lines outside of the gates of estates. They are distinct from strikes in that the stoppages were often spontaneous not highly organized. Usually they were of short duration and did not spread to other industries. The wages paid to coffee pickers remained steady at 10 cents for much of the colonial period. Officially the rate was 15 cents to 20 cents per *debbe* with food.[14] Women respondents maintained that the price they received was 10 cents per *debbe* with one pound of maize meal per day as late as the 1950s. Table 4.1 on work stoppages shows a decided trend to the occurrence of the stoppages in Kenya Colony.

TABLE 4.1 Work Stoppages

Year	*No. of stoppages*	*No. of workers*	*Man days lost**
1948	87	17,287	10,885
1949	71	10,148	24,594
1950	no data	no data	no data
1951	57	6,610	9,671
1952	84	5,957	5,721
1953	39	3,221	2,674
1954	33	1,518	2,026
1955	35	17,852	81,870
1956	38	5,170	28,238
1957	77	21,954	25,391
1958	96	21,395	59,096
1959	67	42,214	431,973
1960	237	72,545	57,860

Source: Kenya National Archives, Colonial Annual Reports 1960, p. 15.
*The official term used to describe stoppages was man hours, however, women were also responsible for these labor actions.

Most years showed an increase over the previous year in numbers of actions and workers involved or man days lost. The years from

1951, 1953 and 1954 show an exception to this pattern because of the Mau Mau emergency.[15] The number of workers involved declined acutely in 1954 when the colonial government staged a massive round up of subversive political elements. During the Mau Mau period (1950–1958) , stoppages were often interpreted as being connected with radical political behavior. A striker or labor activist could find herself detained as a Mau Mau insurgent. Since most strikes and work stoppages occurred in the Central Province, the restrictive measures introduced by the government to control the movements of population, the general suspicion of activists, and strict penalties for anyone who gained the reputation of being an insurrectionist were the most probable reasons for the severe drop in the number of work stoppages.

Often these stoppages lasted little more than one day, although the Mombasa strike of 1947, the Uplands Bacon strike of 1947, and the general strike of 1950 lasted far longer. I have not been able to determine which stoppages actually took place on the coffee estates or how many of them actually took place in Kiambu district. The data for 1960 are somewhat better. Of the 237 stoppages which occurred that year 122 of them took place in the agricultural sector and the majority of those were on the coffee estates in Central Province.[16] Since Kiambu district was the major coffee growing region, it follows that most of the labor actions on the estates were executed in the district.

Even without detailed evidence, it was clear that labor stoppages occurred frequently in Kiambu district. In 1934, coffee pickers staged a stoppage that was serious enough to capture the attention of the DC. Pickers refused to work because they were dissatisfied with their wages. The stoppage was ineffective since wages were not increased. The district officer reported this strike as:

> A native headman of Kibathi's location was convicted in the court of the District Commissioner, Thika, for illegally inducing coffee pickers to leave work. This was part of an attempt by a number of natives of this location to force up the price of coffee picking in the Ruiru area by boycotting the work. A meeting of natives was held in the reserves in November with the object of persuading natives to refuse work unless the price was raised. The meeting, however, was abortive and the natives accepted the price offered and returned to work.[17]

In 1937 coffee pickers created another crisis. The district commissioner reported:

> It can be stated with confidence that there was no attempt to withhold labour for political purposes and many settlers near the reserves have given it as their opinion that labour was going out just as freely as formerly. Nevertheless the native was quick to seize his or her opportunity and went to the farms offering the best wages and conditions forcing others to raise their wages too.

There was a coinciding of coffee picking on various estates and a "squeeze on but not a shortage of labour. All coffee was picked but the settlers were uneasy about the 'crisis'."[18] Whenever possible, workers drifted to the better paying estates. These worker responses were not organized by the trade union movement. They remained independent until 1947, when Chege Kibachia, a trade unionist from Mombasa, reportedly came to Uplands Bacon Factory to organize the strike.[19] A coffee strike was credited to his presence in the district:

> A strike started among the employees of the Uplands Bacon Factory and the employees of the Lari Farm came out in sympathy. The strikers obstinately refused to discuss their grievances and it became apparent that the 'strike' was a political manoeuvre organized by intensive agitation from subversive Kikuyu elements in adjacent reserves. As a result of the tension caused by these inflammatory tactics a riot developed on Uplands Station in which three rioters were killed and six wounded when the Police were ordered to open fire. It is an interesting commentary to note that Chege Kibachia had spent a week working up the Uplands area the day before he was arrested and finally deported.
>
> Later in the same month of September a strike of coffee pickers was organized in the area between the Chania and Ndaruga [rivers]—ostensibly it was organized by the women only and roads were picketed. Although not proven, there is every indication that this strike was organized by Local Native Councillor Solomon Memia and Lawson Mbogua who started the Kibathi agitation. Direct action stopped this strike and the pickers were mostly back at work happily within one week.[20]

Whether Kibachia actually organized the women workers, assisted by Solomon Memia and Lawson Mbogua, is a riddle which cannot be solved from the available data. When questioned about the stoppage, women respondents in Kitambaya (near Ruiru town) claimed that there were no special organizers. According to former

Kikuyu women coffee pickers, they would "just talk" with one another in their homes about the low wages. Women who wanted to convince others to join waited outside the gates of the various estates and spoke to other women about joining in a stoppage.[21]

Some Kikuyu women respondents did, however, claim an influence from the trade union movement:

Q: Why did you decide to strike?
A: We wanted higher salaries.
Q: How much were you getting?
A: We got 7 shillings per month.
Q: Who organized you?
A: The political party did not organize us. There was a man who organized us but I don't know his name. The strike started in Nairobi with the railway workers. When they did so, people in the petrol station also started. Then the ones who worked on the coffee estates said to the headman that they would strike too and the European said that if the headman started the strike he would be taken away. The people said if the headman was taken away we would not work on the estates for 80 days.
Q: How long did the strike last?
A: Two days. We got 25 shillings after the strike.[22]

Another stoppage occurred in 1951 among the coffee pickers in the Gatundu area. The stoppage collapsed after the government threatened to import Meru workers to pick the crop if Kikuyu women continued to refuse to work.[23] The strategy of importing workers from outside of the district was not new. As early as 1927 the DC had suggested to coffee growers that workers be imported to make up for a shortfall in the supply of laborers which was not related to a work stoppage. The DC suggested that the growers organize caravans of motor lorries to bring in women and children from remote parts of the Kiambu Reserve, Embu, Machakos, and Kitui districts.[24] In the 1940s the importation of workers from outside the district was done with the intention of breaking worker solidarity and making work stoppages ineffective.

Women workers did not present a united front to estate owners and government officials. Their general impoverishment meant that they could not afford to totally reject cash-generating labor. The colonial government and the new tax structure meant that women's labor in cash-generating enterprises had become essential to many Kikuyu families whether they were landless or not. Because they became, to a certain extent, dependent on wages to pay taxes and school fees for their children, many women were unwilling to participate in a labor action or be absent from work for long, thus decreasing the solidarity needed for effective labor activism.

Devout religious women also thought such direct action was wrong since it was, according to one respondent, wrong to oppose the Europeans.[25] Women in straitened economic situations or those who were devoutly religious who refused to join a boycott were sometimes threatened by more militant women. The following two testimonies indicate the two poles of thought and action among women workers:

> When the strike started I worked on the Kuwhite estate. We were paid 13 shillings per month and given 30 pounds of maize flour [per month]. Then the Europeans decided to increase the wages by 1 shilling and to stop giving flour. We objected to this and demanded that the wages should be more. We asked that we should be given 50 cents per *debbe*. Each woman had to pick 3 *debbes* per day. We women voluntarily worked on the estates but the chiefs would force women to work to make up the numbers that way. Also the chiefs were bribed by the whites to force women to work. Children starting from the age of 10 and 12 were forced to work on the estates. The women who went on strike were punished by having their wages cut by one day; there was no physical punishment because of the strike.
>
> The estates that I know to have been involved in the strike were Kuwhite, Muhia [now called Ndinota], Kamrefu, Kiora, and Kaface. Three villages would work on one estate. I don't know how many women were involved but we were very many.[26]

This respondent, who was a longtime political activist and Mau Mau organizer, participated in the 1953 work stoppage at the Kuwhite estate. Exactly what role local Mau Mau women played in organizing other women is not clear. Respondents who claimed to have participated in the rebellion expressed strong support for labor activism. Being opposed to Mau Mau tactics did not preclude women from being involved with labor actions. Nonetheless, it is indisputable that in the first few years of the rebellion, Mau Mau women used threats and intimidation to involve other women in work stoppages. The following interview was collected from a staunch Christian woman who took part in the stoppage because she was coerced by Mau Mau women. She claimed that she and her daughter were told that they would be killed if they refused to join the other women:

Q: Did you go to work on the coffee estates?
A: I worked on the estates in 1951.
Q: Did you know anything about a strike?
A: Yes. The women struck because they refused to raise the wages. We were forced to go back to work.
Q: Which estates were involved?
A: Several estates were involved. Muhia was one of them.
Q: How many women were involved?
A: Many more than 100.
Q: Did you take part in the strike?
A: Yes.
Q: How did the women decide to strike?
A: I don't know. I wasn't at the meeting. I was on the church side, so I did not go to the meeting.
Q: How did they convince others to strike?
A: They communicated by word of mouth and the word got out to refuse to work.
Q: Did you get any results? Did you receive better wages?
A: No.
Q: What were your wages at that time?
A: I was paid 45 shillings per month.[27]

Why did women continue to work on the coffee estates despite a grim picture in terms of their treatment and rate of pay? Newspapers, government sources, and my informants all demonstrate that brutality against women occurred and that the rate of pay continued to be low well into the 1950s. One respondent stated that despite the low wage, they worked because they needed the money to pay the taxes. These taxes were imposed directly on women after 1934. Colonialism forced Africans to enter into a cash economy to pay these taxes, but the means to earn cash were limited. Women were essentially limited to work on the coffee estates if they wanted cash. Throughout the colony, the major source of wage labor employment for women was work on the coffee estates. There was a limited amount of work available in harvesting maize and picking pyrethrum. Especially in rural areas, apart from field work, women had few alternatives.[28]

To what extent, however, did women actually control the wages they earned? Were these wages the personal property of the woman or was it controlled by the person(s) in authority over her? If women controlled the expenditure of wages earned, then a side effect of the introduction of women to wage employment on the estates may have been an increase in female autonomy during the colonial period. In 1937, the DC noted that tax payments to the government were:

> [No] longer a family affair in which all members assisted and the result was very apparent in the large number of exemptions which had to be granted, especially in the case of widows and old women. In the past the whole family helped to pay the taxes and when this stopped the head of the family frequently found it difficult or impossible to find the money.[29]

By 1934, as mentioned before, not only were adult males expected to pay taxes, adult women and males over the age of 16 were also taxpayers. The comment by the DC suggest that family cooperation was breaking down, at least with respect to tax paying. Whether this was a result of a general refusal of women and juveniles to contribute their share to the tax burden or whether the male head of households refused to be responsible for the taxes is a question the current data does not yield. What is apparent is that women were not able to meet their share of the tax burden if it was to come out of their own earnings. Women's wages remained at pre-World War II levels; taxes went up; the cost of living went up. Juvenile labor on the coffee estates was also poorly compensated. At the same time, adult males' wages, although increasing for some occupations, generally fell behind the cost of living increases. Family cooperation in paying taxes seems to have stopped because available cash did not meet the level of taxation. Old women and widows began to declare impoverishment to get exemptions from taxation. One woman respondent said that she did not have full control over her wages before she married. When she collected her wages, she and her sisters gave the money to their mother who mother used it to purchase things for them such as cloth for dresses.[30] The available data does not demonstrate a conclusive pattern of who controlled the wages of women and juveniles. Speculation from the limited amount of evidence tends towards a conclusion that juveniles' wages were controlled by their parents, and that married women had full control over their own earnings. Future research might indeed reveal some other pattern.

One of the important benefits of wage labor could have been to increase the mobility of workers. In the pre-colonial period, women's mobility and range of options was limited. A reason for women's economic and political activism was a desire to expand the range of options open to them. To a certain degree, association with the missionaries served this function, and I discuss this in

Chapter 5. Women's involvement in work for Europeans on the coffee estates does not seem to have offered more equality and variety of choice in their economic roles. Working for wages under the conditions determined by cash crop production for the settler estates was less dynamic in changing women's status in society than was participation in the nationalist movement and the introduction of a Christian religious belief system.

Women's wage labor on the coffee estates began early in the colonial period with a marriage of convenience between local planters and local government officials. Gradually the officers became disenchanted with the methods employed by their subordinates, which were encouraged by the planters, to induce and maintain a large pool of women laborers. This disenchantment was emphasized by the missionaries and dramatically exposed by the early African nationalist politicians. Vocal protest led to reform in recruitment and the provision of better treatment of women workers. That the reforms did not, however, contain provisions for increased wages is significant. After the 1930s, women began to voice their own dissatisfaction with their condition once the first factor of violence against women was mostly resolved. The second factor of low wage rates caused women to declare work stoppages against employers who periodically attempted to lower wages and eliminate *posho* when coffee prices declined or inflation eroded their profits. The combination of these factors produced an attitude of defiance in many women workers. The authorities considered women to be bothersome and intractable. Their defiance was manifested in the increase in stoppages from the 1930s, through the end of the colonial period. In that thirty year period, there were many abortive attempts to increase wages through widespread, local, and often short-term labor actions. Of supreme significance is the fact that women directed these labor actions themselves. Up to the 1930s, men, whether African or missionaries, spoke for reform in women's labor conditions. In the 1930s women rejected this passive role and became labor activists themselves. This is illustrated by two statements:

> Harry Thuku is the one who *fought for us* [my emphasis] and stopped us from working like slaves.[31]

And:

> We [women] objected to this and *demanded* [my emphasis] that the wages should be more.[32]

These two statements underline a major transformation in women's attitudes about themselves, about the range of activities they considered suitable for themselves *as women*. They began to confront authority directly through a new political mechanism, the work stoppage, when men's assistance failed them. This change occurred in an era of increased African political activism in Kenya and in Kiambu district. Women were intensely involved in the new militancy and activism. Women's militancy began with labor. In the 1930s, women broadened this militancy and began their own political organization. A solid core of Kikuyu women who learned methods of organizing by orchestrating labor actions refused to be excluded from public life and to be continually relegated to roles which solely encompassed working on the *shambas,* child care, and working on the coffee estates. It may be true that women lost economic status from pre-colonial times to independence, since wage labor and cash income in general may have decreased the importance of their contribution in the maintenance of the family through the supply of the bulk of food produced in their *shambas.* It is certainly true that women acquired a political voice that was loud enough to be of concern to the planters and the government. This is demonstrated by the frequency of the instances and the fact that planters and the government complained about women workers. Their observations are part of the official colonial record. Planters developed a way of decreasing the impact of women's labor actions by importing "strike breakers" from other districts. Women's changing role in the economy is linked to their new relationship to the political associations. A change occurred in the nationalist associations when women gained membership. The EAA had used women's labor and social conditions as a rallying point for other males in their confrontations with the colonial state. In these instances, women's roles were passive. After the 1930s women forced entry as active nationalists in the associations. The processes of women's rise to full membership in the associations will be explored in the following chapters.

Notes

1. Sharon Stichter, "Trade Unionism in Kenya, 1947-1952: The Militant Phase," in *African Labor History*, eds. Peter Gutkind, Robin Cohen and Jean Copans (Beverly Hills/London: Sage Publications, 1978), pp. 155, 161, 163.

2. Sharon Stichter, "The Formation of a Working Class in Kenya," in *The Development of an African Working Class: Studies in Class Formation and Action*, eds. Richard Sandbrook and Robin Cohen (Toronto: University of Toronto Press, 1975), pp. 21-48.

3. Stichter, "Trade Unionism in Kenya, " pp. 157-158, 161.

4. Stichter, "Trade Unionism in Kenya," p. 159; Malcolm Hailey, *An African Survey Revised 1956: A Study of Problems Arising in Africa South of the Sahara* (London: Oxford University Press, 1957), pp. 1447-1448; and Anthony Clayton and Donald Savage, *Government and Labour in Kenya, 1895-1963* (London: Frank Cass, 1974), pp. 331-337, 371.

5. Clayton and Savage, *Government and Labour*, pp. 328-337.

6. Kenya National Archives (KNA). Kiambu (KBU)/114, Annual Reports 1911-1927, p. 8.

7. *East African Standard*, 10 December 1937.

8. Ibid.

9. *East African Standard*, 13 December 1937.

10. Ibid.

11. *East African Standard*, 14 December 1937.

12. *East African Standard*, 30 November 1937.

13. *East African Standard*, 12 December 1947.

14. KNA. Colonial Office Annual Report 1960, p. 15.

15. Ibid.

16. Ibid.

17. KNA. Annual Report (AR)/306/KBU/26, Annual Report 1934, p. 16.

18. KNA. AR/309/KBU/28, Annual Report, p. 18.

19. Kibachia was actually from Kiambu district. He received his education at the elite Alliance High School; he obtained part of his education at the Githunguri School, an independent higher education institute founded by the Kikuyu in response to the circumcision controversy (see Chapter 5). Kibachia was a labor leader in Mombasa from 1945 to 1947. As a result of his labor organization, he was arrested by the government and detained in Baringo district for ten years (1947-1957).

20. KNA. AR/320/KBU/38, Annual Report 1946, pp. 1-2.

21. Interview with Wagara Wainana, Kitambaya, April 29, 1979.

22. Interview with Christine Wangui, Githunguri. May 16, 1979. The strike referred to occurred in 1950 since that is the year of the railway strike. The respondent states that she received a salary of 7 shillings per month and that her wages were raised to 25 shillings. This indicates first that she was a permanent employee rather than a seasonal coffee picker , who was still paid by the *debbe* or piece work rather than a fixed salary. Second, it indicates that the employer was underpaying the permanent employees. Their wages were only 2/3 of the minimum rate for permanent agricultural laborers.

23. Clayton and Savage, *Government and Labour*, p. 311.

24. KNA. Political Record Book (PRB)/38/KBU/114, Annual Report 1927-1928, pp. 1-2.

25. Interview with Tabitha Wambui, Kiambu Town, October 3, 1978.

26. Interview with Virginia Gachiku, Kiambu Town, November 12, 1978.

27. Interview with Tabitha Wambui, Kiambu Town, October 3, 1978. There is some confusion about the wages the respondent claims she received at this time. According to D.J. Penwill, the DC for Kiambu, the standard wage rate in 1956 for coffee workers was 20 to 25 shillings with rations. This standard wage is also corroborated by Clayton and Savage, *Government and Labour*, p. 356.

28. KNA. Native Affairs Department (NAD) Annual Report 1928, p. 100; KNA. NAD Annual Report 1937, pp. 205-206; and NAD Annual Report 1938, p. 113.

29. KNA. NAD Annual Report 1937, p. 3.

30. Interview with Virginia Gachiku, Kiambu Town, April 14, 1979.

31. Interview #1, Rabai, October 1, 1978. Informant requested that her name never appear in any publication.

32. Interview with Virginia Gachiku, Kiambu Town, November 12, 1978.

5

Cultural Transformation: Women and the Missions

After 1910, when most Christian mission stations were in place, missionary influence played a vital role in transforming Kikuyu society. This chapter explores two trends in the relationship between the Kikuyu and the missionaries. The first trend involved missionary service to Kikuyu societies in education and advocacy. Missionaries sometimes used their influence with the government to lobby for African interests. They often interceded in attempts to gain more liberal policies and attitudes towards Africans. Missionaries were also in the forefront of providing a rudimentary level of education. They established schools to teach not only western religion and language but also limited technical skills. These would be necessary to Africans who were forced to alter their lifestyles and work patterns because of the new conditions that had been introduced.

The second set of missionary/Kikuyu relationships was more negative. Quite early in the period of contact, missionaries began to use their special relationship with the government to undermine aspects of African culture leading to modifications of Kikuyu traditional social practices. Because of the missionaries' Eurocentric criticism of Kikuyu culture and their seeming alliance with the colonial government, ideological and cultural conflicts were played out in the political arena as well. Frequently, the colonial administrators were as ethnocentric as were the missionaries; they consistently colluded with the missionaries to change Kikuyu customs. The most drastic and well known case of the cultural conflict between the Kikuyu and the missionaries occurred in the 1920s and 1930s when the missionaries of Central Province banded together to oppose the circumcision of girls. Kikuyu breakaway churches and schools resulted from this, and the smoldering fires of nationalism were revived. The female circumcision issue is connected to Kikuyu women's role transformation. Cultural nationalists defended circumcision as an inalienable rite which marked girls' passage from minor status to full adulthood. Before this chapter proceeds to a discussion of the controversy, however, it is appropriate to review the early years of contact between the missions and Kikuyu women.

The Establishment of Mission Stations

Christian missionary operations in East Africa had two effects on indigenous societies. The first was connected to the slave trade that still existed in the late 19th century. Missionaries fought against the slave trade in East Africa from 1874; they influenced the British government to use its influence to persuade East African rulers to end their support of the slave trade.[1] The missionaries who served on the East African coast helped slaves run away from their masters. They established communities of slaves who received industrial training and worked on mission-run plantations.[2] The second effect of missionaries' presence was the new world view the religion offered. Christianity, for the missionaries, was inseparable from European culture. They insisted that African converts to the Christian faith reject their culture along with their polytheism. Thus, Christian belief was confused with European cultural practices from the late 19th century when Protestant missions began converting coastal peoples.[3] When the missions moved into the interior in the wake of the Imperial British East Africa Company's thrust into the interior, the conflict between European and African culture was already cast in the mold of a conflict between Christianity and heathenism.

In 1898, the Church of Scotland Mission (CSM) station was relocated at Kikuyu on a site to the west of Nairobi, establishing itself in Kiambu district. The Church Missionary Society (CMS) started a mission in Kiambu district in 1900. Other missionary societies soon followed. The American sponsored African Inland Mission (AIM) and the Catholic White Fathers joined the British Protestant missions in the district; by 1902 stations were established at Kiambu town, Limuru, and Mangu.[4] Missionary men and women came to Kiambu district with the object of spreading ideas of

Christianity and "lifting" Africans out of ignorance to the light of western civilization.[5] Conversion was slow between 1898 and 1930. because of the missions' insistence that Africans give up a large part of their own cultures to become Christians. Many Kikuyu believed that the dubious benefits of mission training were not worth the sacrifice of traditional ways of life. They believed that mission training would ultimately be of no practical benefit to them. When the first CMS mission was sent to Kenya, the directors of the mission included a rather revealing statement in their letter of instruction to the missionaries:

> If you would gain access to the people and their confidence and affection they must have your fullest sympathy and love. You will remember that they have not had advantages with which you have been familiar from your childhood. You go to the darkness of heathendom where Satan's seat is: though darkness the Committee are thankful to know, illuminated by a few spots of Gospel light. While firm in the maintenance of the highest standard of truth and purity, you will need the spirit of patience, forbearance, consideration and charity.[6]

From the outset, missionaries had the attitude that they would find many of the African customs to be savage and barbaric. The missionaries travelled to Kenya with the intention to remake the societies they encountered along the lines of Victorian England. In many cases, they were successful. Their first converts were Africans who were cast off and ostracized from their societies.[7] This small group of Christianized Africans made up the original phalanx of African catechists. From the last decade of the nineteenth century, these catechists aided European missionaries in attacking Kikuyu customs, amongst which were the drinking of home-brewed beer, dancing, polygamy, female circumcision, and the belief in witchcraft.[8]

In 1908 the missionaries received government aid in stamping out some Kikuyu customs. Missionaries were able to persuade Governor Sir Percy Girouard that certain Kikuyu customs should be eliminated. Illustrative of this is an address given by Sir Percy when he announced the conversion of the traditional *kiama* into an organization to be known as the Local Native Council (LNC) at a meeting held in Kiambu district. In his address to the traditional *kiama* he condemned the Kikuyu practice of drinking the traditional alcoholic beverage *tembe,* the tradition of rape of women by the *anake,* and the expulsion of dying persons from the villages to expire in the "bush."[9] Sir Percy told the gathered population that no sharp or immediate changes in their traditions was to be instituted.[10] Nevertheless, as early as 1908, the missions and the government were both committed to a campaign to change Kikuyu traditions.

The second cause of the slow rate of conversions was related to the intensity of Kikuyu/missionary contact. The missionaries were so few at first that they could not have made a large impact on the African population in the district which numbered well over 100,000. A total of 15 mission stations were established by the missionary societies in the three Kikuyu districts by 1915.[11] There were eleven mission stations in Kiambu district in 1926.[12] Stations usually had only four missionaries in residence at any one time. This number was reduced when the missionaries were on leave and were not replaced.[13] The second reason for their small measure of success was the diluting effect of intense interdenominational rivalries between the missionaries of different sects.[14] The problem of competition of spheres of influence and interdenominational rivalry was serious enough for a conference of the different missions to be called. After an agreement was reached in 1916 this form of rivalry lessened.[15]

Missionary-Kikuyu Relations, 1898-1927

Initially African response to proselytism was quite mixed. The Kikuyu often viewed the missions with suspicion. The missionaries came into the area in the wake of other Europeans, Arabs, and Swahili porters whose relationships with the Kiambu Kikuyu had been largely negative.[16] Concurrent with the generation of negative Kikuyu/European relations, the missions were responsible for a more positive relationship. The great famine of 1899 was particularly severe in Kikuyu and Kamba country. The missionaries gave aid to the starving population. From a mission station near the IBEAC's abandoned station at Dagoretti, the missionaries of the East African Scottish Industrial Mission cared for many sick and starving Kikuyu and helped to sustain them through the crisis.[17] When the mission station was established at Thogoto in 1900, the society expanded its relief work.[18]

The missions affected Kikuyu society unevenly. Women especially came to regard the missions as a refuge. They ran away to the missions to what they thought would be a freer society.[19] Missionaries praised such action and several saw themselves as liberators who freed women from domestic oppression.[20] Women who tried to run away to join the missionaries were often punished by their families. Some of the first women to seek refuge with the missions joined the CMS facility at Kabete run by Reverend Harry Leakey. Phyllis Wambui's parents beat her to stop her from becoming one of Leakey's first converts. They did not want her to become a Christian and forget traditional ways.[21] Physical punishment did not stop girls like Phyllis from running away to the missions in large numbers. At the AIM mission station at Matara, a girls' home was started and education tailored especially for them was begun. In 1912 a delegation of parents complained to the DC that girls were being alienated from their families. One parent stated that he had lost two daughters to the missions. The missionaries considered the girls to be friendless. However, the father and husband of one of the women complained that even the right to visit her was denied them. The DC's decision was that only truly friendless girls, with no relatives whatsoever, should be allowed to join the missionaries. Altercations over runaway women and girls was the first of several issues where relations between traditional authorities and missionaries became strained. Central to the conflict were attempts to gain control over women.[22]

In the early decades of the twentieth century, missionaries, elders, and fugitive females' male kin battled over who had authority to arrange marriages for these Christianized women. At issue was whether or not they should marry non-Christian Kikuyu. In 1912, the churches and the elders' councils came into conflict over marriage payments and the disposition of Christian widows. The missions argued that bridewealth payments should not be made—such payments were equivalent to selling girls into marriage. The Kikuyu elders countered that if bridewealth was not paid, then the marriage was illegal—the women were concubines. The struggle was resolved through the intervention of the DC who decided in favor of the elders: Christian men would make marriage payments.

From April 25-26, 1912 government officials, missionaries, chiefs, and converts met in Kiambu Town to settle the disagreements over Christian girls' bridewealth.[23] Several converts were opposed to the mission position, proposing that Christianized women follow the tradition of living with the deceased husband's family, even if they were not Christians. Frequently the missions paid bridewealth for girls living at the stations—on behalf of the Christian bridegroom. The converts recommended that initially bridewealth be paid by the missions and that the husband work to repay it. Some missionaries felt that their initial payment of the bridewealth gave them the right to interfere with decisions about a widow's domicile. Converts supported the position that the missionaries should have no say in the matter if the bridewealth had been repaid.

Another point of controversy between missionaries and converts was over widows' remarriage. The missionaries wished to permit remarriage. However, Kikuyu tradition prohibited it for such a practice created a legal tangle over children's allegiance and inheritance rights. The traditionalists argued that the children belonged to the lineage of the deceased husband. A second marriage might involve adoption, confuse the question of land inheritance for the male offspring, and create uncertainty over who should receive or pay bridewealth for the female offspring of the deceased husband. The meeting ended with an agreement on this point at least. Widows were to have rights of remarriage, but the children of the first husband were members of his lineage and would never be members of the second husband's lineage.[24]

In 1913, despite the partial compromise between the churches and the elders over widow's remarriage, conflicts between the two groups were taken to the Attorney General's office. This time, the disagreement concerned the guardianship of Christian women's children. In principle, the courts recognized that Kikuyu law and custom should be respected. However, this would hold only in cases where Kikuyu law was not "repugnant to justice and morality," in opposition to any Protectorate order-in-council, or in violation of any colonial ordinance.[25] The court reserved for itself the power to decide whether a woman could be forced to live with her deceased husband's relatives and upon what grounds such a decision should be made. Most importantly, the court reserved the right of deciding if the offspring of a Christian marriage should be required to live with non-Christian relatives. This decision permitted the removal of the child if it was determined that living with them was detrimental to the child's Christian upbringing.[26] The court rejected the elders' submission that the children should be allowed to live with the next of kin, whether Christian or not. The missions had been intransigent; they held firmly to the position that orphaned children should not reside with non-Christian kin. With the support of the government, missionaries were able to have their views enforced, at least in theory.

Another point of friction between the missions and traditional Kikuyu males over who should control women and marriage customs involved polygyny. If a converted Kikuyu wanted to avoid excommunication or expulsion from the church, he had to comply with the church's requirement of monogamy. This change in marriage customs was insisted on by the mission officers from the earliest years of their presence and proselytism in Kenya. They viewed this change as a beneficial reform. However, many Kikuyu viewed it as yet another attempt to destroy the integrity their customs.

The Circumcision Dispute

The next major assault on Kikuyu culture—the female circumcision controversy—occurred in the late 1920s. Since this became a political issue championed by the nationalist movement it has received more attention in Kenyan historiography than the struggle for jural control of women or the elimination of other Kikuyu customs. Dr. John Arthur of the Nyeri Church Missionary Society station led the anti-circumcision campaign. In 1927 several of the European missionaries followed his lead when he prohibited converts from allowing the circumcision of their female offspring. Church members were forced either to sign a statement condemning the practice or leave the church.[27] Young girls who were members of the church were also required to sign a statement affirming that they would not allow themselves to be circumcised.[28]

The forced signing of these statements was the first salvo in the controversy which swept through the three Kikuyu districts from 1927 to 1933. It radically shifted Kikuyu/mission relations. In the majority of the accounts of the dispute, little attention is given to describing the actual ceremony or how the altercation affected women.[29] The whole episode is treated in political terms, and indeed it had a political side. To both Kikuyu women and men, however, the missionary attitude and intransigence towards circumcision contradicted the basic principle of the conferment of womanhood on females. Tradition dictated that if a girl could not be circumcised then she could not be accepted as an adult;

marriage and full entry into Kikuyu society was denied her. For her entire life she would be considered a minor.

The operation that conferred adult status involved more than the removal of all or part of the clitoris. The whole process of circumcision took several months. The initial part of the ceremony involved the piercing of the young girls' ears so that they could wear the large earrings worn by adult Kikuyu women. The ears were pierced in the lobe and the folds of the ear just above the lobe. After the ears healed, the girls were considered ready for the removal of the clitoris only if their breasts had begun to develop. When the girls gathered to sing songs associated with this rite of passage into adulthood, they were carefully examined by their mothers. Those who had begun to mature, were permitted to participate in the upcoming operation. The parents were responsible for arranging the ceremony. Mothers sought out the most esteemed village elders and requested that the day of the operation be set. When the elders consented, the fathers approached the girls' grandfathers for their agreement to the schedule. When all the parties had given their consent, five goats were taken to the woman known as the circumciser who did the actual cutting.[30] The consultative process involving the girls' mothers, fathers, elders, and grandfathers meant that each group that was in a position of authority over the young girls was asked for their approval for the them to become women—to pass to the next stage of life.

Once this approval had been given, an all night festival was held on the eve of the operation.[31] The next day, groups of six to eight girls went to the river where they ritually bathed. Respondents reported that they were extremely anxious about the operation but suppressed that anxiety and tried to present a stoic demeanor, walking towards the river with fingers tightly curled into their palms. At the river, the girls were divided into two groups, *mugikuyu* and *mukabi*, one named after the Kikuyu and the other after the Masai. After immersing themselves in the water, they proceeded to the homestead that had been chosen for the actual operation. A goat skin was spread outside of the *thingira* (house) for the girls to sit on while the operation was performed. The mother, elder sisters, and paternal aunts held the initiate's arms, and cold water was poured into her lap as the circumciser cut.

After the operation, the newly circumcised women stayed at the homestead until their wounds healed. When healing was complete, they were allowed to return to their own homes.[32] The healing times of the wounds varied. A one month period was usual, however, one woman recounted that she was only allowed an eight day healing period.[33] When they returned, they were ceremonially greeted at the entrance to the homestead by a small girl who escorted them to their parents and family with whom they shared a special meal. For three months following the circumcision ceremony, the young women's health was closely watched. They had only to take care of themselves, and were not allowed to cook, fetch water from the river, or work alongside their mothers and younger sisters in the *shambas*. This leisure time was spent in dressing up in jewelry and clothes and socializing with other recently circumcised women in their village. After the three month period was over, the young women were permitted to visit other villages where they were presented with gifts of jewelry to acknowledge their new status. Until they married, they were allowed to attend the *muchukia* and *mugoya* traditional dances. [34]

The sources for this account of the circumcision process were all elderly women who were born between 1914 and 1930. For all of them, the time immediately after the healing signalled a period of freedom from work filled with the joy of associating with their peer group. Several of the women also recalled fragments of songs they sang to celebrate this transitional period in their lives. This pleasant recollection of the ceremony was not unanimous, however. Some women from Christian families spoke of circumcision as both immoral and physically dangerous for women. Circumcision scarred the birth canal which caused problems during childbirth resulting in extreme and unnecessary pain.[35]

This was a perception the medical missionaries promoted. The attack on circumcision began as early as 1916, well before the confrontation between Europeans and Africans occurred. In a meeting of a conference of representative native churches held July 5-6, 1916 at the Church of Scotland Mission (Kikuyu station), the attendees were asked if the time was ripe for the abolition of female circumcision. Dr. John Arthur gave medical testimony against the practice, stating that it was unnecessary and unhealthy. A delegate from Kabete said that although the operation had not been prohibited, some efforts were being made to keep girls from being circumcised. He also said that some progress had been made in convincing the Kikuyu at Kabete that uncircumcised girls would be able to bear children. The African delegates did not support or oppose the motion but indicated that if European missionaries decided to take action on the issue there would be little opposition.[36]

In the 1919/1920 annual report for Kiambu district, the DC noted that the missionaries were already pressing local authorities to intervene in circumcision cases. The missionaries, led by Dr. John Arthur, were particularly concerned about what they termed "immoral dances" which were a part of the ceremonies. They pressured the government, as well as the LNCs, the Christianized Kikuyu, and the Colonial Office in London, to stop the practice completely.[37] In 1923, missionary influence was strong enough to convince the Colonial Office to take a negative view of circumcision. Part of the Colonial Office survey on the East African territories included this note on circumcision:

> The further bar to Education [of girls] is that most vile tribal custom carried on among the Kikuyu known as "circumcision of girls." According to custom a girl is not marriageable until this rite takes place, neither is she a member of the tribe. Education is bound to try and combat this, and as a result the child girl's owner will do all he can to prevent her acquiring new ideas, for fear she should prove an unsalable article, and he should be left without the money she has represented to him since birth.[38]

The missionaries had less success in persuading the LNCs to view circumcision as a harmful custom. In 1927 missionaries urged the councils to help eliminate circumcision on medical and moral grounds. The Central Province Political Record Book for 1927 noted that circumcision should be stopped because it caused complications during childbirth. Missionary arguments convinced several councils in the three Kikuyu districts to vote for resolutions stipulating the modification of the operation. These resolutions were passed despite the fact that the majority of the Kikuyu resisted ending or changing the custom.[39]

The resolutions had three main features. First, women were only permitted to perform the operation in what was called "minor circumcision."[40] Only a small part of the clitoris could be removed in an effort to prevent scarring of the birth canal. The second feature of the councils' resolution was that women who performed the operation had to be licensed by the government. The final stipulation concerned the age of the girls; they were to be at least thirteen years old before the operation could be performed.[41]

These events were the prelude to the 1928 conflict. Despite the missionaries' position, many Kikuyu—especially women—saw the custom as an indispensable part of women's rite of passage. The government position up to 1929 was that the custom was deplorable but that moderate means of ending the practice should be pursued. This was to be accomplished by such means as prohibiting the major operation and closer control of the circumcisers, educating, Christianizing, and westernizing women.[42] Most of the LNCs in Central Province passed by-laws on the issue; however, the Nyeri district council refused to discuss so intimate a topic.

The enforcement of the by-laws sparked the first flames of the circumcision conflagration. In April 1929, two women from Kiambu district were prosecuted for performing the major operation, and each was fined 30 shillings.[43] Though the fine was relatively small from the court's perception, it represented approximately three months—or more—wages to the women (see Table 3.2). The reaction to the trial made it clear that the councils' by-laws did not have popular support. Opponents also took the position that the district court was not a body which should have had jurisdiction over cases that involved violation of the by-laws.[44]

Fuel was added to the flames of controversy when the missionaries confronted the Kikuyu with an ultimatum in September 1929. The protestant missions fired the first salvo. Dr. Arthur ordered all of the elders in his congregation sign an agreement denouncing female circumcision or face expulsion from the Church. The African Inland Mission and the Gospel Mission quickly followed Dr. Arthur's lead. This offensive backfired. To the missionaries' astonishment, nearly 90% of the Kikuyu left the churches rather than sign these declarations.[45]

Though dismayed by Kikuyu reaction to the ultimatum, the missionaries continued their campaign despite the drastic decline in Kikuyu church membership. The CMS's next move caused a decline in attendance at the mission schools. They required all instructors in the outschools to sign declarations affirming their support for the mission position. Those instructors who refused were dismissed. Again, the strength of Kikuyu opposition to the ultimatum surprised the missions and the government. The CMS lost 80% of its outschool pupils. When the AIM and the Gospel Mission followed the CMS example, they lost even more students than the CMS.[46]

Kikuyu Independent Schools

The Kikuyu revolt against missionary interference, in an issue which revolved around women's status, led to the beginnings of the independent school movement in Kenya. Indeed, independent schools may not have evolved at all had it not been for the struggle over circumcision which forced the Kikuyu to experiment with western-style education. By 1935, Africans controlled a significant portion of rural education. The independent schools were ultimately linked to the political independence movement. In late 1929, a nationalist organization, the Kikuyu Central Association (KCA), sponsored and solicited funds to support the anti-missionary position. District Commissioner S.H. Fazan attributed the KCA's increased influence in the district to their deliberate championship of the pro-circumcision faction.

The circumcision controversy divided the Kikuyu into two factions: those who supported the missionary position and those who wanted to continue the custom in some form or other. According to one respondent, the two factions were so divided that marriages between them were never arranged, although they never fought each other.[47] Some respondents maintained that the two factions created by the controversy persisted into the Mau Mau rebellion; that loyalists were members of families that sided with the missionaries in the 1930s and that the Mau Mau rebels were children of the anti-missionary faction.

The group that supported circumcision began to call itself the Gikuyu and Mumbi group—the Kikuyu legendary progenitors.[48] The Gikuyu and Mumbi faction used the reference to the founding of the Kikuyu as a way of connecting themselves to the Christian Adam and Eve creation legend.[49] This group linked independence in education and circumcision to the demand for the return of alienated land.

In 1930, the Native Affairs Commissioner commented that the greater spirit of independence, defiance, and increased political activity in the district grew out of the events of 1929. Although the commissioner did not attribute all political agitation to the events in the circumcision controversy, he saw the issue as a force that united the Kikuyu. According to the report, circumcision was a question which "banded together pagans and Christians, educated and ignorant in defense of inherited customs."[50] What the commissioner was describing was a resurgence of a broad based cultural nationalism.

Cultural nationalism led to the founding of two types of independent school: the Karing'a and the Independent Schools.[51] The connection was made clear in the 1932 Native Affairs Report: "Private Kikuyu schools, or Independent Schools continue to grow in most districts. This issue had its origin in the circumcision issue."[52] For several years, the DC of Kiambu could not distinguish between these two types of schools. Many Kikuyu women, who were of school age during the 1930s, were also confused by the existence of two distinct independent school systems. When questioned about the Karing'a schools, several respondents identified them as the Independent Schools, claiming that there was no difference between them.[53] There were, however, sharp differences from the outset. By 1933, the Native Affairs Department was able to see the difference in attitude between the two systems.[54]

At first, both types of schools refused any European supervision and rejected any ties with the Education Department. Shortly after they were founded, however, the Independent Schools Association (ISA) tried to get government funding, a process which involved frequent inspection visits by the Department of Education. The Karing'a Schools were perceived to be hostile to the government; they neither sought nor wanted government funding and control. Another major distinction between ISA and the Karing'a Schools was their connection to radical nationalism. The Karing'a Schools had strong ties with the Kikuyu Central Association. In 1937, the DC concluded that "education [in the Karing'a] schools had become subordinated to politics."[55]

By 1932, nine Karing'a Schools had been opened.[56] The usual pattern was for a school to be built and operated close to an existing mission school. To the consternation of the DC, the sponsors of the Karing'a and Independent Schools were well within their rights to operate their institutions. Any person could legally open and operate a school without government approval.[57]

This situation changed after 1933; the Independent Schools began to accept some of the government's overtures for funding and inspection. Several officers, who were on the annual tours required of all government funded schools, visited ISA schools. These officials recognized and accepted that the growth of these schools was indicative of the Kikuyu's desire for their own schools. The inspectors found the teachers to be bright and enthusiastic giving their best efforts to the task of educating the children.[58] The report noted that many of the teachers were not highly qualified according to government standards.

The three school systems competed for students. Kikuyu parents preferred to send their children to the non-mission schools before 1933. The DC noted in 1934 that, "whenever a mission and a Karing'a school are situated close together, the tendency appears to be for the former to increase the number of its pupils at the expense of the latter."[59] This shift towards the mission schools was most probably due to better facilities because of government funding. Schools needed £50 British sterling per year as a minimum operating budget. As late as 1933, neither the government nor LNCs were voting funds for the independent schools. They received no grants-in-aid for equipment, teachers' salaries, or inspections.[60] Parents began to send their children to the better equipped schools; the mission monopoly of government funds made this shift inevitable.

In 1935, the mission schools were no longer the sole recipients of government funds. The official attitude towards the ISA schools had shifted and become conciliatory. This move may have come about as a result of the 1933 inspection tour in which the inspectors had been favorably impressed by the dedication of the ISA teachers. The staff of the DC's office began to meet with ISA representatives to discuss problems. These efforts were in the nature of a disarmament tactic. Local authorities were fearful that opposition to the schools would stimulate political activities and increase Kikuyu resentment and distrust of government.[61]

An important meeting was held between ISA representatives and the government on August 11, 1936. The attendees included the Director of Education, the Chief Native Commissioner, the Provincial Commissioner, the District Commissioners from the three Kikuyu districts, and ISA delegates. This body made decisions which governed the relationships between the ISA, LNC, and the Education Department from 1936 onwards. The new agreement specified that the LNCs would sanction—approve or disapprove—the opening of new schools. The Education Department would certify all schools and provide more adequate inspection of all schools in the three districts. The ISA was ordered to stop enticing teachers away from the mission schools and to only hire teachers who were graduates of mission schools. On the issue of funding, the LNCs were instructed to consider the ISA schools eligible for grants-in-aid. However, all LNC grants were to be subject to final approval by the Department of Education. The level of teachers' salaries were also made subject to the department's approval.[62]

In effect, the agreements buttressed the missionaries position and made the connections between the ISA and the moderate faction of the Kikuyu stronger. The councils were controlled by the moderate government appointed chiefs who now controlled the purse strings of the ISA schools. The balance of power was tipped towards the mission schools when they were protected from losing teachers through competitive hiring. The mission schools were given control of teacher education. Graduates of ISA schools were not considered to be qualified teachers. This policy had political implications as well. The Kikuyu moderates, through their association and training in the mission schools, were less likely to be openly connected to the radical Kikuyu Central Association opinions. For the government and the missions, these agreements solved the problem of radicalism by limiting the nationalists' influence in the schools.

The 1936 concordant between the ISA, the mission schools, and the government was not extended to the seven schools in the Karing'a Association. When a new Karing'a school was opened at Mukui, it was subsequently closed by the government. The reason for the closure was that the Karing'a school violated an agreement made in March 1937 between the government, the president of the Karing'a Association, and the LNC which stipulated that no schools would be opened without LNC approval.[63] The president of the Karing'a Association also promised that the Karing'a schools would not entice pupils away from the mission schools.[64]

Tensions between the government and the Karing'a Schools increased even more in 1938. The Mukui school opened again, and the government closed it along with two Karing'a schools at Ruthimitu and Kahuho. According to the DC, the Karing'a Schools "remained aloof and cooperated as little as possible."[65] The school authorities at Mukui were prosecuted and convicted of failing to obey an order of the Director of Education. They appealed the decision to both the Supreme Court and the Court of Appeal of Eastern Africa. On the second appeal, their sentences were reduced.[66] Yet the troubles were not over. In August of 1938, the Kahuho and Ruthimitu schools were closed again. This time the reasons for the closure was that the schools were not following the syllabus decreed by the Department of Education. Furthermore, the schools refused to allow inspection visits.[67]

The power of school closure and prosecution which the government exercised had two results. First, it forged stronger alliances between the Karing'a Schools and the Kikuyu Central Association.[68] Both associations were able to use what was perceived as arbitrary action by the government to gain wider support among the already disaffected Kikuyu population. The second result of the use of closures was that the leadership of the Karing'a Schools was forced to acknowledge government authority. The Ruthimitu, Kahuho and Mukui schools were reopened in April of 1938 when the Association finally accepted government conditions. The government rebuilt the Mukui school which had been razed during the second closing.[69]

Although, the DC's office softened its position on the Independent Schools and the Karing'a schools, the Department of Education did not change its attitude. The department continued to refuse to give grants-in-aid to schools of either association. More than any other factor, this affected the quality of education in the independent schools. The Department of Education's grants-in-aid were more substantial than those awarded by the LNC. The Department's grants made a significant difference in the number of teachers employed and the size of the facilities. Two of the Church Missionary Society schools at Kikuyu and Kabete stations received grants-in-aid in excess of £7,000 British sterling in 1927.[70]

Despite these obstacles, the independent schools expanded rapidly in the 1930s. In 1929 there were nine independent schools in Kiambu district.[71] By 1938, of the eighty five schools in the district—serving 11,500 students, of whom three thousand were girls—thirteen were ISA schools and ten were Karing'a schools.[72]

The missionaries' aggressive attempts to introduce western forms of worship, education, and cultural practices were met with equally vigorous resistance. New options arose from these conflicts, one of which was the move towards greater independence in education. Late in the 1930s, the Kiambu Kikuyu widened the independence movement to establish a regional teacher training institution.

The Kiambu Kikuyu had a voracious appetite for education. Each year they demanded more and better school facilities from the colonial government and the missionaries. The independent schools movement was one aspect of that growing demand. Kikuyu parents recognized the value of western-style education, however they were adamant that traditional cultural elements be incorporated. They were fully aware that the western elements could provide the necessary tools for young Kikuyu to cope with Europeans—government officials or private employers. The movement to found a teacher training college was another aspect of the increased demand for education. On numerous occasions, the Kiambu Kikuyu asked the government to create a secondary school which would not be under mission control. The government turned down these requests, claiming lack of funds and staff to support secondary education for Africans.[73]

After years of petitioning, the Kiambu Kikuyu took the initiative into their own hands. The growth of the independent schools and the return of Peter Mbiyu Koinange to Kenya made possible the creation of the Githunguri College. Peter Koinange, the son of Senior Chief Koinange, had studied in the United States and earned a Bachelor's degree. When he returned to Kenya, he applied for a teaching position with the Department of Education and was turned down despite his qualifications and the desperate need for qualified teachers. When the Kiambu Kikuyu sent the government a proposal for the founding of a training college, Peter Koinange was put forward as the principle for the college.[74] The college was to be financially independent, and it was to have complete autonomy in appointing teachers. The Kikuyu strongly supported the idea of the college:

> An amazing rapprochement then took place between Christians of all denominations, all sorts and colour of political associations and the ordinary pagan. Very few Government Headmen were strong enough to stand aloof and Koinange [Senior Chief] very certainly lent his influence.[75]

The widely endorsed proposal was a dramatic challenge to the Department of Education's refusal to start a training college. The sponsors of the college scheme were required to comply with the department's regulations, but no other objections to the scheme were raised. In 1937, they were finally able to go ahead with construction plans. A site was chosen near five independent schools at Githunguri town. Many of the pupils from those schools enrolled in the new college. Their ages ranged from six to thirty years. The supporters of the school were diverse: Christian Kikuyu from all denominations, pagans, members of the radical Kikuyu Central Association, and members of the moderate Kikuyu Association. Women supported the founding of the school. Politically active women demanded that females be educated at the college. Their demand for inclusion in the college was merely the most recent expression of their perennial demands for female education.

Female Education

Women were pawns in the struggle for dominance between missionaries and traditional Kikuyu interests. Christian missions and Kikuyu women had a more direct relationship in the area of western-style education. The missionaries were the first Europeans to pay attention to female education. Despite the fact that educating males was always given greater priority, the missionaries began a program of female education well before the government. Funds voted for education by the LNCs were never earmarked for female education. The first requests for female education had been made in 1909. For the next 28 years women used several stratagems to keep the issue of female education alive. Sometimes they appealed to the DC's courts. At other times they simply ran away from their homes and sought refuge at the mission stations where they could enroll in school. The mission run schools of the CMS (Kikuyu station), AIM (Kijabe station), CSM (Kambui station), and CMS (Kabete station) had girls' dormitories.[76] There was an increase in the number of girls educated at the mission schools between 1910 and 1927. At two mission stations of the CSM, the number of girls enrolled rose from 56 in 1910 to 591 in 1927.[77] In 1926, the num-ber of girls in average daily attendance at the 69 mission schools in the district was 1,021. The CMS mission stations at Kabete and Kikuyu were the leaders in girls' education. The Kabete station had 260 female pupils and the Kikuyu station provided instruction for 394 girls.[78]

Most of the instruction given to girls occurred in the rural outschools which played an important role in spreading some knowledge of European culture to the Kikuyu. In these schools an intermediate level of education was provided. The curriculum and technical instruction offered to the students were, of course, shaped by ethnocentric efforts to Europeanize them. Even though the missions educated more girls than the government, the type of education provided for girls was of a lower caliber than that offered to boys. The more ambitious boys' curriculum included reading in Kikuyu and Swahili, dictation in Kikuyu, English and Swahili, writing, arithmetic, nature study, geography, colloquial English reading, history, grammar, and agriculture or manual training.[79] Girls received instruction in the domestic arts: sewing, knitting, childcare, and hygiene. Some received instruction in medical work and agriculture. The largest part of the curriculum was, of course, instruction in Christian doctrine.[80] Essentially they were taught to be good and suitable potential wives for male converts. The girls also worked as agricultural laborers for nearby estates. The missions did not require the girls to work as agricultural laborers on mission owned land. They did, however, work on the *shambas* attached to the missions where food for the mission tables was raised; no payment was given for this work.[81]

Kikuyu women had pressed for more facilities for girls and a higher and more varied level of education. In 1935 a Kikuyu woman presented this very argument in a letter written to the Kikuyu newspaper *Muthitu*. The writer noted that an educated woman needed training in domestic science, horticulture, childcare, and "industry in all things including writing." She claimed that these skills could only be obtained if girls received the *same* (my emphasis) education in secondary schools that was currently available to young men. She commented that Christianized Kikuyu men needed Christian wives and that educated women would be the most helpful and desirable marriage partners despite the commonly held prejudice that educated women restricted men's desires to have plural marriages.[82]

Women activists of all religious persuasions also pushed for higher education for girls. In 1936, Catholic missionaries opened a school exclusively for girls at Limuru in the Kiambaa division of Kiambu district. Soon after this, plans were made to start secondary education for girls at the site of the Alliance High School.[83] A group of women activists took the initiative in 1947 when they founded a girls' wing at the Githunguri school. They financed the girls dormitory and named it *Kiriri* (girls' sleeping place in the mother's house). The women decided to build *Kiriri* without men's help. They travelled from village to village collecting donations.[84] Rebecca Njeri was chosen to be the matron of the dormitory. She later became known as the primary leader of women's resistance in the Mau Mau rebellion. Priscilla Wambaki, also prominent in the Mau Mau leadership, was the treasurer for the project. After the completion of the building, she was placed in charge of stores and supplies for the girls.[85] The course of instruction, set by the women founders, included writing, the domestic arts, and instruction in English and Swahili. Some of the classes were taken coeducationally with the young men at the college where Peter Koinange, Margaret Kenyatta, and Wanjiko wa Wanyee were teachers. Dormitory facilities for girls and boys were run separately.[86]

Women activists also took the lead in selecting the girls for admission. Those girls who passed the secondary school exam were screened by the women's committee. More than sixty female students were enrolled in *Kiriri* from 1947 until the British closed the school early in the Mau Mau emergency because they believed it was a hotbed of nationalism.[87] Women leaders in the *Kiriri* experiment claimed that the girls were not taught radical politics *per se* ; however, many of the most prominent sponsors of the *Kiriri* were actively involved in nationalist politics. A number of them were arrested and detained by the British under the emergency orders as Mau Mau terrorists. Priscilla Wambaki in describing women's role at Githunguri commented that although the girls were not taught to be nationalists or Mau Mau fighters, there was strong nationalist sentiment among the young girls. This sentiment was so high that "some girls decided to take guns to the forest to be with the men to become freedom fighters."[88]

Women's evolution into nationalist fighters is one of several transformations which occurred from 1900 to 1951. These changes were related to the altered traditional social relations between Kikuyu men and women resulting from the intrusion of Christianity and western education. Control over women was a point of conflict between missionaries and Kikuyu males from the beginning of missionary activity in the district. The circumcision controversy was the next point of conflict. Again women were a pivot point in the differences between the two groups of males. In this argument, the colonial government played the uneasy role of mediator. Despite the usual treatment of the controversy in the histories of Kikuyu and Kenyan nationalism, women were not mute about the issues. Many women were in the forefront of the struggle to attain access to education for themselves and their daughters. Moreover, they strove to obtain education that would be equal to that of men's. They sponsored projects to build facilities for girls and contributed funds. They flocked to the schools to enroll as pupils. Some women were teachers themselves. An important development in this situation was the initiative women took in creating a school for girls at Githunguri. The sponsors recognized that girls needed a new education to cope with the economic and political realities colonialism produced. Many of these same women seized a similar initiative in nationalist politics. In 1930, well before the founding of Githunguri, women activists organized themselves with the goal of becoming recognized participants in the Kikuyu Central Association. The core of this group were the ones who founded the *Kiriri*. The story of the self-transformation of this core group is the story of the struggle of women politicians with the male dominated nationalist associations. Success in this struggle led to their involvement in the Mau Mau rebellion. The dynamics of these changes will be taken up in the next three chapters.

Notes

1. F.B. Welbourn, *East African Christian* (London: Oxford University Press, 1965), pp. 64, 104; A.J. Temu, *British Protestant Missions* (London: Longman Group, 1972), pp. 60, 73, 118-119; Roland Oliver, *The Missionary Factor in East Africa* (London: Longman and Green, 1952), pp. 16-18, 26; and Gordon Hudson Mungeam, *British Rule in Kenya, 1895-1912* (Oxford: Clarendon Press, 1966), pp. 65-66.

2. Temu, *British Protestant Missions*, p. 94.

3. Welbourn, *East African Christian*, pp. 13-14, 37, 64; and Temu, *British Protestant Missions*, pp. 107-110.

4. Roland Oliver, *The Missionary Factor*, pp. 169-171.

5. Church Missionary Society Records, "Letter of Instructions to Departing Missionaries," (London: Church Missionary House, 1892) April 1892, G3/A5 L6/310; and Church Missionary Society Records, "Letter to R. Leakey, E. Millar, J.P. NiMission, J.H. Briggs, A.B. Fisher, A. McGregor, and E. Furley," (London: Church Missionary House, 1892), May 2, 1892, G3/A5 L6/306.

6. CMS Records, G3/A5 L6/310. "Letter of Instructions to Departing Missionaries," (London: Church Missionary House, 1892) April 1892, G3/A5 L6/310.

7. Oliver, *The Missionary Factor*, p. 171.

8. Ibid., pp. 201-202.

9. Rape of women was a custom where young men were required to assault the first strange woman they met after the young men were circumcised. This was a part of the ritual of the passage from boyhood to manhood.

10. Kenya National Archives (KNA). Provincial Commissioner (PC)/Central Province (CP)/1/1/1, Central Province Annual Reports 1911-1921, p. 22.

11. Jocelyn Murray, "The Kikuyu Female Circumcision Controversy, with Special Reference to the Church Missionary Society's 'Sphere of Influence,'" (Ph.D. dissertation, University of California, Los Angeles, 1974), p. 39.

12. KNA. Kiambu (KBU)/19, Annual Report 1926, p.16; KNA. Annual Report (AR)/305/KBU/25, Annual Report 1933, p. 16; and KNA. Native Affairs Department (NAD) Annual Report 1936, p. 73. In 1933, there were five mission societies in Kiambu district. In 1936, there were only seven mission societies operating in the Central Province: The Church of Scotland Mission, The Church Missionary Society, the Consolata Catholic Mission, the African Inland Mission, the Gospel Missionary Society, the Catholic Mission of the Holy Ghost Fathers, and the Methodist Mission.

13. Murray, "The Kikuyu Female Circumcision Controversy," pp. 33-44; and Temu, *British Protestant Missions*, p. 72.

14. Temu, *British Protestant Missions*, pp. 103-104; and Welbourn, *East African Christian*, p. 74.

15. Welbourn, *East African Christian*, pp. 74-76; and Temu, *British Protestant Missions*, p. 103.

16. See Chapter 3 for a discussion of the different kinds of travellers and their impact on the Kiambu Kikuyu.

17. Godfrey Muriuki, *A History of the Kikuyu 1500 to 1900* (Nairobi: Oxford University Press, 1974), p. 178.

18. Ibid.

19. Temu, *British Protestant Missions*, pp. 106-107; KNA. AR/275/KBU/10, Annual Report 1916-17, p. 43; KNA. AR/279/KBU/14, Annual Report 1921, pp. 39, 43; and Interview with Martha Waruchu, Kamburu, October 22, 1978.

20. See for example comments in Fr.C. Cagnolio, *The Akikuyu Their Customs, Traditions and Folklore* (Nyeri: The Mission Printing School, 1933); and W.S. Routledge and Katherine Routledge, *With A Prehistoric People: The Akikuyu of British East Africa* (London: Edward Arnold, 1910).

21. Interview with Phyllis Wambui, Rabai, October 10, 1978. The respondent was not sure of the date of her birth. She said she was one of the first three girls to seek refuge at the mission station. When World War I started, she was well past puberty. Despite beatings from her parents, she defiantly continued to go to the church at Kabete headed by Dr. Leakey. She finally left home altogether and lived in the girls' dormitory at the mission station.

22. KNA. KBU/109/Part II (K), Political Record Book 1912, p. 10.

23. Present at the meeting were: C.W. Hobley, Provisional Commissioner for Ukamba Province; C. Lane, Provincial Commissioner, Kenya; G. Northcote, District Commissioner Fort Hall; C.C. Dundas, Acting District Commissioner Kiambu; Chief Kiyanjui; Chief Murara; Chief Mimi; Chief Njiri and other elders. Eight converts from the Scotch Mission (Dagoretti), Italian Mission (Fort Hall), and the French Mission (Kiambu) also attended. KNA. KBU/76, Political Record Book (PRB) 1908-1912, pp. 83-84.

24. KNA. KBU/76, PRB 1908-1912, pp. 85-87.

25. KNA. KBU/77, PRB Volume I 1913-1919, p. 95.

26. Ibid.

27. KNA. NAD Annual Report 1929, pp. 11-12.

28. Interview with Priscilla Wambaki, Ngenda, May 16, 1979.

29. See Roland Oliver *The Missionary Factor;* F.B. Welbourn, *East African Christian;* F.B. Welbourn, *East African Rebels: A Study of Some Independent Churches* (London: S.C.M. Press, 1961); and A.J. Temu, *British Protestant Missions.*

30. Interview #1, Rabai, October 1, 1978. Informant requested that her name never appear in any publication.

31. Interview with Cecelia Wanga, Raibai, December 12, 1978.

32. Interview with Martha Gathoni wa Kamau, Kamburu, October 20, 1978.

33. Interview with Cecelia Wanga, Raibai, December 12, 1978.

34. Ibid.

35. Interview with Martha Waruchu, Kamburu, October 22, 1978.

36. "Minutes of the Meeting of a Conference of Representative Native Churches in Southern Kikuyuland Held at the Church of Scotland Mission, Kikuyu (July 5-6, 1916)," reproduced in G.H. Mungeam, *Kenya Historical Documents, 1884-1923* (Nairobi: East African Publishing House, 1978), pp. 201-204.

37. KNA. AR/278/KBU/13, Annual Report 1919-1920, p. 28.

38. Great Britain, Kenya Colony and Protectorate, Colonial Office (CO)/533/329/95.

39. KNA. PC/CP/1/2/1, PRB, p. 49.

40. The minor operation was the removal of the tip of the clitoris. The major operation involved the removal of the tip of the clitoris as well as the labia.

41. KNA. Kiambu District Miscellaneous Correspondence 1926-30, p. 67; and KNA. PC/CP/1/2/1, PRB 1911-1927, p. 49.

42. KNA. NAD Annual Report 1929, pp. 11-12; and KNA. AR/301/KBU/22, Annual Report 1929, pp. 2-3.

43. KNA. NAD Annual Report 1929, p. 12.

44. KNA. AR/301/KBU/22, Annual Report 1929, p. 2.

45. KNA. NAD Annual Report 1929, p. 12.

46. KNA. AR/301/KBU/22, Annual Report 1929, pp. 3-4.

47. Interview with Maria Njeri, Gatundu, May 15, 1979.

48. In Kikuyu tradition Mogai, the Supreme Being created Gikuyu as the first male on earth and gave him dominion over the earth's resources. Mumbi, a wife for Gikuyu was created after he had received possession of the earth. See Jomo Kenyatta, *Facing Mount Kenya: The Tribal Life of the Gikuyu* (London: Secker and Warburg, 1953; reprint ed., New York: Random House, Inc., 1965), pp. 1-7. This legend was also recounted by a respondent when she described the reasons for the creation of Karing'a schools. Interview with Martha Waruchu, Kamburu, October 22, 1978.

49. Interview with Tabitha Wambui, Kiambu Town, October 3, 1978.

50. KNA. NAD Annual Report 1930, p. 5.

51. Ibid.

52. KNA. NAD Annual Report 1932, p. 11.

53. Interviews with Muthoni Gachage, Tingang'a, January 4, 1979; Tabitha Wambui, Kiambu Town, October 3, 1978; Martha Gathoni wa Kamau, Kamburu, October 20, 1978; Wanjiro (no other name given), Kiambu Town, January 12, 1979; Priscilla Wambaki, Ngenda, May 16, 1979.

54. KNA. NAD Annual Report 1933, p. 57.

55. KNA. AR/317/KBU/29, Annual Report 1938, pp. 18-20.
56. KNA. NAD Annual Report 1932, p. 67.
57. KNA. AR/303/KBU/24 (a), Annual Report 1932, p. 10.
58. KNA. AR/305/KBU/25, Annual Report 1933, p. 16.
59. KNA. AR/305/KBU/26, Annual Report 1934, p. 27.
60. KNA. NAD Annual Report 1933, p. 57.
61. KNA. AR/307/KBU/27, Annual Report 1935, p. 23.
62. KNA. NAD Annual Report 1936, pp. 74-75.
63. Ibid.
64. KNA. AR/309/KBU/28, Annual Report 1937, p. 20.
65. KNA. AR/318/KBU/30, Annual Report 1938, p. 4.
66. Ibid., pp. 18-19.
67. Ibid.
68. Ibid., p. 19.
69. Ibid.
70. KNA. PC/CP/1/2/1, Annual Report 1927, p. 37.
71. KNA. NAD Annual Report 1932, p. 67.
72. KNA. AR/309/KBU/28, Annual Report 1937, p. 20; and KNA. AR/317/KBU/29, Annual Report 1938, p. 20. Only Twenty-three of sixty-three mission schools received government grants.
73. KNA. AR/318/KBU/30, Annual Report 1938, p. 20.
74. Ibid.
75. Ibid.
76. Great Britain, Colonial Office, CO/533/321/96.
77. KNA. PC/CP/1/1/2, Political Record Book 1911-1927, p. 36.
78. KNA. AR/297/KBU/19, Annual Report 1926, p. 16.
79. See Kenya Colony and Protectorate. Education Department, "Department Instructions Governing Native Education in Assisted Schools," (Nairobi: 1921), reproduced in G.H. Mungeam, *Kenya Historical Documents, 1884-1923*, pp. 272-284.
80. Great Britain, Colonial Office, CO/533/321/97.
81. Interview with Phyllis Wambui, Raibai, October 10, 1978.
82. KNA. NAD Annual Report 1936, p. 77; and Great Britain, Colonial Office, CO 533/321/96.
83. KNA. NAD Annual Report 1936, p. 76.
84. Interview with Priscilla Wambaki, Ngenda, May 16, 1979.
85. Ibid.
86. Ibid.
87. Ibid.
88. Ibid.

6

Kikuyu Women and Political Associations, 1920-1947

So far this study has examined Kikuyu women's traditional roles, the changes in them when women became wage laborers, and the effects of missionary attempts to change Kikuyu traditional life. All of these processes contributed to the dynamics of women's transformation and led to women's direct involvement in the politics of nationalism. The circumcision controversy created a situation where the Kikuyu become more aware of the potential effectiveness of political action *as Kikuyu*. It also exposed their need to forge a larger number of links and stronger alliances to combat the cooperation between the church and the colonial officials. This phenomenon is best measured in the success of the independent schools movement. Out of these new coalitions, emerged a demonstration of political independence and an autonomous school system. The political needs of the Kikuyu created opportunities for Kikuyu women to force changes in the traditional Kikuyu social contract. The involvement of the Kikuyu nationalists in the circumcision controversy has frequently been studied. No history of Kenya or of African nationalism during the pre-World War II period is considered complete without a consideration of this topic. Women, however, were not just objects in the struggle between the Kikuyu males and the colonialists. Their involvement in nationalism was more direct and active. The nationalist association known as the Kikuyu Central Association (KCA) was able to gain more Kikuyu support—male and female—as a result of their championship of the circumcision ritual. More supporters rallied to the nationalist position over circumcision than responded to the

KCA over the issues of land alienation, taxation, labor, or access to European education. Although Kikuyu women were concerned about all of these issues, they were not able to force entry into leadership positions or even full membership in the KCA until the controversy occurred. This chapter explores the processes of women's entry into full membership in the associations and examines the goals of the politicized women.

Conflict Between Moderate and Radical Associations

The premier issue of nationalist politics involved access to land. The question of land alienation was a recurrent subject in Kikuyu politics from the earliest days of the British presence when land was alienated (1905) until the end of the colonial era in 1963. The land was sometimes sold to Europeans; in some cases, land was given to British subjects with no purchase price required. A broad spectrum of politically active Kikuyu men were involved. Both the moderate Kikuyu Association (KA) and the more radical East African Association (EAA) tried to regain land. The KA was a quasi-political organization consisting of British appointed chiefs which had been organized before 1920. A letter from the association signed by its Secretary Matthew Njoroge appeared in the *East African Standard* in 1920 stating their position on the return of lands to the Kikuyu.[1] The EAA was formed in 1919 in the African section of Nairobi known as Pangani.[2] It's membership consisted of young, mission educated men who reached maturity in the second decade of colonialism. The two associations used some common tactics in confronting the colonial government. However, there were important differences in their strategies. Both associations questioned officials at *barazas* (Swahili: public meetings convened by officials). Both sent numerous petitions to the Governors of the colony and the Colonial Office in London. However, from 1923 under Senior Chief Koinange's leadership, the Kikuyu Association tried to change government policy through negotiation. The organization had the approval of the Native Affairs Department and several prominent missionaries sat on its advisory board. The DCs from the three Kikuyu districts were ex-officio members of the Kikuyu Association.

The main difference between the East African Association, its predecessor the Young Kikuyu Association, and the moderate

Kikuyu Association was in attitude and method.[3] The more aggressive YKA and EAA favored direct confrontation; they gained another inflammatory issue when the new policies of labor recruitment were instituted in the closing years of World War I.[4] The new labor requirements stipulated massive recruitment of African men to serve in the carrier corps. These men, of whom 160,000 served as porters who carried machine guns, ammunition, and supplies to the front lines, were compulsorily recruited. The methods of recruitment were harsh and came in the form of government raids on African areas. Fighting between the recruiters/raiders and African men sometimes occurred. On the war front, porters had a high mortality rate. Of those who died, only 366 were killed in action. The highest mortality rate for them was caused by disease. The number of porters who died from diseases contracted during the war was 41,942.[5] The EAA also focused on the issue of increased taxation in the World War I era. According to Kikuyu women respondents, the combination of land alienation, forced recruitment of porters, and new levels of taxes became intolerable. These conditions became so unbearable that more Kikuyu men and women became radicalized and joined the EAA. For Tabitha Wambui, Kikuyu protest began when land was alienated because "they took the *shambas* (Swahili: homestead farms) before political parties started. And that is the reason they started fighting."[6] Another respondent reported that political parties began in the district because of government policies of using women and children to build roads and the *kipande* regulations:

> From 1922 to 1923, the school children were called to dig the roads even when they were in dormitories. In the 1914-1918 war the young men were jailed. When they went to fight [as members of the carrier corps] some died because of carrying bullets and guns. They carried them on their heads and took the women's ropes to carry the loads. The anger between the Kikuyu started then. When the war stopped the Kikuyu were given *kipande*. When we were given *kipande* we started to think how we could be free. At that time Kenyatta was a young man and I was schooling at the same school as he at Thogoto. The people started thinking how we could fight the Europeans so that we could be given freedom.[7]

Other respondents ascribed the start of the political movement to a growing perception that the Europeans were ruling them badly and a realization that the Kikuyu had to organize to prevent the British from alienating more land.[8] Land alienation generated some of the most aggressive and long-term African reaction to colonialism and fuelled the nationalist cause for the next forty years. Prominent in the leadership of the East African Association, were James Njoroge, Jessie Kariuki, Job Muchuchu, and Harry Thuku. For the first two years after its founding, the organization was merely a loose association of young men who had been exposed to British culture either through mission education, service in the carrier corps, or employment with the government. Several Ugandans were members of the EAA, and there was at least one African from Nyasa who held the position of treasurer. They claimed to want to redress the grievances of all Africans in the British colonies. Despite that claim, the organization's leadership and membership were dominated by the Kikuyu. Several reasons account for the fact that the most aggressive and likely leaders were Kikuyu. First, the headquarters were in Nairobi, which is near the large, densely populated Kikuyu district of Kiambu. Second, the missionaries had transmitted western-style education to the Kikuyu earlier and on a wider scale than to any other ethnic group in Kenya. Many of the prominent leaders of the nationalist movement received their first intensive culture contact with Europeans at the mission schools. There they absorbed the English language, but perhaps more important, they learned the best way of attacking European domination by learning British principles of control, petition, and litigation. The missions intended to train a new generation of Africans to direct social and economic development along western lines. Unwittingly, they transmitted enough western culture for this new generation to lead Kikuyu society in political agitation.[9]

Harry Thuku, one of the most prominent early leaders, was just such a figure. From his position as a clerk/telephone operator in the Treasury Department, he was able to obtain advance knowledge of developments in government policies that would affect Africans.[10] The East African Association and Harry Thuku leapt into the forefront of association politics in 1921. Thuku was able to capture the loyalty of a great number of Kikuyu and to engender animosity in others. In 1921 and 1922, three crucial events occurred which increased the popularity of the EAA. The first event was the mandatory registration of every male African over the age of sixteen under the new *kipande* or pass laws. The second event was the raising of the Hut Tax from 5 to 10 rupees. And the final change that fanned African resentment of British policies was the across the board reduction of African wages by one-third. The East African Association was able to gain support from many Africans since it spoke out against all of these changes. The increase in support was so apparent that the district officer for Kiambu noted that, "it is becoming increasingly more and more evident that the Wakikuyu are dissatisfied with things as they are."[11] The East African Association expanded its ethnic and geographic base by protesting these shifts in economic policy and the implementation of Labour Circular 1 of 1919.[12] Harry Thuku travelled to the two other Kikuyu districts in 1921 to gain members for the EAA. The DC remarked:

> The activities of ex-convict Harry Thuku have not been confined to this district but seeing that his efforts to obtain subscriptions from local natives have been abortive he is now endeavouring to raise funds from the Fort Hall and Nyeri Districts.[13]

When the Kikuyu Association attempted to isolate the East African Associations' members and stop the spread of the organization, Thuku travelled to the northern portions of the district which was not as strongly influenced by Koinange's association. At one meeting in N'genda, Thuku estimated that 7,000 people showed up to hear him speak.[14] He addressed the two main issues of better conditions for Africans who worked for Europeans and better education for children.[15]

Large crowds turned out to hear the association's program; the crowds were so large that Senior Chief Koinange and the Kikuyu Association became concerned that the East African Association might usurp their authority. They were particularly concerned when Thuku sent a text of the meeting held at Dagoretti in June 1921 (see Chapter 3) to the Colonial Office in London. The text was a record of the labor issues discussed, but the act of sending it to London presented the East African Association as an alternative source of information on Kikuyu political positions and as an alternative authority in the district. By July of 1921 the two associations were locked in a struggle for popular support. Koinange called a meeting of chiefs to try to generate disapproval of the EAA's tactics and filed a formal complaint against the EAA with the government.[16] This did not achieve the desired outcome, for Harry Thuku talked with the chiefs and convinced them that he spoke to the people of real issues which concerned all Kikuyus. He persuaded them to recognize the memo he had sent to the Colonial

Office, since he had gotten more direct action from London than the chiefs had been able to get from the Nairobi government.[17]

The leadership of the Kikuyu Association was only one of three groups who were offended by the EAA activities. The success of Thuku's speaking tours and the growth of his audiences made him notorious with the chiefs' association, the local administrators, and the missionaries. In March 1922 Thuku was arrested for his political agitation and detained at the police station in Nairobi. The next day a crowd gathered and the EAA called for a general strike to protest the arrest.[18] Members of the crowd gathered round the jail loudly called for Thuku's release. According to an eyewitness, the crowd remained fairly calm until Mary Muthoni Nyanjiru, a Kikuyu, galvanized the crowd into action. She accused the crowd of inaction which would not free Thuku. She especially blamed the men for this and told them that they should rush the police station and free Thuku by force of numbers. The crowd surged forward and the British opened fire. An eyewitness to the incident estimated that 56 people were killed. Official British estimates placed the death toll at twenty-one.[19] Thuku recounts the riot in his autobiography:

> [I]. . .could see the Norfolk [Hotel] through my cell window, and I noticed that a large crowd was building up but I did not want to show myself and make them rush the police.[20] I heard later that the city sweepers. . . had refused to work. Other workers also went on strike. But it was the next day that the crowd grew really large, perhaps seven or eight thousand. Military reinforcements were called up to the vicinity, but according to several witnesses it was a peaceful gathering. However, people were pressing nearer and nearer to the police lines, and one woman, Mary Nyanjiru, began to shout that they should get their leader free. The police opened fire from the front, and I heard that some of the settlers who had gathered on the Norfolk Hotel shot at the Africans from behind. Many Africans were killed or wounded, and the death of the woman Mary showed that women were in the forefront of Kenya's fight for freedom.[21]

Mary Muthoni Nyanjiru, the first woman to be killed in a politically motivated challenge to the British, was not just a chance bystander in the crowd. She worked with Thuku in the political association. Mary Nyanjiru was with Thuku in his room in Pangani when he was arrested.[22] Mary's actions have passed into local lore as the beginning of women's political involvement. Wambui Wagarama, who became a political activists in the 1930s, recounted the legend of Mary Nyanjiru: "We were caught again when there was a fight in Nairobi, and the fight was because the women asked for men's pants."[23]

After the riots, Thuku was summarily exiled by Governor Northey to Kisamau. The Young Kikuyu Association and the East African Association were declared illegal organizations. However, the lesson of the partial success of this form of militant protest had been absorbed by the members of the banned associations. This lesson had also been learned by the countless Kikuyu who participated in the mass action, witnessed it, or merely learned of it through the vehicle of rumor. For many years, the district officers of Kiambu showed concern for what they termed "Thukuism." In December 1921, district officer W.F.G. Campbell, detected that the EAA's precedent of mass organization was influencing events and causing a rise in political agitation:

> This movement is at present very uncontrolled and unbalanced. Local natives are being encouraged by political factions. . .to make unreasonable demands, to resent the authority of the Government Officers and Chiefs and. . .the feeling in the Reserves at present is one of unrest and it is not easy to combat propaganda which is skillfully organized and may in time lead to considerable trouble.[24]

Campbell attributed local organizers' success to two factors: their ability to capitalize on grievances in the Reserves over the most recent enforcement of British policy and the mismanagement of the chiefs. The chiefs were, according to Campbell, inclined towards "apathy and incessant victimization of their people." [25]

The conflicts between the chief's organization and the Young Kikuyu Association were pivotal events in the evolution of Kikuyu nationalist politics. This division was the first visible rift in Kikuyu political thought. The chasm widened over the next thirty years. Each controversy drove the moderates and militants further apart. The primary concern of this study is the way Kikuyu women became involved with the militant associations, or more aptly, how the associations were persuaded to include women as full decision-making members when the moderates did not yield to such persuasion. The first issue which foreshadowed the link between women politicians and militant male nationalists was women's labor on the coffee estates. The use of women on the coffee estates and their labor in other enterprises, such as road building projects alongside men, were inflammatory actions instigated by the colonial government. This labor was compulsory, and it was the moderate chiefs who were immediately used to compel women to labor for Europeans.[26]

Women's Involvement with the Political Associations

What is notable about the connection of women's labor issues to the political associations is that it reflected dissatisfactions within the Kikuyu population; many, who previously had reacted passively to increased British control, were pushed to the extreme of becoming political activists. The other important aspect of this connection is that it was the militant politicians, not the moderates, who championed women. Despite this championship, the East African Association did not allow women to become leaders or even to become members. This situation was to change over the next few years when the Kikuyu Central Association was organized and began to make an impact on the nationalist movement. By the mid-1930s women forced some leadership positions for themselves in the KCA. The Kikuyu Central Association was organized from the ashes of the East African Association in 1925. From the beginning, KCA was intended to represent all three Kikuyu districts: Fort Hall, Kiambu, and Nyeri. The first organizational meeting was held in Fort Hall district. Delegates from the three districts attended and representatives from Embu district and Nairobi were also present.[27] The reaction of the Native Affairs Department to the formation of the KCA was far from positive. The Chief Commissioner called the new society "an indeterminate collection of malcontents, with no constitution, no representative authority and no constructive programme (sic) of reform." The commissioner was suspicious of the association and anxious about the effects it could have on the Kikuyu since it had "achieved notoriety and a prominence out of all proportion to its merit or its influence."[28]

The KCA was prominent in the Kikuyu districts because it focused on the issues which continued to chafe the Kikuyu. Their program was far from ambiguous. They agitated for the return of alienated lands, the release of Harry Thuku, and better educational opportunities. Doubtless, the rough treatment that Nairobi rioters had achieved and Thuku's summary exile from any Kikuyu district made the emerging KCA reluctant to reveal the details of their organization and membership to government officials. H.W. Gray, Kiambu DC in 1925, believed that the KCA was not well organized on the district level. When the KCA asked him for permission to meet, Gray attended and recorded these observations:

> The Kikuyu Central Association requested the District Commissioner's permission to hold a meeting at N'genda but no one of importance as far as could be judged turned up, their agent in this District appearing to be a weakling and could not say who the President of the Association is or what its aims and objects are. A number of quite uninfluential semi-missionary natives attended this meeting and as no sense could be obtained from any of them the meeting was a dismal failure in every sense and no attempt was made to call another.[29]

The strength of the chief's organization (the Kikuyu Association) in Kiambu district meant that KCA did not have a very strong base of support. Moreover, the main rural headquarters for the KCA was in Fort Hall district. However, in 1927, the KCA's influence in Kiambu grew. This came about because of the colonial administration's failure to clearly define the boundaries of the Reserves. This issue had been unresolved from the 1910 alienation of land under the Crown Lands Ordinance.[30] From 1910 to 1927, the Kikuyu constantly feared that new land expropriations would occur. The KCA was able to capitalize on these fears when the government proposed to take land from Kikuyu occupants to expand the area of Tigoni township. Although the plans to expand Tigoni were not carried out until 1938, the fear that land would be arbitrarily seized agitated Kikuyu land holders. The other land related fear involved the size of the Reserve. The government had not demarcated the boundaries between the Reserves, Crown Land, and settler farms. Africans feared that they would lose even more land to alienation. At the same time, hut taxation was increased and the number of salt licks for the Reserves were cut back.[31] The Kiambu Kikuyu anxiously questioned the DC about these conditions at the public meeting he convened.[32]

Soon after these changes, a new government inquiry into land holdings was instituted. The Hilton Young Commission was dispatched to Kenya from London with the goal of investigating the possibilities of closer union between the three British territories in East Africa—Kenya, Tanganyika, and Uganda. The KCA and the KA took advantage of these meetings and presented memoranda to the commission on the land issue on February 4, 1928. The moderate and radical associations were in partial agreement. They had similar viewpoints on closer union: both associations were opposed to it because they feared it would result in increased settler control, further erosion of African freedom, and more land appropriation. However, closer union was neither the sole issue the commission considered nor the only concern of the associations. The salient points of agreement were that there should be African representation in the Kenya Legislative Council, not just a European missionary appointed by the government to represent all Africans. The associations also agreed that the total number of persons appointed to represent African interests should be increased to twelve. The KCA wanted all twelve appointees to be Africans, the KA proposed that four should be Africans and that the remaining eight members should be missionaries and British administrators.[33]

The associations also agreed on the *kipande* question. Both wanted to abolish them. They also asked that a larger portion of their taxes be used to provide educational facilities for Africans. The points of agreement were not the only signs that the divide between moderates and militants was closing. M.R. Vidal, DC for Kiambu, observed in 1928 that:

> During the year the division that existed between the younger generation who belong to the [Kikuyu] Central Association and the older generation of chiefs who form the Kikuyu Association has considerably lessened and there are signs that they are now pulling together and putting forward their grievances in a more constitutional manner through the Local Native Council.[34]

The narrowing rift between the male moderate organization and the more militant nationalist association was to deepen in the late twenties. One of the important points of departure involved the role of women in the two organizations. During the turbulent twenties, African politics in Kiambu district were largely male dominated. Though it is true that many of the issues revolved around British treatment of women in labor and under new laws which replaced tradition, women's involvement in protest politics and in the fruitless processes of negotiation was indirect.[35] On the surface, it appeared that women were not very much involved with the new political strategies which were seeping into the Kikuyu land units, since they were excluded from membership in associations by moderates and militants alike. In reality, the changes British colonialism produced impacted women as much as they did males. Women shared the sense of powerlessness and frustration which was one reaction to the sweeping changes. To Kikuyu women of the twenties, British control of their lives seemed to increase almost yearly. The KA and the KCA seemed to present only minor challenges to British policies. Out of this sense of frustration, women entered the political arena as activists.

One of the measures of the failure of the associations to produce changes in colonial policy was the Hilton Young Commission. Neither association influenced the commission; the suggestion of African representation in the government was ignored. Becoming impatient with the tactics sending petitions and memoranda to the government, women activists focused their criticism on the KCA.[36]

The Kikuyu Central Association eagerly sought allies in the 1920s. They tried to gain widespread public support for their ideas and solicited public contributions to finance their operations.[37] Women contributed money to the KCA but were relegated to secondary status. This meant that they were never allowed a voice in decision-making on the central committee; they were not allowed to be agents who disseminated information to rural populations. Thus, both the KA and the KCA replicated the pre-colonial asymmetrical power relations in the new politics. In 1920, a group of women from Kiambu district broke this dynamic. They chose to establish a female power base from which to negotiate for equality with the KCA. From 1930 to 1940, when the KCA was banned by the British, the women activists had some success. Most Kikuyu women identified the issue of female circumcision as an attempt by European missionaries to destroy the integrity of Kikuyu culture. Women, along with men, left the churches, withheld their children from the mission schools, and established independent primary schools for their children. They were especially active in promoting education for girls on the secondary and teacher training levels at Githunguri college. Many women who were aggressive on the issue of girls' education had been noted political activists from the 1930s. They were the first generation of Kiambu women who sought entrance into the nationalist organization as initiators rather than observers of the conflict between Africans and Europeans over the four issues of land, labor, taxation, and education.

The new leadership of the KCA, many of whom had held membership in the old EAA, remained exclusively male.[38] The

KCA spread into the rural areas by organizing meetings at the homes of individuals. At these meetings, the issues were discussed and recruitment of other Kikuyu was planned. These meetings were only open to men, although women prepared the food which was served. As soon as the meeting was opened for serious discussion of issues and tactics, women were told to leave.[39] Many women believed that they, too, should have a voice in politics and an acknowledged role in the association. They sought recognition as something more than mere providers of food for men's meetings. They also believed that they had demonstrated concern over the issues of the day, including the deportation of Harry Thuku. More and more women became disenchanted with their status and reached a turning point in 1930. Kikuyu women split from the KCA and formed their own organization—the Mumbi Central Association.[40] One of the organizers of the association described the decision to leave the men's organization and form an autonomous women's party:

> Starting in 1930 the women were angry because of the cooking and because we were not allowed into the meetings. . . . Women of the village known as Rugigi cooked *jahe, uji,* and killed a goat. Then we went to different villages and started to give oaths. This was in 1930. . . . We went to the villages and organized in each place. . . . Then starting in 1933 we joined the men again. . . . The women told the men we should join together. We killed a goat, made *jahe, uji* and we prepared the thing. We called the men. By 2:00 we took the oath: We will not sell our soil. Don't report a Kikuyu to a European.[41]

This dramatic occurrence had two important features: first, the tactics women used for organization were similar to men's tactics. They organized on the local level in small units and the issues were the same as the KCA's issues. Second, women did not try to diminish the nationalist movement; instead they sought inclusion as concerned, politicized Kikuyu. They did not intend to sustain a permanent autonomous female association free from male control. Their goal was to acquire recognition of the potential value of women's organizational abilities and spheres of influence.[42] They separated from the KCA because they believed that the nationalist movement was hindered by excluding women's talents and ignoring the strength of their commitment. The break was a necessary means of making their point, not an ultimate end of female ambition. The return of the women in 1933, at their own instigation, resulted in a redefinition of the terms of their involvement. More and more, women assumed positions of leadership in rural politics in the district.

Wangui wa Gikuhiu joined KCA when it was first organized. Though an active supporter of Mau Mau, she described herself as "only a member." Women leaders "did the work of talking about how to get the land."[43] Priscilla Wambaki, a leader before Mau Mau and a KANU leader of in her division in the 1970s, recalled the beginning of women's participation in politics:

Q: Were you a member of a political party?
A: Yes, I was a member of KAU.
Q: Did you belong to KCA?
A: KCA was the one before KAU, but I was only a member of KAU.
Q: Did you ever hear of an organization called Mumbi Central Association?
A: I was a member of Mumbi Central Association. I was also a member of KAU.
Q: When did you join Mumbi Central Association?
A: I can't remember the year but I joined it with Wambui Wagarama and I worked with Rebecca Njeri.
Q: What did Mumbi Central Association want to accomplish?
A: Kiama kia Mumbi had the aim to preserve the customs, to not allow them to dissolve. But before we went further the war started. . . . First women were not invited to join Kikuyu Central Association. We met together and decided we didn't like this so we asked the pastor of the church to help us. He did and we raised money and started Mumbi Central Association. We would have dances to raise money and the men could not matter. It was only Mbiu Koinange who was allowed. After a while we joined the men again.
Q: How much money did you raise for *Kiriri*?[44]
A: I don't know since the books were destroyed, but it was much more than 100,000 shillings.
Q: How many oaths did you take?
A: Only children did not take the oath. I won't talk about that. I want to tell how Mbiu helped to build the dormitories so that you can understand the role women played when Mzee [Kenyatta] came from Europe. We met with him. We had not completed the dormitories. We had no windows. He helped us, he was on our side. From that time on he was on our side. If there were no women, then the war would not have been carried on. And the women were mostly girls, because if the men were beaten, they would tell the secrets and the girls would not. Even Mzee knew that the girls played a great part and that is why he gave us Madaraka.[45]

When World War II began, the colonial government proscribed all African political parties using the rationale that African organizations were potential sources of subversive, anti-European activities. A threat of an invasion from Italy seemed to many in the government to be a strong possibility. The KCA had vocally criticized the government from 1925 to 1940 and had sent numerous petitions to Nairobi and London. British officials were anxious to eliminate the KCA within Kenya, since they were opposed to any political body which assumed the voice for African dissatisfactions.[46] Many in government circles considered African leaders to be "adept liars and past masters in sowing the seeds of false rumours."[47] Yet these same leaders were credited with constantly voicing African discontent over land policies, the lack of significant government funding for education, and the imbalance of political power between Africans and Europeans.

With African dissent removed from the scene, the government concentrated its energies on the war from 1940 to 1945. The stage for African political activity was severely limited. In the post-war era, African political activity surged to the forefront of the colony's attention. A new political association, the Kenya African Union (KAU) was formed in Central Province in 1944. It included many of the members of the banned KCA. By 1950, the Kenya government was convinced that KAU was generating a dangerous climate. KAU's membership had grown to include 100,000 Kikuyu.[48]

The legacy of women's forced entry into the militant KCA was a major transformation in women's political roles. From that time onwards, women were formally included in Kenya's political parties, in membership and, to a lesser extent, in leadership roles. KAU had a formal women's wing. So too, did the organization which came to be known as Mau Mau, the Kenya African National Union (KANU) and the Kenya African Democratic Union (KADU). In the Mau Mau movement, the full transformation of women's political roles can be measured. For it was in Mau Mau that women participated in the full spectrum of the organization's activities. They served as recruiters, organizers, spies, soldiers, and prisoners of war. The examination of their activities will be will be taken up in Chapter 7.

Notes

1. Carl Rosberg and John Nottingham, *The Myth of "Mau Mau": Nationalism in Kenya* (New York: Frederick A. Praeger, 1966; reprint ed., New York: Meridian Books, The World Publishing Company, 1970), p. 41.
2. Rosberg and Nottingham, *The Myth of "Mau Mau,"* p. 26.
3. For a more detailed description of the rivalries between the moderate and radical associations see Marshal Clough, "Chiefs and Politicians: Local Politics and Social Change in Kiambu, Kenya," (Ph.D. dissertation, Stanford University, 1978); Rosberg and Nottingham, *The Myth of "Mau Mau;"* John Spencer, "Kau and Mau Mau: Some Connections," *Kenya Historical Review*, 5, 1977, pp. 201-224; and W. McGregor Ross, *Kenya From Within* (London: Allen and Unwin, 1927; reprint ed., 1968).
4. Rosberg and Nottingham, *The Myth of "Mau Mau,"* pp. 12, 27-30.
5. Ibid.
6. Interview with Tabitha Wambui, Kiambu Town, October 3, 1978.
7. Interview with Wambui Wagarama, Kabete, April 29, 1979.
8. Interview with Mary Wanjiko, Kiambu Town, November 22, 1978.
9. F.B. Welbourn, *East African Christian* (London: Oxford University Press, 1965), p. 84.
10. For a fuller account of Harry Thuku's political career see Rosberg and Nottingham, *The Myth of "Mau Mau,"* pp. 35-104; and Harry Thuku, *An Autobiography* (Nairobi: Oxford University Press, 1970), p. 17.
11. Kenya National Archives (KNA): Annual Report(AR)/279/Kiambu (KBU)/14, Annual Report 1921, p. 114.
12. See discussion of the Circular and its effects on labor in Chapters 3 and 4.
13. KNA. AR/279/KBU/14, Annual Report 1921, p. 11.
14. Thuku, *An Autobiography*, p. 92.
15. Ibid.
16. Ibid., p. 25.
17. Ibid., pp. 25-27.
18. Ross, *Kenya From Within*, p. 229.
19. Ross, *Kenya From Within*, p. 223; Rosberg and Nottingham, *The Myth of "Mau Mau,"* p. 52.
20. The Norfolk hotel was situated near the Nairobi jail and a favorite gathering place of Europeans in 1922.
21. Thuku, *An Autobiography*, p. 33. The death of Mary Nyanjiru is also recounted by Job Muchuchu, an eyewitness, in Rosberg and Nottingham, *The Myth of "Mau Mau,"* pp. 51-52.
22. Interview with Mrs. Harry Thuku, Muthiko, December 19, 1978.
23. Interview with Wambui Wagarama, Kabete, April 29, 1979.
24. KNA. AR/279/KBU/14, Annual Reports 1921, pp. 1-2.
25. KNA. AR/279/KBU/14, Annual Report 1921, p. 2.
26. Thuku, *An Autobiography*, p. 16. See the discussion of forced labor in Chapters 3 and 4.

27. D. Mukaro-Ng`anga, *Thirty Years Before Mau Mau: A Study in Rural Resistance and Political Organization in Murang'a District, 1920-1952* (Nairobi: Institute of African Studies, Paper No. 104, 1978).

28. KNA. Native Affairs Department (NAD) Annual Report 1927, p. 2.

29. KNA. KBU/81, Political Record Book (PRB) 1925, p.1.

30. See Chapter 3.

31. KNA. AR/296/KBU/20, Annual Report 1927, p. 2.

32. Ibid.

33. Rosberg and Nottingham, *The Myth of "Mau Mau,"* pp. 93-96.

34. KNA. AR/299/KBU/21, Annual Report 1928, p. 2.

35. See Chapters 3, 4, and 5.

36. Women activists who were interviewed in Kiambu District from 1978-1979 were very critical of the KCA. Few mentioned the KA in their comments about the failures of the tactics of negotiation.

37. KNA. KBU/22, Handing Over Report (HOR) 1929, p. 23.

38. George Bennett, "The Development of Political Organizations in Kenya," *Political Studies*, 2, 1957, pp. 120-125.

39. Interview with Wambui Wagarama, Kabete, April 29, 1979; and interview with Priscilla Wambaki, Ngenda, May 16, 1979.

40. Mumbi is the name of the legendary female progenitor of the Kikuyu.

41. Interview with Wambui Wagarama, Kabete, April 29, 1979.

42. Interview with Nduta wa Kore, Tingang'a, January 13, 1979.

43. Interview with Wangui wa Gikuhi, Ruiru, May 13, 1979.

44. *Kiriri* was the women's dormitory at the Githunguri Independent School which was established by nationalists after the break with church and government controlled education which resulted from the circumcision controversy.

45. Interview with Priscilla Wambaki, Juja, May 23, 1979. Madaraka is the annual independence day celebration. Women's organizations are prominently featured in the day's activities.

46. Bennett, "The Development," p. 128.

47. KNA. KBU/22, HOR 1929, p. 23.

48. Bennett, "The Development," p. 128.

7

Kikuyu Women and the Mau Mau Rebellion

Studies of the Mau Mau movement in Kenya seldom give evidence of women's active participation in the various aspects of the battle against European domination. The major works on Kenyan nationalism and Mau Mau do not place women at the center of the organization. If they are mentioned at all, women are credited with a minimal importance and accomplishments.[1] These descriptions fail to show the historical development of women's involvements in the key issues and events of the nationalist movement; they do not focus on the many achievements and sacrifices of Kikuyu women. Data on the women's involvement in Mau Mau and the importance of their contributions comes from two sources. First, the British colonial government was quite aware of the potential power of women. In the annual reports, DCs frequently chronicled individual political acts by women and wrote of the political mood of Kikuyu women. They often commented on women's impact in sustaining nationalist ideas and activities. Second, oral data collection reveals that there was a nucleus of women in Kiambu district who took on the task of organizing rural resistance to colonialism in Central Province.[2]

Any investigation into the course of Kikuyu nationalism and the Mau Mau movement is incomplete without a consideration of women if it can be demonstrated that women played pivotal roles in either the organization of anti-colonial activities or the dissemination of nationalist ideas. Previous scholarship has centered on male figures—especially on those males who were articulate in the English language. This tendency inaccurately focuses nationalism on the urban areas and ignores the equally powerful impetus for African control which originated in the Reserve areas from rural men and women. An additional area that can be redressed through studying women rebels is the question of a transformation of ideas about women's place in politics. Investigation into women's roles in Mau Mau show a far greater degree of sexual parity within the movement than previous scholarship on the subject has indicated. Women were active in every aspect of the movement and performed vital tasks which sustained the struggle. These ranged from being members of "gangs" in the forest, to serving as participants and organizers of the rural network which channeled supplies and information to the forest armies. Further, women were also incarcerated in the detention camps and jails, processed through the "pipelines," and forced to live in barbed wire enclosed villages during the emergency. Part of the legacy of Mau Mau is that large numbers of the Kenya population credit the rebellion—though it was militarily defeated—with the political victory which produced independence. When this retrospective pride in the rebellion is discussed as a part of Kenya's national heritage, it is absolutely essential that women's contributions be recognized.

Increasingly in the post-colonial era, African women have sought legitimacy within Kenya politics. Women leaders often invoke the untold story of female participation in the most widely known anti-colonial struggle in East Africa as a justification for a larger share of government development plans. A final interesting area of historiography which may be altered as a result of a close scrutiny of women's participation in the rebellion is the ways that our conception of peasant rebellion may be altered. Several scholars on peasant rebellions assert that peasants do not generally rebel against colonial domination. The Mau Mau rebellion is a prime exception to this general assertion. Where there is some demonstration of activist peasant rebellion, little is said of peasant women's roles in resisting colonialism.

The study of women's participation in Mau Mau can be divided into five sections: (a) the growth of political consciousness among women; (b) the role of women in the formation and spread of nationalist parties; (c) the identification of women who were leaders and who were imprisoned as Mau Mau terrorists; (d) women's roles in the Land and Freedom army; (e) the conditions in the Kamiti prison which housed women Mau Mau.[3]

Kikuyu women did not suddenly in 1947 develop a world view that included anti-colonial sentiments. Their involvement in anti-colonialism began in the early years of the twentieth century. At first, their political activism was not focused through association politics. As a result of their isolation, women's political activities up to the 1930s were localized and largely centered on rural issues. Their exclusion from the nationalist associations accounts for this. Women were most concerned about the rural issues of women and children's forced labor on the coffee estates and government road projects. From 1912 through 1930, women protested these labor polices through two means: first, they identified with the East African Association petition which was presented at the Dagoretti meeting in June 1921 and lent their support to the association's ideals.[4] Second, women created and performed protest songs. Women's informal action was directed towards criticizing chiefs and retainers, who were a part of the labor recruitment system, and government policies which promoted the economic exploitation of women workers. Women sang scurrilous songs about the men who abused them. Some of the songs praised Harry Thuku. This type of political song was a precursor of those used in African nationalist politics from 1920 to the end of the Mau Mau period. They were directed against the missionaries during the circumcision controversy which tore asunder the fabric of Kikuyu unity, added fuel to the nationalist movement, and inspired thousands of Kikuyu women to become activists themselves. Shortly after the split and the creation of autonomous Kikuyu churches and schools, women were successful in joining the nationalist associations. This set the stage for their full participation in the anti-colonial struggle through the KAU and Mau Mau.

Kikuyu women joined the nationalist associations to improve their economic status, gain access to the political process, get more education, and regain alienated land. Muthoni wa Gachie, a member of KCA and KAU in the 1940s, recounted women's motives as being political in origin:

Q: When did you join?
A: I joined in April of 1945.
Q: Why did you become a member?
A: So that I could be a politician of the country.
Q: Were there other women who were members?
A: Yes, there was a group of us.
Q: How many?
A: The whole of Central Province.
Q: Were women already members when you joined?
A: Yes, very many were already members.
Q: What did KCA want?

A: We wanted only to make the Europeans go from the country.
Q: What were your responsibilities as a member?
A: I was cooking for visitors and I contributed for Mzee to go to Europe. We were fighting so we could know how to become independent.
Q: Were you a leader?
A: Yes, even I was taken to prison.
Q: How long did you spend in jail?
A: In one year I was jailed three times. This was in 1958. Then I was detained in 1959 for one year. I was detained at Athii River, then I was taken to Embu.[5]

Women's Roles in Organizing Mau Mau

In 1950, the Native Affairs Department noted that there had emerged a violent organization which it termed "Mau Mau." The government quickly moved to curtail and eliminate the movement. The commissioner recorded:

> [Mau Mau] first came to light in Nyeri and Kiambu, when it was found that secret meetings were being held at which an illegal oath, accompanied by appropriately horrid ritual, was being administered to initiates binding them to treat all Government servants as enemies, to disobey Government orders and eventually to evict all Europeans from the country.[6]

The government reacted to the perceived threat of Mau Mau by arresting the oath takers and declaring the organization to be illegal. Despite these measures, the society grew rapidly over the next two years. Hundreds of thousands of Kikuyu took the oath of allegiance to the new party, fled to the forest to conduct a guerrilla war against the Europeans, and conducted what amounted to a civil war against those Kikuyu who remained loyal to the colonial government and/or allowed themselves to be co-opted into the Homeguard forces.[7]

Kikuyu women participated in significant numbers in nearly every aspect of the war waged by the Land and Freedom army. Women who had been instrumental in forming the Mumbi Central Association were in the vanguard of what became thousands of women who were identified as subversives by the government.[8] These women were recognized rural leaders; they administered oaths and were among the first of the Kikuyu leaders to be jailed by the British under the Emergency Orders of October 1952. These orders gave the government martial law powers. The situation was declared to be an emergency because of the massive oathing ceremonies held by the Kikuyu, the spread of the Land and Freedom army from the urban areas into the rural districts, and the rise of violence against Loyalist Kikuyu. In Kiambu district, Senior Chief Waruhiu, a prominent pro-government spokesman, was assassinated. His murder was the event which precipitated the announcement of the state of emergency and the British declaration of war against the Land and Freedom army.[9] Nduta wa Kore and Wambui Wagarama, who were past secretary and president of the Mumbi Central Association, were immediately arrested under the Emergency orders:

> [At] the starting of Mau Mau. . .the leaders were taken to Kapenguria. Mzee (Kenyatta) was caught and jailed. All the leaders were jailed, even I and my husband were jailed on the same day.[10]
>
> And the woman who was the leader was Wambui (Wagarama). There were many women (in this group) but I don't know how many since we didn't count them. Up until 1952 I was a leader. I was jailed in 1952 in Githunguri. . .because of being a politician. . . . I stayed in jail for one month and two weeks. The second time I was taken to Kamiti, that was in 1953. They said that I was organizing the women and put me in jail.[11]

Wagara Wainana also described herself as a leader of Mau Mau. She was able to avoid being placed in detention:

Q: When did you take your first oath?
A: About 1948.
Q: How many did you take?
A: Only two.
Q: Were you a member of the Mau Mau committee?
A: I was a committee member of KAU and of Mau Mau.
Q: Which area did you represent?
A: I represented Karura (Muthurura) Kiambaa.
Q: Was your husband involved in politics?
A: Yes.
Q: How was it that you were not put in prison?
A: I was not detained because my husband was beaten. My co-wife's son was also detained. The co-wife was sick so that there was no one left so that the Europeans left me to care for the sick.
Q: Did they know that you were an active Mau Mau?
A: They knew but not who the actual person was unless the other Kikuyu told them.[12]

These foremothers of female activism were not the only women's leaders who were jailed under the Emergency Orders. Rebecca Njeri Kairi, Mary Wanjiko, and Priscilla Wambaki were other well-known Kiambu who were signaled out by the government as subversive influences.[13] The officials pinpointed what appears to have been the top layer of a hierarchy of female influence in the district. From the 1930s, these women had created a network which transmitted information and money throughout the district. The chain of command had two women who were almost equally influential in the district. Six women, representing the six divisions in the district, were responsible to the two district leaders. The eight women leaders who carried the major responsibility for organizing women in the entire district were:

District Organizers	
Rebecca Njeri Kairi	Wambui Wagarama

Priscilla Wambaki	Mary Wanjiko	Nduta wa Kore	Virginia Gachege	Margo wa Mimi	Mary Nyarurui

(Division Level Organizers)

Rebecca Njeri Kairi merited special mention in the district annual report as: "Ex-woman leader of Mau Mau, close associate of Kinyatta (sic) vitriolic tongue, friend of Kiano and Mboya, stirring up all the hate she can."[14] This description of Rebecca in the official records is important in that it shows that women activists were not invisible to the local officials. Because of their high visibility, they were as quickly identified as were the male leaders. The 1952 arrests were designed to decapitate the movement, to eliminate the most influential members. The district officers had kept watch on female leadership and included them in the first blow against Mau Mau. The network which these women created and operated included one in every four women of the district who were influenced to cooperate in some way with KAU.[15] Eighty thousand Kikuyu were detained during the Emergency.[16] Towards the end of the Emergency in 1956, there were still 16,386 Kikuyu from Central Province who were awaiting release from the detention camps and jails. One-third of the detainees in the camps came from Kiambu district.[17]

The reasons for women's imprisonment as Mau Mau were clear. British officials and western observers, who were either in Kenya during the Emergency or shortly thereafter, frequently noted women's importance to the rebellion. Women were very active in the secret oathing ceremonies and in the clandestine network that supplied materials to the forest fighters.[18] In the first example, women were highly visible at the oathing ceremonies. The oath was a declaration of allegiance. Oath takers swore to fight to regain Kikuyu land and expel Europeans from Kenya. In traditional society, women and children never took oaths. However, the Mumbi Central Association and KAU used oaths to invoke women's loyalty. Later, the Mau Mau organization used the oath irrespective of age and sex.[19] Women administered oaths. This represented a major change in their authority. There were six oaths. The first was known as the "A" oath and the second was the "B-Batuni" oath. These two were given to all initiates after a goat had been slaughtered and its blood drunk by the oath takers.[20] These two oaths were often given to large groups of women, children and men.[21] The advanced oaths were taken by individuals who demonstrated a high degree of commitment to the rebellion. Leaders took the most advanced oaths, those more minimally involved took only the first oath of secrecy.[22] Mass oathing ceremonies were held in the first few years after the founding and spread of KAU when large numbers of Kikuyu were required to demonstrate loyalty to the party. These ceremonies were conducted by men and women.[23] In 1950, the Kiambu DC reported to his superiors that men were no longer administering oaths of loyalty to Mau Mau. Women, however were proceeding with the work of oath-giving:

> For a woman to administer a Muma [sic] oath would be utterly contrary to Kikuyu custom—although it must be admitted that until the Dedan oaths were started it was also unknown for a woman to have a Muma oath.[24]

A break with past custom in giving and taking oaths was one of the many changes in gender roles nationalism introduced for women. Phyllis Wanjiko wa Mimi, the women's wing leader who was responsible for the area from Ndumberi to Tingang'a, often gave the oath to mixed groups of men, women, and children in the *shamba* near her homestead.[25] The usual procedure was for a woman to contact friends, relatives, and neighbors and ask them to join KAU. Before the declaration of the Emergency, this was openly done. After the October arrests of the leaders and the proscription of KAU, greater secrecy was used. Operation Anvil, a massive military operation, was launched against Mau Mau in 1954.[26] Thereafter, Mau Mau oath givers used even greater caution. As a result of "Anvil", thousands of Kiambu Kikuyu were imprisoned under the detention orders. Over 375 from the Gatundu division found themselves in prison. During the operation, the British tried to separate the rebels from loyal Kikuyu and those who were not involved at all. Nearly 8,000 women were detained in the prison facility at Kamiti where a special installation was built for women Mau Mau.[27]

The Female "Passive" Wing

Perhaps the most crucial area of women's involvement in the rebellion was their contributions in the supply lines of the organization. The rebellion could not have endured for seven years without the supplies of information, food, medicine, and guns that flowed from the towns and Reserves into the forest. From the first days of the uprising, women were the primary source of these items. The DC of Kiambu observed:

> In September, the Chura location appeared to become a centre of the Mau Mau central committee, and every Itura had its own sub-committee, nor did they lack a women's section. The latter throughout may well be described as the "eyes and ears of Mau Mau."[28]

In the Native Affairs Department report for 1953, women's importance and the diverse tasks they performed in the rebellion were recorded. They supplied food to the fighters when they came near the villages; women also carried food into the forest and several were captured dressed as Mau Mau soldiers.[29]

Although women were well-known participants in the rebellion, the strength of their commitment perplexed British officials. Europeans generally portrayed the rebellion as violent, bestial, unchristian, and uncivilized. They were shocked by women's prominence in the movement. Since the British males were accustomed to the 1950s' English ideal of docile female behavior, women's participation was more unacceptable to them than was men's. Also, Kikuyu women had not been noted for participation in criminal activities. During the first fifty years of British rule in Kenya, female crime had been so low that no jail facilities were built for them because "The extent of Female crime, both adult and juvenile before the Emergency presented no problem."[30] Government officials were shocked by Kikuyu women's "truculence." In 1953, the Native Affairs Department tried to account for this phenomena:

> The attitude of the women of the tribe towards the Emergency was, in general particularly distressing. Perhaps owning to the divergences in educational standards between the sexes, the primitive and indigenous cult of Mau Mau has had for many a powerful appeal. There have been instances of female relatives being privy to the murder of their loyal menfolk.[31]

Other reports included comments on how much women were attached to the rebellion:

> [there was] a reputation for particularly tough women who are certainly the backbone of the sublocation. Their truculent attitude is most noticeable at barazas.[32]

Women did, indeed, provide a backbone for Mau Mau. Since the women's chain of command had been established as early as the 1940s, the leadership in the hierarchy knew the degree of commitment of women in the entire district and had an efficient means of increasing the numbers of women who were associated with Mau Mau. They were also able to acquire necessary items quickly. When the freedom fighters took to the forests, this network was already in full operation. The funnelling of supplies and the arrangement of safe hiding places became women's responsibility because of their superior organization. Former women activists explained the operation of the network in great detail. Each district had a central committee that was responsible for arranging safe places and smuggling supplies. One woman was chosen to be responsible for the coordination of women's activities, it was she who was contacted by the central committee and told when supplies were needed. She would then contact her division leaders and they obtained whatever was required from women under their commands:

Q: Did you go to the forest?
A: No, I didn't go.
Q: Did you help the forest fighters?
A: Yes.
Q: How did you help?
A: I gave them food, money, everything.
Q: Where were the fighters you helped located?
A: They were in Ndeiya forest. They came from Ndeiya to Muguga, from Muguga they went to the (Abedares) forest. People from all these areas cooked for them.
Q: How would you know when to prepare the food?
A: They would send one of the fighters from the forest to say that they would be there at a certain hour and that we should prepare.[33]

Women easily channeled food to the forest fighters. But medicines, doctor's services, and ammunition were also needed. With the exception of doctor's services, women were the major suppliers. Some women, who did not consider themselves to be formal Mau Mau members but who identified with the goals of the rebellion, were able to supply these goods because their of special place in the colonial regime. On crucial occasions, a nurse's aide at Kiambu hospital entered into the network when she smuggled medicine out of the hospital and gave it to a Mau Mau woman:

Q: Where did you live at the time of the Emergency?
A: I lived in the hospital. . . . I was a nurse at the Kiambu hospital. I was there from 1950 until 1957.
Q: Did you ever cook for the Mau Mau?
A: No, but I gave them medicines.
Q: Were you ever caught giving medicine?
A: No, I was giving them secretly.
Q: How did you get the medicines to the fighters?
A: The fighters came secretly at night to get the medicines and then they would go back to their camps.[34]

Other women recounted the methods used for smuggling:

When the war started we thought of some people going to the forest. We were cooking food and taking it to the forest. We carried guns. If we gave it to her (pointing to Phyllis Wanjiko wa Mimi) she would take it to the forest. We went during the night. During the day the Homeguard came to collect us. We were brought here to dig the ground with our hands. Some were killed. Others were jailed for some years. Then from there the war slowly came to an end.[35]

Yet another respondent described how women braved arrest, imprisonment, and punishment:

Q: Did you ever help the forest fighters?
A: Yes, I helped with food and took food to the forest. If they could cook, the young girls would carry the food. I, myself, carried the food.
Q: Where was this forest?
A: They were not in a forest. They would stay in a house and food would be taken to them.
Q: How long did you help?
A: I helped from the start of Mau Mau until the end of it. We were troubled very much by giving them food.
Q: Were you ever beaten because of your activities?
A: Yes, very much.
Q: Were you jailed?
A: No.
Q: Were you punished in other ways?
A: There were many ways, men were castrated, women had bottles put into their private parts. . . . This happened to me. Others were detained. There were books for registering yourself as Mau Mau. It was a big book. I kept the book. When I knew what was going on, I burnt the book and that is how I escaped.
Q: How many names were in the book?
A: Two thousand names.
Q: Was that only for Kambui?
A: Yes, it was there at Kambui.
Q: Was the group mixed?
A: Yes, it was men and women.[36]

As record keeper, Veronica Njoki said that those who were recruited into the movement were men and women, children were not used as part of the "passive wing.'" Only those who were aware of the dangers of participation and who demonstrated commitment were registered and relied on for supplies.[37]

Women's Roles in the Forest Camps

These are a few of the experiences of the thousands of women who made up the "passive wing." Though the British called them "passive" they were actively involved in the war; they operated with full knowledge that they risked torture and imprisonment if they were detected. Other than this type of involvement, women also participated to the extent of joining the guerilla camps in th forests. While there, they had two roles. The first was caring foı the communities in exile and the second was serving as soldiers Life in the forests was precarious at the best of times. Women whc were the "homemakers," were especially at risk after the Britisł began to send forces into the forests to destroy the guerilla camps The King's African Rifles, the Homeguard forces, and pseudo-gangs dressed to appear as Mau Mau could accidentally stumbl‹ upon groups of women and children in the forest while the Maı Mau fighting units were on a mission. Despite these dangers women raised their families in the camps. A forest camp wa: established in the once heavily forested area just outside of Nairobi (now named the Nairobi City Park). The government was aware oı the camp. Security forces made repeated attempts to discover it: location and halt the flow of goods into the camp from the Kiambu Reserve and Nairobi.

> Whilst. . .last year *Mau Mau* activities overshadowed the whole area, yet 1955 this overcast was well pierced, and a definitely clearer outlook appeared over the troubled areas. . .due to the intense activity of all Security forces. . .[and] "Anvil". . .which so greatly improved the situation in Nairobi was reflected in Kiambu, though the "forest" of Nairobi still remained the headquarters of *Mau Mau* early in the year. But it soon became clear that contact between the forest and the *Mau Mau* part of Nairobi was getting very tenuous, and later on it virtually ceased.[38]

Elizabeth Wanjiko spent one year in the Nairobi guerilla camp with her husband, but their four children stayed in the Reserves with their grandmother. The camp broke up when British forces intensified their search for it and captured many of the fighters:

Q: Was there a large group in the forest?

A: Yes, there were very many of us and I left the forest at the time my husband was jailed.

Q: Was the camp ever attacked by the Europeans?

A: The Europeans kept searching to see how they could destroy us. They stopped coming to the forest at the time my husband was detained.

Q: Did you live in the forest after he was detained?

A: My husband was taken during the night, the following morning I went home. I never returned to the forest but the fighters continued to help me. . . . They brought me money so I could educate my children.

Q: How long was your husband detained?
A: Seven years. He was caught at the beginning, that was just after Mzee was detained. . . . He was taken in the forest, he was not alone. There were very many men with him. The women were hiding in another place and the women were the ones who knew what was going on. . . . Because the men were detained, the wives went each to their own homes.
Q: What was life like in the forest?
A: The houses were just huts that we built out of junk so that if you saw a policeman coming you could leave it. We were just putting rubbish together. There were no *shambas*. Food came from the homes [in the villages]. We washed and hung clothes near the streams, the camp was built near the stream but if not then the fighters would bring water in their cars.[39]

John Diuni was the leader of the camp while Elizabeth was in the forest. The camp followed the traditional male/female division of labor. The freedom fighters had an efficient supply network, but they also stole food and supplies when these failed them. Medicines were smuggled into the forest camp by sympathetic doctors who ventured into the camps to treat the sick. Their visits were made on a regular basis and no special summons for help was necessary to arrange these visits.[40] Forest fighters often kept close ties after British attack forces destroyed their camps. Once Elizabeth Wanjiko left the forest after the men were captured she joined in the passive wing of Mau Mau and sent supplies to other groups in the forest camps.

Other women formed part of the fighting forces. The number of armed women in the rebellion is impossible to estimate from the available data. There was more than a random one or two female soldiers for special mention of them is made in the district reports. The capture of a woman warrior was rare, but it did occur. One such warrior, Elizabeth Gachika, described herself as a "freedom fighter." She took her first oath in 1951. In 1952, some Kikuyu living in her village reported her to the authorities. She was arrested and sentenced to three months in jail. Along with thirty five other oath-takers, she was detained and sent to the Nairobi jail.[41]

After Elizabeth Gachika was released from her three month term in the Nairobi jail, she decided to join one of the established forest camps in the Nyandura (Abedares) forest. This camp had a mixed population of from 200 to 300 people who had come from Kiambu, Meru, or Nyeri districts. Like other women in the forest, she performed domestic labor of cooking and smuggling food. In this particular camp, there was no strict division of male/female labor so that Elizabeth also participated in the military operations with male warriors. From 1953 to 1955, Elizabeth was a Mau Mau soldier:

> Q: Did the women take part in the actual fighting?
> A: We were doing just like men. We could shoot and so forth. If the Europeans came into the forest, they would be beaten even by two fighters and then removed because the Europeans could not see the ones who were not fighting. . . . I shot many. . . . I went with the men on raids. The man with me refused to shoot. I took the gun and shot and then we ran away. Another woman who was with me would go to look for Europeans and if they yelled we would shoot them. We were the ones who fought for freedom, not the ones who told you about the cooking.
> Q: Did the men feel resentment because of your shooting?
> A: Men were the ones who were giving us strength to fight. It was the men who wanted us to continue to ask [for freedom]. . . . With this fight we were all together. . . . Even when we took the oath, we were men and women together. Even when I was detained I was told that Mzee was detained and that I should not worry. Chief Waruhiu was shot and the following morning I was taken to jail. . . . He was shot because of going against the Kikuyu and following the word of Europeans. The work of killing people like Waruhiu was the work of women and girls. Women were doing a lot of work. Girls are very tough.[42]

She left the camp:

> Because I was shot. When I was caught and removed from the forest by the Europeans who come from far countries. . . . I was taken first to a camp at Nyandara, near the boundary of the forest (British facility), then I was taken to Gatundu, then to Ndumberi and then to the Kiambu police station and from there to Kamiti prison. . . . They didn't take me to the hospital, even when I was brought to Kiambu, they refused to help me. I got bandages at Kamiti.[43]

Conditions in the Prisons

When the Emergency officially ended in 1956, of the 27,841 Kikuyu who were still in the detention camps, 3,103 were women.[44] Women's known activism sparked a response from the government. They were arrested, detained, and interrogated in large numbers. The following tables reveal the number of women imprisoned during the Mau Mau period and the correlation with the numbers of Africans detained in the camps. Of the 13,265 females admitted to Prison in 1955, 1,714 were discharged from prison custody, 11,467 were sentenced to imprisonment (9,961 of these were first offenders, the balance were repeat offenders).[45] Table 7.1 gives the number of African, Asian, and European women who were admitted to jails and prisons camps in the years of the Mau Mau emergency. The data includes women who were admitted for crimes unconnected with Mau Mau offenses. Therefore, at this point in the analysis, it is not possible to tell exactly how many women were admitted to prisons because of political activism or a suspicion of being involved with the Mau Mau rebellion. However, data from 1953 reveals that nearly all the women prisoners were African. Reporting on the disposal of 242 women admitted to prisons, the Prison Department noted that none were Asian or European. Only two of the African women prisoners were not native to Kenya.[46] Before the Emergency, the amount of female crime in Kenya was so slight that no particular facilities were built. To the surprise of the colonial government, when Mau Mau activities became pronounced, women's leadership and participation were on such a large scale that the prison system had to build a facility to house them. The Kamiti prison was extended to accommodate the upsurge in women prisoners and detainees; the camp included 1,335 women prisoners and 1,010 women detainees by the end of 1954.[47]

TABLE 7.1 Women Admitted to Prisons, 1952-1958

Year	*Number*	*Number Sentenced*	*Recidivists*	*First Offenders*
1952	347	n/a	n/a	n/a
1953	4 ,415	3,132	55	3,077
1954	9,609	8,494	290	8,204
1955	13,265	11,467	1,506	9,961
1956	8,900	7,906	1,627	6,279
1957	8,854	7,472	2,068	5,404
1958	7,295	5,976	1,873	4,103

Source: Kenya Colony and Protectorate. Kenya Prisons. Annual Report, 1953, p. 8; Kenya Prisons, Annual Report, 1956, p. 8-9; Kenya Prisons, Annual Report, 1958, p. 10.

TABLE 7.2 Africans Admitted to Detention Camps, 1948-1957

Year	*Number*
1948	16,369
1949	16,637
1950	18,037
1951	18,257
1952	23,201
1953	32,862
1954	25,979
1955	30,247
1956	41,441
1957	53,080

Source: Kenya Colony and Protectorate. Annual Report on the Treatment of Offenders, 1957, p. 2.

Women were also detained in other facilities. The Athii River detention camp, which was built in 1953 to contain violators of the Emergency Regulations, had ten compounds containing 1,429 detainees. One of the compounds was reserved for 27 female detainees held there.[48] Most women prisoners were Kikuyu who were sentenced to prison terms because of violations of the Emergency regulations.[49] A high ratio of the African women who were sentenced to prison were first time offenders (see Table 7.1). The data from Table 7.2 gives figures on those who were admitted to detention camps. Detainees were convicted of more serious Mau Mau activities. Whether a woman was in prison or a detention camp, sentences ranged from short terms of one or two months to the full duration of the Emergency.

TABLE 7.3 Staff Employed by the Prisons Department

	1953	*1954*	*1955*
European	125	314	422
Asia	50	81	95
African	3,025	10,630	11,850

Source: Great Britain Colonial Office Report on the Colony and Protectorate of Kenya/1954, p. 116; Kenya Colony and Protectorate. Kenya Prisons. AR/1955, p. 2.

TABLE 7.4 Lengths of Sentences

Length of Sentence	*1952 Admission on conviction*	*% of total admissions*	*1953 Admission on conviction*	*% of total admissions*
1 month or less	638	3.1	796	1.87
1 to 6 months	15,051	68.1	22,668	53.25
6 months to 2 years	4,232	20.1	11,402	26.77
2 to 3 years	387	1.9	1,190	2.79
3 years or more	1,318	6.4	6,526	15.32

Source: Kenya Colony and Protectorate. Report on the Treatment of Offenders for the Year 1953, p. 6.

The camps were not merely holding facilities. Prisoners were required to work and submit to a socialization process whose goal was to persuade them to renounce Mau Mau or be "cleansed."[50] The 50 prisons, 40 prison camps, and 32 detention camps in Kenya were staffed by Europeans, Asians, and Africans (see Table 7.3). The Community Development organization was also involved in rehabilitating prisoners.[51] At Kamiti the department was given some control over the detainees' "leisure time."[52] Nearly 300 women attended classes and were instructed in animal husbandry, hygiene, health, agriculture, and local government.[53] However, these classes were not the most important aspect of the organization's anti-Mau Mau work. The department also ran childcare facilities for women prisoners and detainees.[54] Most of the government's success in converting Mau Mau detainees in 1955 and 1956 was among female prisoners in Kamiti prison. Several facilities for women were maintained in the colony, but Kamiti was for the "hardcore" Mau Mau women.[55] In 1956 the prison released 1,194 women leaving 1,384 women in the camp. In 1957, 4,220 women were released, and 174 women Mau Mau remained in detention. Many "hardcore" Mau Mau women were not released until 1960. The rehabilitation efforts among women were so successful that by 1957 Mau Mau detainees were:

> Processed straight to their homes on release and have not passed through the pipe line camps in their own areas as is the case with men. This is a tribute to the thorough and successful rehabilitation work undertaken at the camps.[56]

Community Development officers were aided in their work of detaching women from Mau Mau by Christian missionaries. The Christian Council of Kenya sent representatives to the camps to hold Christian services and "cleanse" women prisoners of their radical beliefs.[57] The Department categorized prisoners according to the strength of their attachment to Mau Mau and response to rehabilitation. The "Y" category were those who were responding to socialization.[58] Most Kamiti women prisoners were considered to be in the "Y" category of rebels.

Conditions for women Mau Mau and/or Mau Mau suspects were similar to those for males who were arrested and detained. Oral interviews with former Mau Mau female prisoners reveal a system which tolerated and routinely used harsh treatment to enforce discipline and destroy women's loyalty to the rebellion.[59]

TABLE 7.5 Discipline of Prisoners

Punishments	*1950*	*1951*	*1952*	*1953*	*1954*
Penal Diet	22	44	57	470	63
Reduced Diet	221	107	61	98	99
Solitary Confinement	22	42	48	34	32
Solitary Confinement and Penal Diet	256	229	243	282	336
Reduced Diet and Loss of Remission	23	5	1	31	31
Reduced Diet and Solitary Confinement	-	-	2	6	3
Totals	544	427	412	921	564

Source: Kenya Colony and Protectorate. Kenya Prisons. AR/1954, p. 11.

Women in Kamiti were required to work for the prison system.[60] Light work of raising vegetables and fruit was given as a reward for cooperating with the rehabilitation program.[61] This usually took the form of taking a pledge renouncing Mau Mau and giving information about Mau Mau activity in the prisons and elsewhere. More intransigent Mau Mau were required to work on road-building and quarrying stone. The prison commandant reported in 1955 that 199,000 running feet of stone was quarried by Kamiti prisoners.[62] Once the stones were quarried and dressed, women prisoners transported them by head. In 1954, women prisoners helped in terracing the 35 acre prison farm. The value of the labor extracted from women prisoners and detainees through the cultivation of the 197,305 lbs. of vegetables they raised in 1956 was £1,973.[63] Other forms of punishment included isolation, the withholding of food allotments, and corporal punishment. In the 1954 report on the prisons, 439 prisoners were disciplined by having their food withheld.

Former women prisoners at Kamiti described the systematic use of terror, physical punishment, and forced labor. They were given inadequate food and clothing in the camps. Muthoni wa Gachie spent four and one-half years at Kamiti under these conditions. Her experiences were consistent with those recounted by other respondents.

Q: Were you a leader?
A: Yes, even I was taken to prison. . . . They came to my house to get me because I was a leader. They took me to Tingang'a and I was beaten there. . . . I was taken to Kiambu the next day and I stayed there for three days. After that I was taken in a lorry to Kamiti. I still have the manacles they put on me. My number in prison was 800. . . . We were doing heavy work, being beaten and punished. We had to carry stones on our heads.[64] When we were in detention the work was only to be beaten, given hard work and not enough food. We spent one week digging trees with other women.
Q: Why were you detained?
A: Because I was speaking about the government.
Q: What did you say?
A: I was saying that Europeans should be taken to their homes and our children should be given education.
Q: How did the Europeans know about you?
A: Other people reported me.
Q: Were you married then?
A: Yes.
Q: Did your children go to detention with you?
A: No, they were not in detention with me but they suffered because they lacked food, clothing, and education.
Q: Was your husband involved?
A: He was also jailed but not put into detention.
Q: Who took care of the children while you were in jail and detention?
A: Only God. Our homes were burnt, cattle were taken, we were left with no clothing and wore banana leaves. Even that woman gave birth on the way. We had nothing to help the child. We removed the headscarf to carry the child. Bottles were put in our private parts as a punishment.
Q: Where were you detained that they did these things?
A: Just here at Githunguri. The Homeguards were doing this.

Q: Did they do this to make you admit Mau Mau?
A: They were doing this so that the Europeans could give them something.[65]

Mary Wanjiko, who was detained in the first months of the Emergency also described the conditions in the camps: "We were punished, beaten, forced to carry stones, and doing all kinds of work. We were guarded by the police."[66] Some women were only kept in jail for short periods of one week to three months. In jail, they were subjected to beatings. These were accompanied by constant questions about their Mau Mau connections and about whether they had taken the oaths. Women who were detained in the prison camps for periods of one year to nine years reported more brutal treatment than those who were detained merely on suspicion and released after a few weeks. In the prisons, they were only given water and a few beans a day. Rations of milk, meat, and even maize meal were withheld from them. According to these survivors, they had to work on road-building projects in the vicinity of the prisons, without tools and under guard. While in prison, some women gave birth; many of the children died from malnutrition and lack of adequate care. The following excerpt from one former prisoner illustrates the treatment Mau Mau women received:

> When we were brought from the Rift Valley we never knew anybody. I was caught with Koinange's family and taken to jail at Githunguri. When we had stayed there for one month we were taken to Nairobi (a group of women), then we were taken to Kisumu by train. We stayed one year and two months and then in February of 1956 I was taken to Kamiti. . . . I was released in 1958 and all those years I was being questioned. I was beaten, some had teeth broken, some were made lame and some were badly wounded. We were all women and when we were taken to jail we were examined by the doctor. If you were pregnant then it would be written down so it would be known if you were expecting before you came in. It would be known if you had it in prison. If not, we would know who from. We took care of the children in prison—those who were born and brought there. We built nurseries for them. . . . At Kamiti we worked for ourselves. We had gardens where we grew cabbages, beans, potatoes, and so forth. During the punishment, those who said they didn't take the oath were working in the *shambas*, those who said they did take the oath had to carry soil on their heads with a basin. The would pile it up in one place and then take it away the next week.[67]

A few women leaders believed that they were given especially harsh treatment because they were leaders.

Q: Were you detained?
A: Yes.
Q: Where were you taken?
A: I was taken to Kajado in Masailand.
Q: When was this?
A: It was in 1952. That was the time when Mzee was detained with Rebecca Njeri. . . . I was in detention for one year then I was taken to the Athii River [camp]. . . . At Kajado only the women leaders were detained. Men were there also but the women were kept separate. We were not forced to work but kept locked in our rooms. There we were beaten but not too much. But when we were taken to the Athii River, we were beaten very much. All of the members of KAU—men and women— were detained. Women were not many at Athii River, we were about 200, but the men were uncountable. Those who were involved in politics or any other movement but not the church were taken to Kamiti. This was in 1954 and only women were there. We were beaten and very many died. During that time people were hanged in great numbers and we buried many there. We were not afraid of the corpses, even if we were doing this job we were still beaten. We could see some corpses with the blood from the beating still on them. During the time of getting food in the prison the young girls would pull the carts, they were tied three by three to the carts in order to pull them to where they were to get the food and then they had to pull the carts back to Kamiti. Even now, I remember what was done when I see a young girl like you. . . . We would leave the prison to dig the terraces. We took breakfast at five a.m. We had *uji,* the girls would bring it from two miles away, then we took the *jembes* and basins to dig the terraces, we were only women. . . . We got *ugali* with boiled beans or boiled cabbage. We worked up to three then we took supper at four. After that we were locked in the house and on one could go to wash. We were fed *ugali* and it was not well cooked. If there were no beans or cabbage we got only one boiled potato with the *ugali.*[68]
Q: Was there any meat, eggs, milk or tea?
A: No! Even the children couldn't get these things. I am disappointed to hear that many people believe that women did nothing in the war, we buried the bodies. The children of Kamiti were tied with ropes together to be guarded while we women worked. They gradually died off. It was due to hunger. We suffered a lot from hunger. . . . Kamiti was a hell prison. Some were dying, some were beaten to death, sometimes they died after work. We were happy when someone died because we said "Now she is free!" I was still in Kamiti in 1956.[69]

Former prisoners described these prison conditions in the 1970s. In the 1950s the British government was well aware of some of the abuses that took place in the prisons. The fact that women were a significant portion of the prison population and that they were not accorded any special treatment because of gender is little known and rarely mentioned in the historiography of Mau Mau. These facts were not hidden from public view during the Emergency. Indeed, the treatment of women prisoners caused a minor scandal in 1956 in Kenya and England. Eileen Fletcher, a Quaker who worked for a year in the Kamiti prison, stunned the House of Commons in London with information about women's treatment. In an interview with the London weekly, *Tribune*, given in late May, 1956, Miss Fletcher described conditions under which women and even girls of eleven and twelve were held at Kamiti. They were not being rehabilitated, as the prison system was purportedly designed to do but were exposed to what Miss Fletcher called "stark terror":

> Girl prisoners who sang Mau Mau hymns were sentenced to 16 days solitary confinement. . . . I saw girls come out and I can tell you that even now it sometimes keeps me awake at night when I remember the look of stark terror on their faces. Not only were children aged eleven and twelve given life sentences, but young girl prisoners had to work at stone breaking as part of their ordinary prison labour. In one prison, women who only had one blanket to wear asked "What would your Queen think if she saw us wearing blankets?"[70]

Eileen Fletcher charged the prison administrators with being too severe in their punishment; she also testified that several young girls were extralegally held in the prison camp for they were underaged when they were arrested:

> I have seen African children in British goals sentenced to life imprisonment for consorting with armed persons and unlawful possession of ammunition. . . . In a woman's prison less than a year ago I saw 21 young people—including 11 and 12 year olds—who were condemned to this inhuman punishment for supposed Mau Mau offenses.[71]

According to Fletcher's evidence, the young girls' cases were reviewed every four years and the commandant of the prison expected that the juveniles would serve a minimum of eight years in prison.[72] These serious charges emotionally focused on the treatment of young girls who, along with women were not generally known to be in prison for their involvement with Mau Mau. Fletcher's newspaper interviews touched off a flurry of countercharges against her. Her accuracy and trustworthiness were questioned in government circles both in Nairobi and in London. Within five days of the interview in the *Tribune,* a spokesman for the Governor of Kenya gave an interview to the *Daily Chronicle* in Nairobi. He claimed that Miss Fletcher had resigned after working in the camps for only seven months and that her statements were filled with "lies and hearsay."[73] Miss Fletcher added more charges when she replied to the statements printed in the *Chronicle.* She wrote that to her knowledge:

> As Kenya had no approved school for girls, the courts had no alternative but to send them to prison—which they are entitled to do under the Juveniles Ordinance in the case of girls over 14.[74]

Fletcher reiterated that some of the girls in prison were as young as eleven and that official records supported her statements. Female prisoners in Kamiti were supervised by a European male commandant and a staff of European women. African men and women were also wardens in the facility. The European women police officers carried canes on their rounds which they made with patrol dogs.[75]

In the midst of the publicity war between the Governor's office in Kenya and Eileen Fletcher in London, Mr. Fenner-Brockway, a Labour Party member of Parliament, promised that consideration would be given to Fletcher's statements in a House of Commons sessions debate.[76] Both the British government and the colonial administration were embarrassed by the incident. Over the next few months, the Colonial Secretary initiated investigations and tried to defuse the situation. On June 29, 1956, Alan Lennox-Boyd, the Secretary for the Colonies, publicly denied Fletcher's charges. He said that her statements might have had some truth to them in 1954, but that reforms had been made in the year since her service with the penal institution.[77] Twelve days later, Sir Eboo Pirbhu, a member of a visiting committee at Kamiti, also said that conditions in the prison had improved in the year since Miss Fletcher had resigned from her job with the Rehabilitation Department.[78] Finally, in 1956, information was released about Kamiti through Lady Baring, wife of the Governor. After touring the prison, she told newspaper reporters that she saw no evidence of hardship in the camp; the women were well taken care of and eager to renounce their Mau Mau affiliation.[79]

When Lady Baring visited Kamiti there were 2,598 female prisoners in the facility. During a two and one-half hour tour, she observed one European officer, three European women officers, and four hundred African male and female wardens. Mau Mau regalia was displayed for her and she was present when women detainees were interrogated. The newspaper accounts of the visit focused on the fact that women prisoners who wanted to renounce their association with the rebellion were coerced by other prisoners. Omitting any reference to conditions in the prison, it concluded with:

> Today no vestige of intimidation remains at Kamiti. Most women are eager to cast off Mau Mau and return to normal life as quickly as possible.[80]

For six months, these charges and countercharges, the harshness of the treatment, and the age of the girls were hotly debated in the newspapers and in the House of Commons. During the course of the furor, the Colonial Secretary's office was forced to admit that harsh treatment had occurred. Further, the office had to affirm that in violation of the penal code, long periods of solitary confinement were given. The most damaging evidence was that some girls had been sentenced to life imprisonment when they were under age fourteen at the time of sentencing. The government had denied this at first, but the discovery that the prison records had been altered to conceal the true conditions at Kamiti created a scandal. Thereafter, annual reports on the conditions in the prisons included detailed information on the treatment of prisoners and the punishment or dismissal staff for their mistreatment of prisoners. With much embarrassment, the government promised further investigations and remedies. Late in 1956, the government admitted to the errors in reporting and promised a full investigation; they reminded the reading public that the girls:

> Of whom we are talking as if they were juveniles in the strict sense of the term have themselves played a terrifying role in the Mau Mau conspiracy.[81]

Mr. G.H. Heaton, author of the 1956 government report on prisons and detention camps in Kenya, commended the rehabilitation camps for their "excellent results."[82] No mention was made of any of Miss Fletcher's allegations; the conditions described to me by women prisoners also do not appear in the report on Kamiti prison. The scandal at Kamiti was allowed to die an administrative death. Greater administrative attention to reporting on prison conditions was not enough, however, to ensure the end of abuse. The major scandal of the murder of eleven male detainees at the Hola camp facility in 1959 finally brought an end to the detention system and the "pipeline" process of gradually releasing detainees into lesser and lesser high security facilities until finally they were released to their home villages.[83] The prisoners were killed while being punished at the Hola camp.[84] At first, tactics similar to those used in the Kamiti scandal were employed to explain the deaths. Officials first claimed that the eleven men had died because they had drunk contaminated water. Finally, statements were issued which confirmed that the prisoners had been beaten to death. The Hola camp incident caused stringent investigation of the entire prison and rehabilitation system; the Kamiti scandal did not. Although reports of brutalities against women appeared three years before the deaths of the men at Hola, the only response the government made in 1956 was a series of gestures designed to convince the public in England that women were "eager to cast off Mau Mau." Public knowledge of brutalities against men ended the entire scheme.

Far from being eager to cast off Mau Mau, women activists displayed a depth of commitment to the nationalist cause; they persistently participated in the rebellion with great courage in the face of real suffering and possible death. Women's formal involvement in nationalist organizations developed gradually from the 1930s to the 1950s. Their commitment to gaining greater economic, political, and social control began when the colonial state intruded into the district and slowly extended its control. With each new change, women voiced their dissatisfactions and finally organized a concerted resistance to the government policies of land alienation, the dismantling of traditional culture, and the co-optation of women into the wage labor force. As women's protest grew from passive and reactive forms to full scale rebellion, they sought inclusion in the nationalist associations. When this was denied, women changed their tactics. Until 1930, women's demonstrations had been localized and episodic; after 1930, they organized formal networks. The first configuration was a corollary to male protest.

After 1933, when the vigor of women's organizational abilities had been demonstrated, the male nationalists accepted them as full participators in resistance. The last stage of women's protest which resulted in their transformation came against the backdrop of the failure of the tactics of nationalist negotiation with the British. Peaceful means of improving African conditions in Kenya were viewed by many in the nationalist associations as futile and violent anti-colonial resistance in the form of the Mau Mau rebellion began in the 1950s. Through their partnership with men in the Mau Mau rebellion, women experienced their greatest role transformations.

By their own estimation, one-fourth of the adult female population in Kiambu district participated in various aspects of the Mau Mau rebellion. Women were highly visible and active in the smuggling network, as soldiers, and as residents of the forest camps. They were interned in Kamiti prison and in municipal jails because of the strength of their opposition and their high visibility. An important feature of the story of women's roles in the nationalist rebellion is the division of allegiance that women experienced as a group. This paralleled the division in Kikuyu society on nationalist issues that have been amply demonstrated by other research into Kikuyu nationalism. Some Kikuyu women remained loyal to the British. Such women were sometimes the victims of Mau Mau women. The Loyalist women were sometimes co-opted by the colonial government to rehabilitate Mau Mau women detainees. This division was not only a factor in women's solidarity, it was also present within families. The collected oral data reveals that nearly all of the most highly active women were married to or otherwise related to men involved with Mau Mau. There is also a trend for women who were not a part of the leadership to be involved in Mau Mau activities when their husbands or other male relatives were not. A few respondents indicated that their husbands knew and disapproved of their activities with the freedom fighters. However, their spouses did not betray them by reporting them to the Homeguard forces or colonial officials.

If men knew of this high level of commitment during the 1950s, we must assume on ongoing knowledge about women and nationalism—and specifically about women and Mau Mau—from that time period to the present. An important historiographic question is why such intense participation has been ignored or slighted in accounts of the rebellion. Perhaps the explanation for this oversight in the historiography on Mau Mau revolves around the resources used in reconstructing the history of the period. If the research problem is set up to correlate western education and fluency in English with political activism, then minimally educated rural women would not appear to be important participants. Western education was distributed inequitably between women and men, thus women were less fluent in English than men and perhaps more rooted in Kikuyu traditions of subsistence based agriculture. One of the other research flaws that has led to women's exclusion from studies on nationalism is the tendency to focus on urban centers more than on the rural areas. Males migrated to the urban centers in much larger numbers than did women. Because they were confined to the rural areas by a lack of real employment in the urban centers, women staged their labor protest against rural economic conditions. Men's labor protest occurred chiefly in the urban centers.

A final reason for women's nonappearance in the historiography on Mau Mau may be a cross-cultural assumption about the nature of male/female political roles. In traditional Kikuyu society, the public arena for decision-making and the conduct of intersocietal conflict (wars) was almost totally a male preserve. Prominent Kikuyu women were excluded from this arena and only allowed to oversee "women's matters." The society created under colonialism layered another male dominated society over the Kikuyu's own. Those who have studied the dynamics of the disruptions and transformations created by the British in Kenya may have uncritically accepted the stereotypical norms which divided roles and political relationships in ways which were similar to the pre-colonial Kikuyu gender divisions. Thus, these scholars construct a schema which was blind to the changes in gender roles that resulted from the skewing of traditional political and economic relationships in the crisis packed colonial era. This schema includes characteristic male strategies of visible, public oriented activities often physically expressed through warfare. Female strategies were limited to peer pressure and secret networking. After the colonial state assumed the previously Kikuyu male sphere of decision-making and refused to share it with Kikuyu men in any significant fashion, African politics became extreme and eventually violent. This process of the radicalization of the nationalist movement created an opportunity for an entry point for Kikuyu women. Women took advantage of the crack in the facade of male domination. They transformed their roles in Kikuyu society through their activism over a thirty year period. When viewed through the lens of accepted western and African ideas about the role of women, the dynamics of Kikuyu nationalism can only be misinterpreted. Moreover, under these assumptions, women form but a small part of the nationalist forces. These assumptions must be thrown out, for they obscure women's roles and conceal a major part of the true nature of Mau Mau which was largely a rural rebellion of minimally westernized Kikuyu men and women.

Notes

1. See Carl Rosberg and John Nottingham, *The Myth of "Mau Mau": Nationalism in Kenya* (New York: Frederick A. Praeger, 1966; reprint ed., New York: Meridian Books, The World Publishing Company, 1970); Robert Tignor, *The Colonial Transformation of Kenya: The Kamba, Kikuyu and Maasai from 1900-1939* (Princeton: Princeton University Press, 1976); Martin Kilson, "Land and the Kikuyu," *Journal of Negro History*, 40, 1956, pp. 103-153; Robert Buijtenhuis, *Mau Mau Twenty Years After: The Myth and Survivors* (Hague: Mouton, 1973); and Robert Buijtenhuis, *Essays on Mau Mau: Contributions to Mau Mau Historiography* (Leiden: African Studies Centre No. 17, 1982).

2. See Chapter 6 on the Mumbi Central Association.

3. The Land and Freedom army is the name which Mau Mau fighters gave to themselves. Mau Mau is a nonsensical word in Kikuyu which was created by the British to describe the militant freedom fighters.

4. See Chapter 3.

5. Interview with Muthoni wa Gachie, Githunguri, January 10, 1979.

6. Kenya National Archives (KNA). Native Affairs Department (NAD) Annual Report (AR) 1950, p. 2.

7. The Homeguard were Kikuyu who were considered loyal to the British and who were recruited to serve the British as soldiers and police in their fight against Mau Mau.

8. Interview with Nduta wa Kore,Tingang'a, January 13, 1979.

9. Rosberg and Nottingham, *The Myth of "Mau Mau,"* pp. 271-279.

10. Interview with Wambui Wagarama, Kabete, April 29, 1979.

11. Interview with Nduta wa Kore, Tingang'a, January 13, 1979.

12. Interview with Wagara Wainana, Kitambaya, April 29, 1978.

13. All of these women were identified through the colonial archives and by men and women in the district during the period of research as being in the forefront of the political movement. All except Rebecca Njeri Kairi and Mary Nyaruiru were interviewed. Mary Nyaruiru could not be located during the research period. Rebecca Kairi unfortunately succumbed to a mental breakdown just weeks before our scheduled interview session.

14. KNA. Kiambu (KBU)/50, Handing Over Report (HOR)1955, p. 8.

15. Interview with Wambui Wagarama, Kabete, April 29, 1979.

16. Jeremy Murray-Brown, *Kenyatta* (London: Allen and Unwin, 1972), p. 273.

17. KNA. KBU/50, HOR 1955, p. 2.

18. L.S.B. Leakey, *Mau Mau and the Kikuyu* (London: Methuen, 1952), p. ix; T.F.C. Bewes, *Kikuyu Conflicts: Mau Mau and the Christian Witness* (London: Highway Press, 1953), p. 56.

19. Greet Sluiter [Kershaw], *Confidential Report on Migrant Labour and Connected Matters in Four Villages in the Kiambu Reserve of Kenya* (Nairobi: Department of Social Service, Training and Research of the Christian Council of Kenya, 1957), pp. 73-82; and KNA. AR/333/KBU/45, Annual Report 1954, p. 3.

20. "A" oath: Even if we are cut, we will not leave our soil. If anyone asks about the soil and the oath, we will not tell. "B" oath: If I become a freedom fighter, I will not tell. Even if my mother is guilty of betraying the Mau Mau, I will tell it.

21. Information on the widespread administration of the oath is sometimes contradictory. Some nationalist said that everyone was given an oath, others claim that only those who could understand the meaning of the words took the oaths.

22. Interview with Phyllis Wanjiko (Margo) wa Mimi, Tingang'a, December 20, 1978.

23. Interview with Phyllis Wanjiko (Margo) wa Mimi, Tingang'a, December 20, 1978; interview with Priscilla Wambaki, Ngenda, May 16, 1979; interview with Mary Wanjiko, Kiambu Town, November 22, 1978.

24. Quoted in F.D. Corfield, *Historical Survey of the Origins and Growth of Mau Mau* (London: HMSO Cmnd 1030, 1960), p. 90.

25. Interview with Phyllis Wanjiko wa Mimi, Tingang'a, December 20, 1978; interview with Muthoni Gichege, Tingang'a, January 4, 1979.

26. Operation Anvil was started in April of 1954. Its purpose was to round up Mau Mau leadership and operatives in Nairobi. As a result of the operation, over 27,000 Kikuyu were arrested and sent to the detention camps. See Rosberg and Nottingham, *The Myth of "Mau Mau,"* pp. 302-303, 335.

27. Interview with Wangui wa Gikuyi, Ruiru, May 13, 1979.

28. KNA. AR/326/KBU/44, Annual Report 1953, p. 1.

29. KNA. NAD. AR/1953, p. 25.

30. Kenya Colony and Protectorate, "Report on the General Administration of Prisons and Detention Camps in Kenya," by G.H. Heaton (Nairobi: Government Printer, 1956), p. 3.

31. KNA. NAD. AR/1953, p. 25.

32. KNA. KBU/50, HOR 1955, p. 8.

33. Interview with Hannah Wandia, Thika, May 24, 1979.

34. Interview with Elizabeth Warimu, Ndumberi, October 18, 1978.

35. Interview with Muthoni wa Gachege, Tingang'a, January 4, 1979.

36. Interview with Veronica Njoki, Githunguri, May 20, 1979.

37. Ibid.

38. KNA. NAD. AR/1956, p. 31.

39. Interview with Elizabeth Wanjiko, Tingang'a, December 29, 1978.

40. Ibid.

41. So many women were caught and convicted of participating in Mau Mau that a special prison facility was built for them at Kamiti. Once the new prison

was completed, the length of women's sentences increased. Some women remained in prison until 1960.

42. Interview with Elizabeth Gachika, Kiambu Town, January 7, 1979.

43. Ibid.

44. *Daily Chronicle*, (Nairobi), 7 September 1956.

45. Kenya Colony and Protectorate (KCP). Treatment of Offenders AR/1957 p.10.

46. KCP. Kenya Prisons. Report on the Treatment of Offenders. AR/1953 p. 51.

47. KCP. Report on the General Administration of Prisons and Detention Camps in Kenya, p. 3; KCP. Report on the Treatment of Offenders. AR/1954, p. 4; KCP. Report on the Treatment of Prisoners for the Year 1954. AR/1954, p. 4.

48. KCP. Report on the Treatment of Offenders. AR/1953, pp. 16-17.

49. KCP. Treatment of Offenders. AR/1956, pp. 8-9.

50. KCP. Community Development Department (CDD). AR/1954, pp. 21-24; KCP. CDD. AR/1955, pp. 22-26.

51. KCP. Treatment of Offenders. AR/1955, p. 2.

52. KCP. Treatment of Offenders. AR/1956, p. 2.

53. KCP. CDD. AR/1955, pp. 25-26.

54. KCP. CDD. AR/1956, p. 6.

55. KCP. CDD. AR/1954, p. 30.

56. KCP. CDD. AR/1956, p. 4.

57. KCP. CDD. AR/1955, pp. 22-23.

58. There were four categories: (1) Z1 - Mau Mau leaders who refused to respond to the rehabilitation program (2) Z2 - Rank and file who refused to renounce Mau Mau (3) Y - Those who responded to rehabilitation and (4) X - Those who were rehabilitated and placed on parole. See KCP. CDD. AR/1956, pp. 3-6.

59. Interview with Tabitha Mumbi, Thika, May 24, 1979; interview with Elizabeth Gachika, Kiambu Town, January 7, 1979; interview with Nduta wa Kore, Tingang'a, January 13, 1979; interview with Wambui Wagarama, Kabete, April 29, 1979.

60. KCP. Report on the Treatment of Offenders. AR/1953, pp. 4-5; KCP. Report on the Treatment of Offenders. AR/1955, pp. 16, 18.

61. Convict labor was an important source of both income and supplies for the Department of Prisons. In 1953, the value of the agricultural produce raised by prisoners totaled £10,220. The amount of revenue received from prison industries amounted to £150,595 and £15,897 was given to the system as payment in using convict labor on the East African Railway, Harbour Administration, and other authorities. See KCP. Report on the Treatment of Prisoners. AR/1953, pp. 14-15. In Kamiti, the value of vegetables raised by female prisoners was £1,973 in 1956; KCP. Treatment of Offenders. AR/1956, pp. 14-15.

62. KCP. Treatment of Offenders. AR/1955, p. 15.

63. KCP. Treatment of Offenders. AR/1956, p. 14.

64. Interview with Muthoni Gachie,Tingang'a, January 4, 1979.

65. Interview with Muthoni wa Gachie, Githunguri, January 10, 1979.

66. Interview with Mary Wanjiko, Kiambu Town, November 22, 1978.

67. Interview with Tabitha Mumbi, Thika, May 24, 1979. When the Emergency was declared, European settlers in the Rift Valley expelled Kikuyu families who had worked for them as squatters. The squatters were sent to Kiambu, Murang'a, and Nyeri districts.

68. Both *ugali* and *uji* are boiled ground maize meal.

69. Interview with Priscilla Wambaki, Juja, May 23, 1979.

70. *Daily Chronicle,* (Nairobi), 31 May 1956.

71. *Tribune* (London), 25 May 1956.

72. Ibid.

73 *Daily Chronicle,* (Nairobi), 31 May 1956.

74. Ibid. Approved schools were institutions maintained by the government for juvenile delinquents.

75. Ibid.

76. Ibid.

77. *Daily Chronicle,* (Nairobi), 29 June 1956.

78. *Daily Chronicle,* (Nairobi), 12 July 1956.

79. *Daily Chronicle,* (Nairobi), 7 September 1956.

80. Ibid.

81. *Tribune,* (London), 16 November 1956.

82. Kenya Colony and Protectorate, "Report on the General Administration of Prisons and Detention Camps in Kenya," by G.H. Heaton (Nairobi: Government Printer, 1956), pp. 2-4.

83. KNA. "Records of Proceedings and Evidence into the Deaths of Eleven Mau Mau Detainees at Hola Camp in Kenya, 1959"; Rosberg and Nottingham, *The Myth of "Mau Mau,"* pp. 335-344.

84. KNA. "Record of Proceedings and Evidence in the Inquiry into the Deaths of Eleven Mau Mau Detainees at Hola Camp in Kenya, 1959"; Rosberg and Nottingham, *The Myth of "Mau Mau,"* pp. 334-344.

8

The Mau Mau Rebellion, Kikuyu Women, and Social Change

This chapter explores the reasons for the scarcity of information about women in the Mau Mau rebellion in the historiography of Kenyan nationalism. Over the past thirty years, historians of Mau Mau have generated a large body of scholarship. Noticeably absent from these considerations is the female dimension, since the major portion of the scholarship never poses questions which illuminate or acknowledge women's participation. Counterfactually, the rebellion is cast as a struggle between African and European males, hiding some of its significant aspects. First, it ignores women's initiative and concerns for change, concealing colonialism's deleterious effects on women, changes in their status, and their protests against economic and cultural changes. The second aspect that ignoring women's political activism hides is its function in creating a new political tradition. In post-colonial Kenya, the creation of women politicians has been partly explained as being justified because of women's participation in and sacrifices during the rebellion. This chapter critiques the current scholarship on Kikuyu nationalism, and it poses and answers the questions of the extent of women's involvement in militant nationalism and how women's involvement produced a tradition of female leadership in post-Mau Mau Kenya.

The Historiography of Mau Mau

In his 1982 work, *Essays on Mau Mau: Contributions to Mau Mau Historiography*, Robert Buijenthuis surveys the state of scholarship on the Mau Mau rebellion from the 1950s to the 1980s.[1] Researchers and participants in Mau Mau have posed and answered fundamental questions such as: what were the origins of Mau Mau, what were its patterns of recruitment, and what defined membership? A second level of questions attempt to delineate the political, ideological, and personality connections of Mau Mau to nationalist associations in the pre-1948 period. Third, the historiography has focused on the different phases of the Mau Mau rebellion. A fourth concern has been how the colonial state in Kenya and the British government marshalled their forces to counter and defeat Mau Mau. These question were largely explored from the 1950s to the 1970s. Beginning in the 1970s, questions of class and local level analysis came into vogue. Typical questions were: Which of the Kikuyu districts in the Central province of Kenya contributed members of the rank and file versus member of the Mau Mau leadership? Can Mau Mau be interpreted as a conflict or civil war between rural/urban populations and elite mass/sectors of society? And is Mau Mau best understood as labor conflict which evolved between the lumpenproletariat and skilled workers in the trade unions?

All of these questions have deepened our understanding of the multifaceted nature of Mau Mau and have revealed cleavages in Kikuyu society. Some of the cleavages began in the pre-colonial period. Many others were introduced under the colonial regime. While debate rages over some of these issues, in particular over local level differences and the variations in participation in Mau Mau according to class status, the scholarly jury on Mau Mau still does not illuminate women's contributions to the rebellion in particular and Kenyan nationalism in general. Women are not examined in the earlier Mau Mau studies.[2] With the exception of a few works such as Tabitha Kanogo's recent book on Mau Mau and squatters in the Rift Valley, scholarship of the 1980s merely accords women token acknowledgement as Mau Mau participants in the "passive wing" of the organization.[3] By not asking the question about women's contribution to Kenyan nationalism and Mau Mau, the analysis continues to project a perception that it was a conflict between males; the conflicting dyads which are created are: Africans versus Europeans, nationalist versus loyalists, mass versus elites, rural versus urban, and lumpenproletariat versus trade union members. The state of the scholarship, therefore, ignores an important aspect of Kenyan nationalism: the development of nationalist sentiment and activity among women from the 1920s and the colonial state's response to women's nationalism.

The government's response was to alter social policy. The centerpiece of this was the creation of a department whose policies and programs were directed specifically to wean women from Mau Mau. These policies were developed in response to two needs. The first was to isolate the military force of Mau Mau and defeat them by attacking and cutting off their popular support which the British called the "passive wing." This "wing" was composed largely of women. Their function was to supply information, smuggle arms, food, clothing, and medicine to the guerilla army and to maintain the lines of transit for recruits travelling from the urban and rural sectors of the Central Province to join the military forces in the forest. The use of the phrase "passive wing" hides the military and psychological importance of this type of activity. More aptly, the women and men who were the support troops of Mau Mau should be termed the non-combatant forces. The British government treated them as a serious threat to be contended with.

The second part of the new social policy was a program aimed at capturing the loyalty of the Kikuyu. This involved the villagisation program and a full-blown propaganda campaign whose major purpose was to detach women from Mau Mau. Women's activism received special attention since key government officials believed that women were "far more rabid and fanatical than the males" and more violent in their support of Mau Mau.[4] The social policy response to women's perceived "fanaticism" was the beginning of the design and application of institutions whose goals were to address the problems of lack of mass education, adequate programs for health care, access to a clean and reliable water supply, and childcare facilities. The policy acknowledged, perhaps for the first time, that the colonial government had a primary responsibility for the welfare of rural populations. The Community Development Department, which was created in 1954, addressed these problems; it was given a large annual budget of £250,000 and a staff which included Africans as well as Europeans.[5]

This Department was part of the British struggle to control women. Before the 1920s, the contest over who would control women—African or European males—revolved around jural issues: chiefly the control of marriage laws. The colonial state, of course won the contest.[6] Other conflicts of this nature revolved around the control of female circumcision and women's wage labor.[7]

Women's massive participation in Mau Mau contributed to the rebellion's initial psychological, if not military, successes. A total of 34,147 women were sentenced to prison for violation of the Emergency Regulations between 1952 and 1958.[8] Thousands of these women were repeat violators of the regulations against taking oaths and aiding the forest fighters by supplying food, guns, and information. Therefore, for both the British and the nationalists, wooing women's loyalty was an essential element of winning the war.

The Image of Women Nationalists

Though current historiography barely touches upon women's contributions to the rebellion, it was widespread and effective in sustaining Mau Mau. When women's activism is described in the pro-colonial historiography, two portrayals of women emerge. They project women as either victims of Mau Mau or prostitutes who, through personal contact with male nationalists, were drawn to Mau Mau while resident in Nairobi. The view of women as victims of Mau Mau originates from the colonial record. Women are presented by colonial officials as physical and psychological victims of atavism. The first type of victimization characterizes women as being forcibly compelled to take the oath of allegiance to Mau Mau. A special branch report on intimidation in oathing recounted the forced oathing of a Catholic Kikuyu woman which occurred in 1952. She was stripped naked, severely beaten to the point of unconsciousness and upon her revival, compelled to "drink blood from a bottle, and perform the other disgusting rites constituting the Mau Mau ceremony."[9] Another 1952 incident contributed to the view of women as prey. In Nyeri, the District Commissioner reported that forcible oathings of women and children were wide-spread.[10] Further fuel is added to the image of women as victims by writers who were openly antagonistic to Mau Mau. In *State of Emergency*, F. Majadalany painted women's attraction to Mau Mau as being caused by a misdirected hero worship of nationalists described as "young thugs and criminals." Women nationalists were relegated to the role of "adoring female hangers-on." According to the author women nationalist moved their prostitution activities from the urban areas to the forest camps:

> When the fighting gangs were formed each included its quota of women, and though their first function was to act as pack transport (with some concubinage on the side) many of them became ferocious and implacable fighters too."[11]

Both Corfield and Majadalany ascribe irrationality and bestiality to Mau Mau. One of their measures of its extremity is incidents of attacks on Loyalist women.[12] In the Lari Massacre (March 26, 1953), eighty-four Loyalists were killed. Two-thirds of the victims were women. During 1952, Mau Mau military actions killed twenty-three Loyalists of whom two were women and three were children.[13] While the rebellion was in progress, a popular British tactic was to portray women as the principle war casualties. However, women were ninety-eight of the 1,024 Kikuyu who were killed by the Mau Mau.[14] This figure represents actual deaths and does not, of course, account for victimization which stopped short of death ranging from harassment to threats and beatings.

The image of women nationalists as prostitute originates from the district and provincial reports. Women nationalists began to be described as prostitutes by the colonial officials when the Kenya African Union successfully staged mass rallies in the Central Province. For example, a mass rally was held in Nyeri on July 26, 1952 and was described by the DC:

> Over 20,000 men, women and children attended. K.A.U. insinuated over 40 bus loads of Nairobi thugs and prostitutes, who were clearly under instructions to excite the crowd.[15]

In describing the participation of the Meru in Mau Mau, J.T. Kamunchulah repeats the theme of a connection between prostitution and women's activism. He attributes the success of the Mau Mau in acquiring arms from government soldiers between 1950 and 1952 to:

> A network of communication with prostitutes, who lay "tender traps" for African *askaris*, of ambushing the African *askaris* in dark streets and abducting and later suffocating them to death.[16]

Women, Nationalism, and the Colonial Infrastructure

What these views suggest is that women were attracted to Mau Mau for reasons other than rational political ones and that only those women who were pariahs in European and African society were liable to be seduced by Mau Mau nationalism. These images of detribalized women being the initial female contingent of Mau Mau are counterfactual. In the first year of the Emergency, local level British officials noticed that large numbers of women were actively involved in Mau Mau. The accepted explanation of women's attraction to Mau Mau was that their lesser exposure to British institutions, such as the Christian missionary schools, and their exclusion from employment in the settler economy had left them more "primitive" than males who had been westernized.[17] Indeed, Kikuyu women were not as tied to the day-to-day structures of colonial rule as were men. Nonetheless, they were affected by colonialism. In the pre-colonial period women farmed land which was later alienated by the Crown Lands Act (1902). Loss of land produced scarcity. Consequently, women as well as men were affected by overpopulation and pressures on the land which the introduction of the settler economy and state induced. In the areas dominated by the settler economy, women were an important part of the labor force. They were seasonal laborers and were used extensively in the production of coffee, the leading settler export from Kenya.[18]

Missionaries intensively recruited women. They viewed themselves as the champions for alleviating women's misery through stamping out customs which they perceived as a devaluation of the status of women and harmful to them. In the Eurocentric view, these included the payment of bridewealth, prohibitions on remarriage of widows and female circumcision. Though the mission efforts at educating women always received a lower priority than those directed towards males, the rural schools and churches focused on persuading women to accept western mores, customs, and values.[19]

Colonial laws also were directed towards women. The effect of land alienation has already been mentioned. Other colonial laws such as Communal Labor (1908) and the Hut and Poll Tax (1910, 1934) caused resentment and their combination with the nationalist issues of mission opposition to female circumcision, unfair labor practices, taxation, lack of adequate education, and no voice in politics drew women to the nationalist associations and ideology.

Affected by the all the colonial laws, women also registered their protest against these laws well before the rebellion. The colonial officials did not, however, treat women's resistance as an integral part of the tide of protest that was rising in Kenya from the 1920s. The government had several indicators of women's activism. These events, such as a women's strike on the coffee estates in 1947 were dismissed as being caused by male outside agitators.[20] Another major incident of women's resistance occurred in 1947 and 1948 when women of Fort Hall district participated in what was termed "The Revolt of the Women." This was a protest against the scheme to compel women to dig terraces in their fields for the purpose of soil conservation. According to the Corfield report, this was initiated by the Kenya African Union. At a large meeting, an agreement was reached that women would not participate in the government scheme. Women's unanimous support for this meant that none of them showed up for the communal labor, and "by the end of August all communal labour was virtually at a standstill."[21] The Corfield report consistently interpreted women's agitation as aberrant:

> During the earlier part of the year [1948] agitation against soil conservation continued in Fort Hall district and led to a minor political upheaval known as "The Revolt of the Women" in two locations of that district. Disruptive elements outside the district continued to agitate against the co-operation of women in soil conservation work, and this later led to a full-scale descent of the women themselves to district headquarters. This as the District Commissioner commented, marked a growing tendency which was entirely alien to normal Kikuyu custom, indicating that agitators had been at work.[22]

In 1950, the Kiambu DC reported to his superiors that men were no longer administering oaths of loyalty to Mau Mau. Women, however were proceeding with the work of oath-giving. A break with past custom in giving and taking oaths was one of the many changes in gender roles nationalism introduced for women.

The Impact of Social Policy on Women's Nationalism

When the last of the Mau Mau women detainees were released and returned to their villages in 1960, they discovered that the colonial government had radically altered village life as a part of its war against Mau Mau. The campaign against women was achieved in the villagisation program. Initially begun as a punitive measure, the project became a centerpiece of social and military policy.[23] The turning point in achieving success in defeating Mau Mau on the home front was achieved when activists, or those merely suspected of being activists, were rounded up. The entire Kikuyu population was semi-imprisoned during the Mau Mau emergency in the guarded villages. The centrality of the villagisation program for defeat of the Mau Mau forces was recognized in official circles. Addressing the legislative assembly in Kenya in 1955, the Governor, Sir Evelyn Baring stated that:

> It has been possible in many areas to arrange a system of movement control by which villagers going to work on their *shambas,* or herding their cattle, do so under escort from either the Tribal Police or the Watch and Ward Units. It is the establishment of this system which in many areas has broken the physical contact with the gangs. The individual gangsters must often have hidden in a hole in a sisal hedge and have slipped out for a few minutes to tell a woman working in her field that food must be left at a certain place at a certain time or else there would be trouble. In this way the fear of the terrorist was maintained. Now, there can be no absolute certainty, but it appears probable that the new system has in most areas broken that physical contact and dissipated that fear.
> ... As a result too, the flow of information from the villagers has greatly improved.[24]

The rupture of the physical contact between villagers and Mau Mau fighters meant that women who were not imprisoned during the Mau Mau emergency had their own intensive encounters with the colonial regime. The object of the intensive contact was, of course, to defuse nationalism and curtail Mau Mau activities. Just as was true in the prisons and detention camps, the centerpiece of policy was the withholding and granting of benefits to sway the non-combatant wing away from radical nationalism. One of the consequences of being identified as Mau Mau was loss of land. The land of members of Mau Mau was confiscated and allocated it to "deserving Loyalists."[25]

The instrument for this policy, the Community Development Department, was thought to have potential for creating a true social revolution in the villages. The major goal was:

> To teach the women in the new villages a new way of life and to show them that the possibilities of community life in a smaller area offer better opportunities for improved homes than the old scattered villages—as indeed they do.[26]

The relocation scheme that involved the forced relocation of the entire Kikuyu population of the three Kikuyu districts in Central Province was begun in 1954 and began to be phased out in 1958.[27] More than 80,000 Kikuyu households were uprooted in Kiambu District between 1954 and 1955. Also, more than 17,000 Kikuyu squatters, who were ejected from the Rift Valley by settler farmers, joined the population of the Kikuyu districts and were required to live in the new villages.[28] For Kiambu district, the focus of this research, this involved over 300,000 men, women, and children. They were compelled to build new villages and tear down or abandon their homesteads. They lived behind barbed-wire fences, under guard, and under curfew. In order to farm, Kikuyu women were escorted to their fields by the Homeguard. All persons had to be back behind the barbed-wire fences before 4:00 p.m. each day.[29] In 1955, threats of confiscation of land and the imposition of a 24 hour curfew were used in Kiambu district to break the "passive wing." Abuse of villagers under the authority of the Homeguard were reported. Milka Ngina who spent the Emergency in the guarded villages recalled:

> A: We were beaten and forced to dig the terraces. They beat us very much and it was the Homeguard who did the beating.
> Q: Did you take the oath?
> A: Yes, I took very many and we were beaten when we took the oath.
> Q: Were you put into detention?
> A: Some women were detained but not all of them.
> Q: Did Kenya become independent because of Mau Mau?
> A: Yes, because they bought the freedom with blood.
> Q: Did others in your family take the oath?
> A: All the Kikuyu took the oath at that time.
> Q: Was there any fighting around your home?
> A: Yes.
> Q: What happened?
> A: We were beaten by the Homeguard because the Mau Mau passed through our homes. I myself was almost beaten to death.

Q: Why did the Homeguard help the British?
A: We were beaten by the Homeguard because the Mau Mau were not on good terms with the Homeguard and those who were giving food were on good terms with the Mau Mau.[30]

Catherine Wajiru, who lived in Embu during the Emergency, was also exposed to the civil war between Mau Mau supporters and Loyalist Kikuyu.

Q: Did you help the freedom fighters?
A: Yes.
Q: How did you help?
A: I gave them cooked food.
Q: Does that mean that there were freedom fighters in Embu?
A: Yes, they were there because they were living in the forest near us.
Q: Were you happy to give them food?
A: We gave them food because we had no security and if we refused to give them food, they could beat us.
Q: Were you living near Embu people?
A: Yes, we were mixed. We built the homes in the same place and we worked on the *shambas* with other groups.
Q: Did the Embu give food?
A: Yes, they did. They stopped giving them food when the villages were built but before that the Mau Mau would take goats and even cows by force. Also we were beaten by the colonials if they found that we were giving food. There were spies called Homeguard who would tell when you helped.
Q: Were you beaten?
A: Yes, I was beaten very much and my husband died during that time because of the beating.[31]

Being placed in the villages sometimes meant that families were uprooted several times. Another consequence of the villagisation scheme was a return to a forced labor system. This was the fate of Wagara Wainana's village when they were compelled to help construct the new facilities.

Q: Did you get put into the villagisation program?
A: Yes, we built the villages.
Q: Did you carry on the work of Mau Mau from the villages?
A: Yes, we continued after that. We women were taken to a place and forced to do work for nothing. This place was called Kianjogu. . . . We did digging and we didn't know the reason we were doing this digging. We dug all around the camp, sweeping, and clearing the camp. Then we were taken to another camp. We stayed in Kianjogu for seven months. Then we were taken to a village for

> four years and then I went to my farm. This was in 1955. We were only fighting and in the end were were helped by God. . . . When Kenyatta came back from England he called us all together and organized us. I took food to the Mau Mau. We also took guns. When I was taking food, I was hiding from the Europeans when another one of us saw the police, she started screaming, and ran down to the river. I grabbed her by the throat so that we could not be heard. When the soldiers came near, I ran away and the other one was screaming again. Then the other one was caught and put into detention.[32]

The villagisation program was successful in demoralizing the non-combatant wing. The African Affairs Department recorded that:

> The withdrawal of the surrender terms on 10th July was combined with local propaganda, so that at the end of June and the beginning of July the volume of confession swelled to such a degree that the teams were unable to cope. A very great deal of Mau Mau funds was handed in as well as guns and ammunition. The threat of confiscation of land, together with the imposition of 24-hour curfews also had a considerable effect in breaking the last efforts of the Mau Mau to conceal information. The confession teams in the settled areas. . .had an extremely difficult job to begin with. . . . They subsequently achieved remarkable and effective results in breaking the passive wings on the farms and discovering the main gang bases or food depots.[33]

The major point of contact between the Kikuyu and the government under these semi-concentration camp conditions was through the Community Development Department. Initially most of the Department's annual budget of £250,000 was spent on the work of Emergency rehabilitation.[34] The rural rehabilitation program focused on women and children because the majority of men were "either serving sentences, detained, working in the home guard, operating in the forests or living in the towns."[35] The Department's major vehicle for influencing women was through the Maendeleo ya Wanawake clubs.[36] The clubs had begun in the late 1940s but did not have significant membership until the Emergency. Membership in the organization expanded tremendously during the Emergency years since it could be the crucial difference between survival and starvation under the villagisation program. The work of the clubs included running day nurseries, making and supervising the distribution of soup, distributing milk to hungry children, and "caring for children whose parents were missing or dead."[37] These humanitarian efforts were not unaffected by the Emergency since the:

> Work of Maendeleo clubs [was] hampered by subversive propaganda and additional communal work necessary in the rehabilitation of and fortifying villages.[38]

The clubs were only able to meet after the four o'clock curfew. Nonetheless, the Department used the clubs as "an effective instrument against subversive elements."[39] The Department measured its success through the rise of membership. In 1954, Maendeleo membership reached a total of 36,970 members in 508 clubs (see Table 8.1). The 45 clubs in Kiambu had a membership of 5,050.[40] More than fifty percent of the membership of the clubs were in the three Kikuyu districts of Central Province and Nairobi where Mau Mau activities were greatest.

In addition to administering to the needy, the Community Development programs were "responsible for internal broadcasting, libraries, the distribution of papers, classes, *barazas*, recreation, and instruction in various forms."[41] The purpose of the education component of the program was to counteract Mau Mau by providing a course of "general knowledge".[42] Typically, this included bringing books, pamphlets, and a film truck to villages. This information stressed the positive benefits of colonialism for Kenya and the evils of Mau Mau.[43]

In the guarded villages, the clubs were used to aid the security forces. Club members gathered information about Mau Mau activities and tried to persuade Mau Mau adherents to abandon the movement.[44] Women were told that they had to become allied with the government rather than with Mau Mau. If they chose to remain publicly sympathetic to Mau Mau, they lost access to the services which the clubs offered.[45]

> Where the backbone of *Maendeleo* clubs had been in existence since 1951-53, the club members have. . . been of value to the Security forces giving information freely and persuading others to give up *Mau Mau*. In at least one case they played an important part in the capture of a *Mau Mau* general. The women realized that the ideals of *Maendeleo* and *Mau Mau* were incompatible and they would have to choose between them. . . .The numbers of clubs and members in these areas are on the increase as more and more realize that *Mau Mau* has brought nothing but distress and sorrow.[46]

The persuasive message resulted in tremendous growth in membership for the clubs. In 1955, the number of clubs increased to 596 with a membership of 43,000.[47] The benefits of belonging or simply being associated with the clubs was particularly crucial in 1955/56 when famine struck Kiambu district.[48] The curfew caused food scarcity; the women had fewer hours available to them in which to fetch water and fuel and to cultivate their fields.[49] During the famine, the Kiambu 107 clubs operated soup kitchens and increased their issuance of milk.[50] Total club membership reached 34,500 fully paid members in 1956. In addition, there were 11,500 women who benefitted from the club services who were not able to pay the membership fees.[51] By the end of 1957, there were 986 clubs with 33,613 fully paid members.[52]

One of the goals of the Community Development Department was to train Africans to be good citizens according to British standards. A by-product of this for women was their representation on the village and district councils. By 1955, the Community Development Department anticipated that women's voices would have more weight in village affairs because: "Maendeleo members [were] coming forward to take their place on locational and District Councils in greater numbers."[53]

TABLE 8.1 Maendeleo Ya Wanawake Clubs

District	*Clubs*	*Members*
Army Camp	8	400
Kiambu	45	5,050
Fort Hall	35	3,250
Nyeri	100	7,500
Embu	25	1,250
Meru		20
Settled Areas	10	300
Naivasha	1	45
Thompson's Falls	1	85
Nairobi	5	400
Machakos	94	10,000
Other Districts	183	8,510
Total	508	36,810

Source: Kenya Colony and Protectorate. Community Development Department. AR/1954, p. 13.

Viewing Mau Mau from the female perspective adds several important aspects to the understanding of the rebellion. Such an angle illuminates an oft repeated statement that landless and less affluent Kikuyu were more likely to take part in Mau Mau whereas the more affluent Kikuyu publicly took sides with the British and joined the Loyalist forces as Homeguards. In some families, women were deeply involved in Mau Mau when males publicly disassociated themselves from it. There are two possible explanations for this phenomena. First, women's involvement with Mau Mau cut across "class" lines. Wives of prominent Kikuyu were jailed. At least one Kikuyu woman organizer was the wife of a chief. Second, women's involvement in radical nationalism expresses the ambiguity of prominent families' identification with Mau Mau sentiments. Males of prominent families might have silently supported Mau Mau and maintained a public face of being Loyalists. If men openly supported the rebellion, the consequence was loss of land and privileges. This may have led to a perception that it was marginally safer for women to carry out the family's commitment to Mau Mau. The entire family need not have been impoverished by supporting the rebellion; a nationalist female, if arrested and detained, could be easily discredited and disowned. Whether this was deliberate family policy among a number of families is, of course, unknown. If families deliberately chose to allow female members to openly sympathize with Mau Mau while males publicly disowned any association with the movement, this may explain some of the curious features of Mau Mau the government reported and that were uncovered in oral interviews. Specifically, it may explain the government's contention that women were more rabid and fanatical, that men had stopped giving oaths and women were assuming these responsibilities. It may also explain the government assertion that women of Loyalist families were involved with Mau Mau activities. Mau Mau women also reported to the author that their husbands, though considered to be loyal to the government, knew of the aid they gave to the Mau Mau rebels and did not report them.

Women's participation in the violent Mau Mau revolt focused government attention on the need to use some of its resources to develop programs to serve women and their needs. In order to defeat Mau Mau militarily, it was crucial for the British to isolate the Mau Mau army from its non-combatant section. Mere isolation, however, was not sufficient. The non-combatant force, led and organized by women to a large degree, had to be engaged with force and persuasion. Thus, women were jailed in increased numbers between 1954 and 1957. The increase in the number of women imprisoned occurs at the same time that military victory over Mau Mau occurs. It is my contention that this was not mere coincidence but that success in the war against women was a necessary ingredient in the war against Mau Mau. The special strategy which was created to detach women, who could not be identified as guilty of violations of the Emergency regulations, was to mount a campaign of propaganda and education designed to convince them that disassociation from Mau Mau held positive rewards. First, the entire Kikuyu population was relocated to villages which were closely supervised by the Security Forces, the Homeguard and the new Community Development Department. Within three years of this policy, a drop in Mau Mau activities occurred. The British government started a social revolution of providing an extensive social services program. Women were the first to be experimented upon since the government recognized that they had to be detached from Mau Mau for final victory to occur. This had consequences for post-Mau Mau Kenya. The creation of the Community Development Department was the precursor of the Community Development Program in independent Kenya and the Women's Bureau. The contemporary vigorous Maendeleo ya Wanawake clubs also owe their growth to women's vigorous nationalism during Mau Mau. In the 1980s, there were over six thousand Maendeleo clubs. The Maendeleo is Kenya's largest women's organization.[54]

One of the reasons for the lack of development of an analysis of women's nationalism, their participation in and importance to Mau Mau in the historiography of Kenya is that scholars followed the line taken by the colonial government. Until thousands of women were imprisoned for Mau Mau offenses, colonial administrators dismissed incidents which indicated that women were actively involved in resisting colonial policy. In the case of labor stoppages and protests against terracing, district officers maintained that women's activism was caused by male outside agitators. Therefore, psychologically, the administrators were unprepared for women's protest; it seemed to them to be sudden, fanatical, and unexpected.

Historians of Mau Mau have also treated women's nationalism as incidental to the main currents of nationalism. Their sources for the story of the origin, growth, and spread of Mau Mau as well as its internal structure and goals have been almost exclusively male ones, whether these were Europeans or Africans. The use of this perceptive lens created the false paradigm that politics was almost solely a male concern. Consequently, the questions posed to respondents and the official records focus on the actions of males. When males did comment on women's involvement, these did not seem to be a major thread of the rebellion. In searching for answers to a political dilemma, scholars have naturally looked to those departments which had responsibility for political and economic issues. The full story of the colonial battle against women's nationalism is not revealed in government political record books, though important indicators occur. In the social services area, even more revealing data surfaces. Since the colonial officials were trapped in their 1950s perceptions of women, they relegated policies dealing with women to community development. As the Community Development report noted, the voice of women began to be heard during the Mau Mau rebellion. Women had spoken loudly through their nationalists political and labor actions for over twenty years in colonial Kenya. When they took up arms and supported violent rebellion their voices, began to be heard. The legacy for contemporary Kenyans is to acknowledge women as equal partners. Kenyan women have held appointed and elected office on the local and national level during the first 25 years of independence. They have never attained political office which is commensurate with their numbers in the population, nor with their importance in the nationalist struggle. In the twenty years from the attainment of independence, women did not hold even 2% of the elected positions. Their share of appointed positions was a mere 18%.[55] Access to political positions is possible for women, parity has not been approached. Such a role for women would have been impossible in the pre-colonial period. Through the crucible of rebellion, Kenyan women forged access to fuller participation in public affairs and decision making.

Notes

1. Robert Buijtenhuis, *Essays on Mau Mau: Contributions to Mau Mau Historiography* (Leiden: African Studies Centre No. 17, 1982).

2. See Carl Rosberg and John Nottingham, *The Myth of "Mau Mau": Nationalism in Kenya* (New York: Frederick A. Praeger, 1966; reprint ed., New York: Meridian Books, The World Publishing Company, 1970); Robert Tignor, *The Colonial Transformation of Kenya The Kamba, Kikuyu and Maasai from 1900 -1939* (Princeton: Princeton University Press,1976); Martin Kilson, "Land and the Kikuyu," *Journal of Negro History*, 40, 1956, pp. 103-153; Robert Buijtenhuis, *Mau*

Mau Twenty Years After: The Myth and Survivors (Mouton: The Hague Press,1973); Robert Buijtenhuis, *Essays on Mau Mau:*; Tabitha Kanogo, *Squatters and the Roots of Mau Mau 1905-1963* (Columbus: Ohio University Press, 1987); Donald Barnett and Karari Njama, *Mau Mau from Within an Analysis of Kenya's Peasant Revolt* (New York: Monthly Review Press, 1966); Anthony Clayton and Donald Savage, *Government and Labor in Kenya, 1895-1963* (London: Frank Cass,1974); Frank Furedi, "The Social Composition of the Mau Mau Movement," *Journal of Peasant Studies* 1 (4) July, 1974, pp. 486-505; Frank Furedi, "The Kikuyu Squatters in the Rift Valley, 1918-1929," *Hadith* 5, 1975, pp. 177-194; M. Tamarkin, "Loyalist in Nakuru During the Mau Mau Revolt and its Aftermath," *Asian and African Studies* 12 (2), 1978, pp. 247-261; Michael Coray, "The Kenya Land Commission and the Kikuyu of Kiambu," *Agricultural History* 52 (1), 1978, pp. 179-193; John Newsinger, "Revolt and Repression in Kenya: The 'Mau Mau' Rebellion, 1952-1960," *Science and Society* 45 (3), 1981, pp. 159-185; Sharon Stichter, " Workers, Trade Unions, and the Mau Mau Rebellion," *Canadian Journal of African Studies*, 9 (2) 1975, pp. 259-275; M. Tamarkin, "Mau Mau in Nakuru," *Journal of African History* 17 (1), 1976, pp. 119-134; L.S.B. Leakey, *Mau Mau and the Kikuyu* (London: Methuen & Company, 1952); L.S.B. Leakey, *Defeating Mau Mau* (London: Methuen & Company, 1954) ; F. Majadalany, *State of Emergency. The Full Story of Mau Mau* (Boston: Houghton Mifflin Company, 1963); B.A. Ogot, *Politics and Nationalism in Colonial Kenya* (Nairobi: East African Publishing House, 1972); M.P.K. Sorrenson, *Land Reform in the Kikuyu Country* (London: Oxford University Press, 1967); Tabitha Kanogo, "Rift Valley Squatters and Mau Mau," *Kenya Historical Review*, 5 1977, pp. 243-253.

3. Kanogo, *Squatters and the Roots of Mau Mau.*
4. Kenya National Archives (KNA). Native Affairs Department (NAD). Annual Report (AR)/1953, p. 25. Kenya Colony and Protectorate (KCP). Community Development Department (CDD). AR/1956, p. 4.
5. Great Britain. Colonial Office Report on the Colony and Protectorate of Kenya, 1954, p. 80. The original Community Development staff included 24 European Rehabilitation Officers and 37 African Rehabilitation Officers.
6. KNA. Kiambu (KBU)/109/Part II (K), Political Record Book (PRB), 1912. p. 10; KNA. KBU/76, PRB 1908-1912, pp. 85-87.
7. For female circumcision see KNA. NAD. AR/1929, pp. 11-12; Rosberg and Nottingham, *The Myth of "Mau Mau,"* pp. 106-125; Jocelyn Murray, "The Kikuyu Female Circumcision Controversy, with Special Reference to the Church Missionary Society's 'Sphere of Influence,'" Ph.D. dissertation, University of California, Los Angeles, 1974, *passim*..
8. See Chapter 7, Table 7.1.
9. F.D. Corfield, *Historical Survey of the Origins and Growth of Mau Mau.* Cmnd. 1030 (London: HMSO , 1960), pp. 155-156.
10. Ibid., p. 134.
11. Majadalany, *State of Emergency*, p. 60.
12. Corfield, *Historical Survey*, p. 101.
13. Corfield, *Historical Survey*, p. 157; Majadalany, *State of Emergency*, pp. 137-147.
14. Buijtenhuis, *Essays on Mau Mau*, p. 184.

15. Quoted in Corfield, *Historical Survey*, pp. 136-137.

16. J.T. Kamunchulah, "The Meru Participation in Mau Mau," *Kenya Historical Review* 3 (2), 1975, p. 193.

17. KNA. NAD. AR/1953, p. 25; KNA. African Affairs Department (AAD). Central Province (CP). AR/1953, p. 27.

18. KNA. NAD AR/1926, p. 87; KNA. NAD AR/1925, p. 64; KNA. NAD AR/1926, p. 79.

19. A.J. Temu, *British Protestant Missions* (London: Longman Group,1972), pp. 106-107.

20. KNA. AR/320/KBU/38/1946, pp. 1-2.

21. Corfield , *Historical Survey*, p. 67.

22. Ibid., p. 77.

23. KCP. AAD. CP. AR/1954, p. 3.

24. KCP. Legislative Council Debates, October 18, 1955, p. 4.

25. KCP. AAD. CP. AR/1954, p. 52; KCP. AAD. CP. AR/1955, p. 51.

26. KCP. CDD. AR/1954, p. 31.

27. KCP. CDD. AR/1958, p. 7.

28. KCP. AAD. CP. AR/1955, pp. 35, 51.

29. KNA. CDD. AR/1957, p. 33; KNA. AAD. AR/1954, p. 33.

30. Interview with Milka Ngina, Kiambu Town, May 11, 1979.

31. Interview with Catherine Wajiru, Kitambaya, May 11, 1979.

32. Interview with Wagara Wainana, Kitambaya, April 29, 1978.

33. KCP. AAD. AR/1955, p. 37.

34. KCP. CDD. AR/1955, p. 1.

35. KCP. CDD. AR/1954, p. 31.

36. Translation: Progress among women.

37. KCP. CDD. AR/1955, p. 7.

38. Ibid.

39. KCP. CDD. AR/1954, pp. 12-13.

40. Ibid., p. 13.

41. KCP. CDD. AR/1955, p. 25.

42. Ibid.

43. KCP. CDD. AR/1952, p. 9; KCP. CDD. AR/1956, pp. 1-10.

44. KCP. CDD. AR/1955, p. 7.

45. Ibid.

46. Ibid.

47. Ibid., p. 12.

48. KCP. AAD. CP. AR/1955, p. 48.

49. The connection to the Emergency conditions and the famine in the district is clear. No mention is made in the colonial records of famine in other parts of Kenya in 1956.

50. KCP. CDD. AR/1956, pp. 13-14.

51. Ibid., p. 10.

52. KCP. CDD. AR/1957, p. 8.

53. KCP. CDD. AR/1955, p. 6.

54. Abel Ndumbu, *Out of My Rib: A View of Women in Development* (Nairobi: Development Horizons, 1985) , p. 86.

55. *Women of Kenya Review and Evaluation of Progress* (Nairobi: East African Literature Bureau, 1985, p. 42.

9

Conclusion

This study was begun with the intention of investigating the possibilities and significance of political activism among Kikuyu women of Kiambu district in the colonial era. The second question posed was how women's position in society was changed by their colonial experience. In the first instance, scholars had assumed that women were politically passive. But this research demonstrates where and how women were active participants, rather than merely acted upon or used to broaden a platform of a particular association. A major contribution is the retrieval of an unsuspected history of evolution of women's roles that transformed them. The fact that early nationalists used women's exploitation as wage laborers in their confrontations with the government has been represented as evidence of women's indirect involvement. These interpretations of the labor issue are myopic. For although the issue of their exploitation was aired, the solutions did not alleviate women's labor grievances. Therefore, Kikuyu women became active organizers, staging their own protests against serving as a cheap labor force for the planter class. These took several forms. They ranged from verbalizing their dissatisfaction through abusive songs to planning and carrying out work stoppages. Sometimes these work stoppages coincided with other labor protest; most often, women's labor protest was independent.

Women's labor action and labor consciousness is amply demonstrated in this inquiry. However, there is another aspect of women's involvement in wage labor that could be addressed in future research. Data needs to be collected on what effect the redirection of women's indigenous labor into wage labor had on the self-sufficiency of traditional agriculture. The implications of this kind of study are that examining societies where women were the primary farmers when settler cash crop farming was introduced may reveal, first that a decline in food production occurs when cash crop farming replaces women's food production; second, it will may quantify how much women's labor subsidizes cash crop farming through comparing women's wage rates, costs of production, and market prices with the cost of importing food to replace domestic food production. The implications for national development are that more resources should be made available to women farmers, even though the crops they produce have no great export value. Women's transformation to wage laborers in the colonial era could have started the decline of Kenya's food production. State support for women's farming could revive it.

The economic sector is an important area of change for women. A second area that shows social change for women is cultural practices. Few accounts of the circumcision controversy and its aftermath include women as direct participants. On one level, the controversy was a confrontation over who would control Kikuyu culture through the vehicle of controlling women's bodies. The missionaries were involved with a struggle with Kikuyu males for control of culture from the early twentieth century. However, Kikuyu nationalists quickly linked this to issues of self-rule and economic survival. The KCA was able to influence large numbers of Kikuyu into making this linkage. The result was a widening split of the Kikuyu into two opposing factions. The division remained a factor in later political unrest and accounts for the state of civil war between the Kikuyu during the Mau Mau rebellion. The effect of the controversy on women's transformation was to embroil them as participants in the struggle between Christian and traditional forces. This shifted women's relation to the church. Before the controversy, many women had viewed the church and western religion as a refuge from the burdens of traditional life. In the course of the dispute, thousands of women abandoned the church and turned circumcision from a custom into a cause. The subsequent battle created two changes. First, the membership of the nationalist association grew. The new configuration included men who had not attached themselves to the association before 1928 and women who became formal members of the association. Second, independent churches and schools were established. In the independent schools, females were allowed more access to western-style education. The most significant aspect of this, from the perspective of women's transformation, is that they participated in planning, designing, and administering the new schools. Women's relationship to the Githunguri Teacher Training College demonstrates this relationship best, since prominent nationalist women designed and created a special facility for girls.

Both the labor issue and the circumcision controversy reveal a shift in women's structural relationship to decision-making and leadership before 1940. Events after World War II brought this change to full maturity. Women sought first class membership in the nationalist organizations from the 1930s. At first, this status was denied to them. Kikuyu Central Association leaders, who were experiencing their own transformation, did not realize that women's roles were changing dramatically. The KCA was forced to appreciate this change when women nationalists compelled them to accommodate their political ambitions. The struggle between male and female nationalists was internal and hidden from the observations of non-Kikuyu and perhaps later generations of Kikuyu nationalists. The only sources for this struggle are the women who claim to have initiated it and achieved their goal of being recognized as valuable and near equal political allies. The results of this can be seen in the existence of a women's wing in the organizational structure of KAU and Mau Mau. Women were the leaders of these wings.

The evolution of women's structural relationship to decision-making was from a passive role to an activist one in the large confrontation between Kikuyu and settler, African and European. In this process of movement from secondary to primary participation, these pioneer women became advocates and examples for the transformation of customary gender roles. The new set of relations broke down male political privilege. Women earned this through sacrifice. The gender shifts in power and authority occurred at the same time as major changes were disrupting Kikuyu society. Indeed, had this not been true, women's leverage would have been greatly reduced. The three major areas of transformation: labor, politics, and gender relationships can be plotted out in five stages.

Women's Transformation Model

In Stage 1 of the model, women had economic responsibility, some control over routing resources, but were allowed few means of achieving real economic independence because the acquisition of land—the ultimate symbol of independence in society—was closed to them. The social contract created by the male-dominated structures limited women's political role, since they were barred from membership in the ruling councils. The contract confined their social role to control over "women's things." Nonetheless, women did have some informal ways of softening male control through group criticism of male authority figures and offenders. Like politics, warfare was the sole province of men.

Stage 2 occurred after 1895 when the colonial state was introduced. Colonialism redistributed power, wealth, and authority. Kikuyu males were largely locked out of the structures and processes of control. The British controlled land, labor, the political structure, and strongly influenced the view of women in society.

Stage 1 Pre-colonial

Politics:	No political power
Land:	No land ownership
Work:	Women farmers; women traders; women have domestic role
View Of Women:	Women's roles asymmetrical and complementary to men's
Military:	Women don't wage war

Stage 2 Colonialism's Impact

Politics:	Men lose political power
Land:	Land alienation
Work:	Taxation; forced labor/wage labor; women farmers; women traders; women maintain domestic role
View of Women:	British view women as dependent
Military:	British control warfare

Stage 3 Anti-colonial Reaction

Politics:	Political parties formed
Land:	Kikuyu try to regain land
Work:	Labor protest
View of Women:	Male nationalist view women as focus of protest

	Stage 4 Women as Agents of Change
Politics:	Women form political party; nationalist associations incorporate women; women assume leadership role in managing resources and people; women assume ritual authority in oathing
Land:	Kikuyu try to regain land
Work:	Women organize work stoppages
View of Women:	Male nationalists view women as allies
Military:	Women wage war

	Stage 5 Conditions after Independence
Politics:	Women vote; women hold political office
Land:	Women own land
Work:	Women wage laborers; women have domestic responsibility; women traders
View of Women:	Women are men's legal equals
Military:	Women in armed forces

In Stage 3, the voice for negotiation with the British was assumed by male Kikuyu, both radical and moderate. No significant female initiated protest is discernable at this stage. However, this period did not cover many years. Perhaps the best date for its end is 1922 when the British disbanded the first all male nationalist organization.

Women's roles in society began to be transformed through their own organizational initiative in Stage 4. Women tried to re-structure the relationships of power, increase their access to wealth, and attain political authority. In this stage, women's political protest was parallel to men's and independent. Women formed their own political association, organized independent labor actions against the planter class, and negotiated with male nationalists for access to the radical political party. What is important about women's protest in this stage is that both European males and Kikuyu males were the focus of women's grievances. Both maintained male-dominated political structures that women sought to change. Women also lodged protest against Kikuyu male authority figures whose position derived from their service to the colonial regime as chiefs, retainers, and members of the Local Native Councils. Moderates, as represented by the Kikuyu

Association, never moved towards changing their definition of gender roles; the settler/ government alliance was equally oblivious to changes in women's position in decision-making and economic control. Women achieved their greatest success in having their interests considered with the radical males who belonged to the Kikuyu Central Association and later the Kenya African Union. During this stage of transformation which lasts from 1930 to 1960, women gained partnership status in the nationalist associations and the Land and Freedom army. Significantly, a recognized and effective female leadership became visible. They directed women's political activities and mobilized thousands of women to participate in mass actions. In a significant break with past traditions, women assumed responsibilities for making war in Stage 4. Women's warring capabilities were recognized by males, Kikuyu and British alike. Mau Mau men served with women soldiers. However, women's use of violence as a means of changing their conditions was perceived as a threat by the British. This produced a brutal repression which took the forms of jailing, torturing, and killing female Mau Mau soldiers.

Stage 5 marks the independence period, where women's position in society is defined by legal equality. They have access to participation in political affairs through voting and holding political office, if they can get elected or appointed. Women can own land, which is still the major means of becoming economically independent for many. Also, women are involved in wage labor in the agricultural as well as the industrial sectors. And finally, they are members of the various branches of the armed forces. Women's position in all of these categories are continuations of the status they achieved in the later years of colonialism. Many of the changes are limited. Women do not have a high rate of participation in government, nor do they control a major portion of the wealth of the nation.

While Kikuyu women's nationalist issues were the same as men's, there are some important contrasts in the processes through which women and men became activists. The two most significant factors that determined women's route to prominent radical activism were the failure of the colonial state to institute means to co-opt women and male radicals' desperate search for allies. The British coopted male Kikuyu authority to give legitimacy to the colonial state when the traditional council of elders became an agent of colonialism (the Local Native Councils). Although the councils were stripped of their pre-colonial functions of war-making, full governance, and adjudication, they were a lower level of the colonial bureaucracy with limited jurisdiction over tax collection, labor recruitment, and education. The chief's councils were salaried and served as the primary voice of the government to the people.

The British did not attempt to bring women's councils into the colonial bureaucracy, nor did they try to coopt women's authority structures to serve the state. But the women's council was also altered by colonialism. This conversion was one women initiated themselves. It is at this level of transformation that the women's model diverges sharply from men's. Though the chiefs were often critics and opponents of the colonial government, they were essentially allied with it and viewed as collaborators. Women's authority was not structurally allied with the colonial regime. Part of this devolved from the fact that women had an unequal structural relationship to power in the pre-colonial era. The largest cause of this was British assumption that women had no place in governance.

Before and during the colonial era, women's subordination to male power structures meant that when they attempted to influence men, they did so as politically disaffected groups and individuals. In the pre-colonial era, their protest took the form of group censure of men through ritual cursing and mockery (scurrilous songs). Thus, the forms of women's protest were oppositional and confrontational even before the British arrived. Women continued to use mockery as a means of political expression against the British. However, under colonialism they enlarged the scope of protest.

Of course, women's radical political action was coterminous with men's. Colonialism created radical male political factions because it ruptured the process of political change. Pre-colonial authority structures accommodated younger males by admitting them to the circles of power in phases (junior warrior to senior elder) and purchase. Moreover, leadership was periodically handed over to the next generation. Thus, young men's political ambitions were delayed but gratified. This served to check revolt among the young since they knew that they could attain the highest levels of authority in society through orthodox means. Colonialism eliminated this process. Suddenly, elders were appointed by an alien government and these appointments lasted beyond the normal period of the generational change over. Consequently, young men's political ambitions were frustrated. As a group, young men were in open conflict with the colonial government and, for the first time, in open conflict with older Kikuyu for access to political control. Young men's reactions were to create the alternative structure of the nationalist associations.

Young men's structural relationship to controlling insitutions became similar to what women's had been in the pre-colonial period; they adopted women's strategies of protest and opposition. In the 1930s and 1940s, men participated in the female tradition of *muthirigo* and criticism of elders. Just as women had been forced to establish a separate legitimacy as critics of male rule, so did young men struggle to establish their separate legitimacy as critics of colonial rule by Europeans and moderate Kikuyu chiefs. Another interesting convergence in the pattern of radical males' and women's nationalism is the location of protest. Up to the circumcision controversy there was an important difference, for male nationalists concentrated on the urban areas. The strength of the chiefs' influence in the rural areas limited nationalists' ability to gain followers. When the circumcision controversy exploded, male nationalists were able to change this. In the rural areas, they encountered politicized women who, because of the differences in male/female migration patterns, had not moved to the Nairobi. The traditional women's council became a rural instrument that voiced political disaffection. In the process of achieving this, they gained the legitimacy as representatives of Kikuyu interests that the elders had relinquished when they joined the colonial forces. These conditions made nationalists turn to women as allies once women demonstrated their organizing and recruiting skills. The young nationalists benefited by linking themselves to women's political protests. Together as alternative sources of legitimacy, the radical males and prominent women promoted political organization on the issues of land, labor, education, and political empowerment. The rurally based protest was activist from the beginning, ultimately it turned to violence. The moderate males eschewed violence as a means of achieving social change. Therefore, it can be asserted that Kikuyu women's activism from the 1930s onwards drew on their pre-colonial tradition of opposition to the status quo. Since the elders' councils did not have this tradition, the male nationalists were women's logical allies.

Perhaps it was the recognition of the threat posed by female dissidence that caused the independent Kenya government to allow women the possibility of achieving power, status, and wealth. In independent Kenya, women can own property outside of their household possessions. A few women have achieved political office. KANU insists that women be involved in the political process on the district and national level. Each district has a women's wing under female leadership. These concessions are recognitions of the potential value of female power.

However, women's transformation is not complete. Women's social and economic issues still do not receive priority rating in national policy. Nonetheless, the legacy of female activism provides models, ideals, and opportunity for future transformation. While the historiography on Kenyan nationalism is mute on the subject, politicians in the post-colonial era concede women's power potential.

Glossary

age set	those circumcised at the same time
ahoi (*muhoi*, s.)	client with cultivation rights
anake	warriors
athami (*muthami*, s.)	client with cultivation and building rights
baraza (*Kiswahili*)	public meeting convened by officials
debbe	unit of measurement weighing thirty pounds
ene	land ownership rights
Gikuyu	legendary male founder of the Kikuyu
gikwa	yam
Githunguri	teacher training college begun by the Kikuyu
gutaramira ng'ania	ritual cursing
hinga	Kikuyu women who spoke Masai usually of Masai origin through adoption
irigu	banana
jembe	hoe
kana	baby girl
karego	small girl
Karing'a Association	Kikuyu independent schools
kiama	council of elders
kiama kia atumia	women's council
kiama kia kamatimu	junior elders council (marriage a prerequisite)
kiama kia maturanguru	junior elders council (circumcision of first child a prerequisite)
kigwa	sugar cane
kihingo	economic self-help organization
kipande	fingerprint and work registration Africans were required to wear
kiriri	girl's sleeping place in mother's house; name given to girls' wing at Githunguri school
mbari	lineage
mboco	kidney bean
mtama (*Kiswahili*)	millet
muchukia	traditional dance attended after circumcision
mugikuyu	circumcision age set name for females
mugoya	traditional dance attended after circumcision
muhai	mother of young children
muhiki	betrothed or married woman with a child
mukabi	circumcision age set name for females

Mumbi	legendary female founder of the Kikuyu
munyago	digging stick
muthurigo	protest songs, often of a ribald nature
mutumia	mother of one or more initiated children
mwembe	maize
mwere	bullrush millet
nduma	edible arum
Ngai	god
ngwaci	sweet potato
njahi	lablab bean
posho (*Kiswahili*)	food allotment--usually maize meal
Reserve	land remaining under African ownership after land alienation occurred
shamba (*Kiswahili*)	homestead farm
squatters	Africans receiving cultivation rights on European farms in exchange for labor
tembe	traditionally brewed beer
thahu	ritually unclean
theti	old woman
thingiri	Kikuyu house
thoroko	cowpea
ugali	thick maize meal porridge
uji	thin--sometimes fermented--maize meal porridge
Agikuyu (*Mugikuyu*, s.)	ethnic name given to the descendents of Kikuyu and Mumbi
Wandorobo	indigenous occupants of land south of the Chania River

Abbreviations

AAD	African Affairs Department
AIM	African Inland Mission
AR	Annual Report
CDD	Community Development Department
CMS	Church Missionary Society
CO	Colonial Office
CP	Central Province
CSM	Church of Scotland Mission
DC	District Commissioner
DPRB	Dagoretti Political Record Book
EAA	East African Association
EAS	East African Standard
HOR	Handing Over Report
IBEAC	Imperial British East Africa Company
ISA	Independent Schools Association
KA	Kikuyu Association
KADU	Kenya African Democratic Union
KANU	Kenya African National Union
KAU	Kenya African Union
KBU	Kiambu (district)
KCA	Kikuyu Central Association
KCP	Kenya Colony and Protectorate
KNA	Kenya National Archives
LNC	Local Native Council
MCA	Mumbi Central Association
NAD	Native Affairs Department
PC	Provincial Commissioner
PRB	Political Record Book
PRO	Public Records Office, Kew England
YKA	Young Kikuyu Association

References

Aaronovitch, S. and K. 1947. *Crisis in Kenya*. London: Lawrence and Wishart.

Abbott, Susan. 1974. Full-time Farmers and Weekend Wives: Change and Stress Among Rural Kikuyu Women. Ph.D. dissertation, University of North Carolina.

____. 1975. "Women's Importance for Kenyan Rural Development." *Community Development Journal* 10 (February): 179-182.

____. 1976. "Full-time Farmers and Week-end Wives: An Analysis of Altering Conjugal Roles." *Journal of Marriage and the Family* 38: 165-174.

Abdalla, Raqiya Haji Dualeh. 1982. *Sisters in Affliction: Circumcision and Infibulation of Women in Africa.* Westport, Connecticut: Zed Press.

Abour, C. Ojwando. 1971. *White Highlands No More.* Nairobi: Pan African Researchers.

African World. 1955, September. London.

Alpers, Edward A. 1975. *Ivory and Slaves: Changing Patterns of International Trade in East and Central Africa to the Later Nineteenth Century.* London: Heinemann.

Altrincham, Lord. 1955. *Kenya's Opportunities: Memories, Hopes and Ideas.* London: Faber and Faber.

Ardener, Shirley. 1973. "Sexual Insult and Female Militancy." *Man* 8 (September): 422-440.

Atieno-Odhiambo, E.S. 1973. "A Portrait of the Missionaries in Kenya Before 1939." *Kenya Historical Review* 1: 1-13.

____. 1975. *Paradox of Collaboration and Other Essays.* Nairobi: East African Literature Bureau.

Barnett, Donald. 1963. *Mau Mau: The Structural Integration and Disintegration of Aberdare Guerilla Forces.* Los Angeles: University of California Press.

____., ed. 1973. *The Hardcore: The Story of Ngugi Kabiro.* Richmond, British Columbia: The Liberation Support Movement Press.

____., ed. 1973. *Man in the Middle: The Story of Ngugi Kabiro.* Richmond, British Columbia: The Liberation Support Movement Press.

____., ed. 1974. *The Urban Guerilla: The Story of Muhamed Mathu.* Richmond, British Columbia: Support Movement Press.

Barnett, Donald and Karari Njama . 1966. *Mau Mau from Within: An Analysis of Kenya's Peasant Revolt.* New York: Monthly Review Press.

Barr, Jean. 1975. "Making the Invisible Visible: African Women in Politics and Policy." *African Studies Review* 18 (December): 19-27.

Beattie, J.H.M. 1956. "Ethnographic and Sociological Research in East Africa." *Africa* 26: 265-276.

Beech, Mervyn W.H. 1913. "Suicide Among the Akikuyu of East Africa." *Man* 13: 56-57.

____. 1917. Kikuyu Systems of Land Tenure. Oxford: Rhodes House.

____. 1917. "The Kikuyu System of Land Tenure." *Journal of the African Society* 17: 46-59, 136-144.

Bennett, George. 1957. "The Development of Political Organizations in Kenya." *Political Studies* 2: 113-130.

____. 1963. *Kenya, A Political History: The Colonial Period.* London: Oxford University Press.

Beraki, Joseph. 1979. Charismatic Leadership in the Nationalist Movements in Ghana and Kenya: A Comparative Study. Ph.D. dissertation, United States International University, San Diego.

Berg-Scholossen, Dirk. 1979. The Social and Economic Bases of Politics in Kenya: A Structural and Cultural Analysis. Ph.D dissertation, University of California, Berkeley.

Bewes, T.F.C. 1953. *Kikuyu Conflicts: Mau Mau and the Christian Witness.* London: Highway Press.

Bienen, Henry. 1974. *Kenya: The Politics of Participation and Control.* Princeton: Princeton University Press.

Blackburne-Maze, C.I. 1913. *Journals of My African Travels.* Maidstone: W.E. Thorpe and Son.

Blundell, Michael. 1964. *So Rough a Wind: The Kenya Memoirs.* London: Weidenfeld and Nicholson.

Boahen, A. Abu. 1962. "The Caravan Trade in the Nineteenth Century." *Journal of African History* 3: 349-359.

Bohannon, Paul. 1959. "The Impact of Money on an African Subsistence Economy." *Journal of Economic History* 19 (December): 491-503.

Bohannon, Paul and G. Dalton, eds. 1962. *Markets in Africa.* Evanston: Northwestern University Press.

Boserup, Ester. 1970. *Women's Role in Economic Development.* New York: St. Martin's Press.

Bowles, B.D. 1973. *The Interpretation of Nationalist Movements in East Africa.* Nairobi: Conference of the Historical Asssociation of Kenya,.

Boyes, John. 1911. *King of the Wa-Kikuyu.* London: Methuen and Co.

Brett, E.A. 1973. *Colonialism and Underdevelopment in East Africa.* London: Heinemann.

Buell, R.L. 1928 [1965]. *The Native Problem in Africa.* Hamden: Archon Books.

Buijra, Janet. 1975. "Women Entrepreneurs in Early Nairobi." *Canadian Journal of African Studies* 9: 213-234.

Buijtenhuis, Robert. 1973. *Mau Mau Twenty Years After: The Myth and Survivors.* The Hague-Paris: Mouton.

____. 1982. *Essays on Mau Mau: Contributions to Mau Mau Historiography.* Paper No. 17. Leiden: African Studies Centre

Bunche, Ralph J. 1939. "The Land Equation in Kenya." *Journal of Negro History*: (January) : 41-42.

Bunyasi, J.S. Makokha. 1973. "Labor in the Kenya Coffee Industry: An Economic Analysis." M.A. Thesis, University of Nairobi.

Cagnolio, Fr. C. 1933. *The Akikuyu: Their Customs, Traditions and Folklore.* Nyeri, Kenya: The Mission Printing School.

Carey-Jones, N.S. 1966. *The Anatomy of Uhuru: An Essay on Kenya's Independence.* Manchester: Manchester University Press.

Carlebach, Julius. United Nations, Economic Commission for Africa. 16 July 1963. *The Position of Women in Kenya.* (E/CN. 14/URB/9).

Carter, Gwendolyn, ed. 1966. *National Unity and Regionalism in Eight African States.* Ithaca, New York: Cornell University Press.

Cavendish, Richard, ed., 1970-1972. *Man, Myth and Magic: Enclyclopedia of the Supernatural.* 7 vols. London: Purnell for BPC Publishing.

Cavichi, Edmondo. 1977. *Problems of Change in Kikuyu Tribal Society.* Bologna: EMI.

Charle, Edwin. 1970. "Political Systems and Economic Performance in Some African Societies." *Economic Development and Cultural Change* 18, Part I (July): 575-597.

Chidzero, B.T.C. 1960. "African Nationalism in East and Central Africa." *International Affairs* 36 (October): 464-475.

Christian Science Monitor. Boston. 1951-1959.

Ciancaneli, Penelope. 1980. "Exchange, Reproduction and Sex Subordination Among the Kikuyu of East Africa." *The Review of Radical Political Economics* 12 (Summer): 25-36.

Clayton, Anthony. 1976. *Counter Insurgency in Kenya, 1952-60: A Study of Military Operations Against Mau Mau.* Nairobi: Transafrica Publishers.

Clayton, Anthony and Donald Savage. 1974. *Government and Labour in Kenya, 1895-1963.* London: Frank Cass.

Clough, Marshall S. 1978. Chiefs and Politicians: Local Politics and Social Change in Kiambu, Kenya. Ph.D. dissertation, Stanford University.

Clough, Marshall S. and Kennell A. Jackson. 1975. *A Bibliography on Mau Mau.* Sacramento: Mimeographed.

____. 1975. *Mau Mau Syllabus.* Sacramento: Mimeographed.

Coleman, James S. 1954. "Nationalism in Tropical Africa." *The American Political Science Review* 48 (June): 404-426.

Coleman, James S. and Carl Rosberg, eds. 1964. *Political Parties and National Integration in Tropical Africa.* Berkeley: University of California Press.

Collier, Jane F. 1974. "Women in Politics." in Michelle Zimbalist Rosaldo and Louise Lamphere , eds., *Women, Culture and Society.* Pp. 89-96. Stanford: Stanford University Press.

Colony and Protectorate of Kenya. 1956. *Inspection of Prison Establishments, Sessional Paper No. 7.* Nairobi: Government Printer.

Cone, L.W. and J.F. Lispcomb. 1972. *The History of Kenya Agriculture.* Nairobi: University Press of Africa.

Cooper, Fred. 1980. *From Slaves to Squatters: Plantation Labor and Agriculture in Zanzibar and Coastal Kenya, 1890-1925.* New Haven: Yale University Press.

Coray, Michael. 1978. "The Kenya Land Commission and the Kikuyu of Kiambu." *Agricultural History* 52 (1): 179-193.

Corfield, F.D. 1960. *Historical Survey of the Origins and Growth of Mau Mau.* HMSO. London: Cmnd 1030.

Corydon Papers. n.d. Papers of Sir Robert Corydon. 18 boxes. Oxford: Rhodes House Library.

Coupland, Reginald (Sir). 1967. *The Exploitation of East Africa, 1856-1890: The Slave Trade and the Scramble.* Evanston: Northwestern University Press.

Curtin, Philip. 1966. "Varieties of Nationalisms in Modern Africa." *The Review of Politics* 28 (April): 143-153.

Cutrufelli, Maria Rosa. 1983. *Women of Africa: Roots of Oppression.* London: Zed Press.

Daily Chronicle. 1956-1957. Nairobi.

Dalton, George. 1961. "Economic Theory and Primitive Society." *American Anthropologist* 63: 1-25.

____. 1969. "Theoretical Issues in Economic Anthropology." *Current Anthropology* 10: 63-102.

Davison, Jean. 1989. *Voices from Mutira : Lives of Rurual Gikuyu Women.* Boulder & London: Lynne Rienner Publishers.

Dilley, Ruth. 1934. *British Policy in Kenya Colony.* Seattle: University of Washington.

Dobbs, Cecil Moore. Memoranda, Correspondence, Etc. of Service in Kenya. MSS Afri.s.S15. Oxford: Rhodes House Library.

Dobbs, M.W. 1964. Recollections of Kenya 1906-1931. Oxford: Rhodes House Library.

Dobson, B. 1954. "Women's Place in East Africa." *Corono* 6: 454-457.

Dundas, Charles R. 1908. "Kikuyu Rika." *Man* 8: 180-182.

____. 1913. "The Organization of Some Bantu Tribes in East Africa." *Journal of the Royal Anthropological Institute of Great Britain and Ireland* 45: 236-306.

Dywer, Daisey Hilse. 1982. "Outside the Courts: Extra-Legal Strategies for Subordinating Women," in Margaret Jean Hay and Marica Wright, eds., *African Women and the Law: Historical Perspectives.* Pp. 90-109. Boston: University Papers on Africa, VIII.

East African Standard. 1920-1959. Nairobi.

Edari, R.S. 1971. *Ethnic Relations Prospects for National Integration in Kenya.* Evanston: Northwestern University Press.

Evans, M.N. 1955. "Local Government in the African Areas of Kenya." *Journal of African Administration* 7 (July): 123-127.

Fabian Colonial Bureau. 1944. *Kenya: White Man's Country? Report to the Colonial Bureau.* London: Fabian Publications.

Fanon, Frantz. 1965. *Studies in a Dying Colonialism.* New York: Monthly Review Press.

Fazan, Sidney Herbert. 1956. Loyalist versus Mau Mau. Oxford: Rhodes House.

____. 1968. Kenya Native Affairs. Oxford: Rhodes House.

Ferraro, Gary. 1970. *Kikuyu Kinship Interaction in Nairobi and Rural Kiambu.* Nairobi: Nairobi University Cultural Division.

Finnegan, Ruth. 1970. *Oral Literature in Africa.* Oxford: The Clarendon Press.

Fisher, Jeanne. 1964. *The Anatomy of Kikuyu Domesticity and Husbandry.* London: Department of Technical Cooperation.

Fletcher, Eileen. 1956. *The Truth About Kenya.* London: Movement for Colonial Freedom.

Frankel, S.H. 1953. *The Economic Impact on Underdeveloped Societies: Essays on International Investment and Social Change.* Boston: Harvard University Press.

Furedi, Frank. 1973. "The African Crowd in Nairobi Popular Movements and Elite Politics." *Journal of African History,* 14: 275-209.

____. 1974. "The Social Composition of the Mau Mau Movement." *Journal of Peasant Studies* 1 (4) July: 486-505.

____. 1975. "The Kikuyu Squatters in the Rift Valley, 1918-1929," in B.A. Ogot, ed., *Hadith 5: Economic and Social History of East Africa*: 177-194. Nairobi: East African Publishing House.

____. 1989. *The Mau Mau War in Perspective.* London: James Currey.

Furley, Q.W. 1972. "The Historiography of Mau Mau." *Hadith 4:* 105-133.

Gachie, Muthoni wa. 1979. Tingang'a. Interview, January 10.

Gachika, Elizabeth. 1979. Kiambu Town. Interview, January 7.

Gachiko, Virginia. 1978. Rabai. Interview, November 16.

Gachiku, Virginia. 1978. Kiambu Town. Interview, November 12, and April 14.

Gadsen, Fay. 1980. "The African Press in Kenya, 1945-1952." *Journal of African History* 21: 515-535.

Gatheru, R.M. 1964. *Child of Two Worlds: A Kikuyu's Story.* New York: Praeger.

Gaturu, Violet Nyambura. 1973. *Modern Marriages Among the Kikuyu.* Kampala: Makere University Department of Sociology.

Gichage, Muthoni. 1979. Tingang'a. Interview, January 4.

Giching'a Njoki wa. 1979. Ruiru. Interview, May 16.

Gikoyo, Gucu. 1979. *We Fought for Freedom.* Nairobi: East African Publishing House.

Gikuhi, Wangui wa. 1979. Ruiru. Interview, May 13.

Gluckman, Max. 1941. "Economy of the Central Barotse Plain." *Rhodes-Livingstone Papers* No. 7.

Goody, Jack. 1976. *Production and Reproduction: A Comparative Study of the Domestic Domain.* Cambridge: Cambridge University Press.

Gorden-Brown, A., ed. 1954. *Yearbook and Guide to East Africa.* London: Robert Hale.

Gordon, David Frank. 1981. Colonial Crises, Decolonization and the State: The Case of Kenya. Ph.D. dissertation, University of Michigan.

Gray, Richard and David Birmingham. 1970. *Pre-colonial African Trade: Essays on Trade in Central and Eastern Africa Before 1900.* Oxford: Oxford University Press.

Great Britain. Colonial Offfice. 1920. 533/248/644-647. Compulsory Labour. June 17.

____. 1920. 533/247/860. Letter to Viscount Milner, Secretary of State for the Colonies from C.E. Wilson, Foreign Secretary, Baptist Missionary Society Regarding Recruitment of Native Labour for Farm and Government Work. July 20.

____. 1920. 533/249/92. Letter from Primitive Methodist Missionary Society to Lord Milner, Secretary for the Colonies Regarding Native Labour. July 23.

____. 1920. 533/249/94. Native Labour. Letter from London Missionary Society to Secretary for the Colonies. July 26.

____. 1920. 533/249/240. Native Labour. Letter from the Anti-Slavery and Aborigines Protection Society to Under Secretary of State. August 24.

____. 1920. 533/249/388-389. Native Labour. Letter from the AntiSlavery and Aborigines Protection Society to the Under Secretary of State, Colonial Office. October 22.

____. 920. 533/249/446. Native Labour. Letter from the United Free Church of Scotland, Greencock Presbytery to Viscount Milner, Secretary of State of the Colonies. November 4.

____. 1920. 533/249/537-539. Native Labour. Letter from the Conference of Missionary Societies to Milner. December 21.

____. 1920. 533/248/586-588. Increase in Native Taxation. Letter from J.W. Arthur, the Alliance of Missionary Societies in British East Africa to Secretary of State for the Colonies. May 10.

____. 1920. 533/248/499. Forced Labour. Letter from J.S. Middleton, Labour Party Secretary, to Milner, Secretary of State for the Colonies. April 22.

____. 1923. 533/319/419-423. Native Labour in Kenya, Uganda and Zanzibar.

____. 1924. 533/319/8-12. Advisory Committee on Native Education in Tropical Africa. January 9.

____. 1924. 533/338/378-380. Report by Major Fischer on his Journey to the East African Dependencies with the Phelps-Stoke Education Commission.

____. 1924. 533/319/462-464. Native Policy. November 3.

____. 1924. 533/319/464-480. Kenya Colony: Its Early Settlement and Native Problems. May 3.

____. 1924. 533/321/531-532. Letter from Major Fischer to Mrs Hooper Regarding Education of Native Girls in Kenya. September.

____. 1924. 533/321/90-112. Memorandum on the Education of Native Girls Prepared by M. Cicely Hooper, Fort Hall. August 1.

____. 1924. 533/321/75-76. Education for African Girls. July 8.

____. 1925. 533/352/521. Report prepared by Orr, Director of Education in Kenya Colony: Women's Education.

____. 1954. Report on the Colony and Protectorate of Kenya. HMSO. London.

____. 1959. "Records of Proceedings and Evidence in the Inquiry into the Deaths of Eleven Mau Mau Detainees at Hola Camp in Kenya." Cmnd. 778.

Great Britain. 1955. East Africa Royal Commission Report 1953-1955. Cmnd. 9475.

Great Britain. 1956. Parliament. Parliamentary Debates. (House of Commons) 555 (June 6): 1088-1211.

____. 1956. Parliament. Parliamentary Debates. (House of Commons) 555 (June 11-22): 564-571.

____. 1956. Parliament. Parliamentary Debates. (House of Commons) 555 (June 20): 1409-1416.

Gregory, John Walter. 1901. *The Foundations of British East Africa.* London: H. Marshall.

____. 1952. *The Great Rift Valley.* E.D. Loftus, ed. Nairobi: East African Literature Bureau.

Gutkind, Peter, Robin Cohen and Jean Copans, eds. 1978. *African Labor History.* Beverly Hills/London: Sage Publications.

Hafkin, Nancy J. and Edna G. Bay, eds. 1976. *Women in Africa: Studies in Social and Economic Change.* Stanford: Stanford University Press.

Hailey, Malcolm (Lord). 1938. *An African Survey: A Study of Problems Arising in Africa South of the Sahara.* London: Oxford University Press.

____. 1957. *An African Survey Revised 1956: A Study of Problems Arising in Africa South of the Sahara.* London: Oxford University Press.

Hansen, Emmanuel. 1977. *Frantz Fanon: Social and Political Thought.* Columbus: Ohio State University Press.

Harbeson, John Willis. 1970. Nationalism and Nation-building in Kenya. Ph.D. dissertation, University of Wisconsin.

____. 1971. "Land Reform and Politics in Kenya." *Journal of Modern African Studies* 9 (August): 232-251.

Harlow, Vincent, E.M. Chilver and Alison Smith, eds. *History of East Africa*. Vol II. Oxford: Oxford University Press.

Hay, Margaret Jean and Sharon Stichter, eds. 1984. *African Women South of the Sahara*. London/ New York: Longman.

Helm, June. 1961/1962. "The Ecological Approach in Anthropology." *American Journal of Sociology* 67: 630-639.

Herskovits, M.J. 1962. *The Human Factor in Changing Africa*. New York: Alfred A. Knopf.

Hill, M.E. 1956. *Planters Progress: The Story of Coffee in Kenya*. Nairobi: Coffee Board of Kenya.

Hill, Polly. 1963. "Markets in Africa." *The Journal of Modern African Studies* 1: 441-453.

____. 1969. "Hidden Trade in Hausaland." *Man* 4 (September): 392-409.

Historical Association of Kenya. 1972. *Politics and Nationalism in Colonial Kenya*. Nairobi: East African Publishing House.

Hobley, C.W. 1967. *Bantu Beliefs and Magic*. London: Frank Cass &Co. Ltd.

____. 1910 [1971]. *Ethnology of A-kamba an Other East African Tribes*. London: Cass.

____. 1929. *Kenya, From Chartered Company to Crown Colony*. London: H.F. G. Witherby.

Hodgkin, Thomas. 1961. *African Political Parties*. London: Penguin Africa Series.

Hollander, Roberta. 1979. Out of Tradition: The Position of Women in Kenya and Tanzania During the Pre-colonial, Colonial and Post-independence Eras. Ph.D. dissertation, The American University.

Hooper, Cicely. 1935. *New Patches: Women's Customs and Changes in Africa*. London: The Livingston Press.

Hopkins, A.G. 1973. *An Economic History of West Africa*. London: Longman.

Hosken, Fran P. 1980. *Female Sexual Mutilations: The Facts and Proposals for Action*. Lexington, Connecticut: Human Rights/Health Action Network.

Huxley, E. 1968. *White Man's Country: Lord Delamere and the Making of Kenya*. 2 Vols. New York: F.A. Praeger.

Huxley, Elspeth and Margery Perham. 1944. *Race and Politics in Kenya: A Correspondence Between Elspeth Huxley and Margery Perham*. 2nd ed. London: Faber and Faber.

Iliffe, John. 1975. "The Creation of Group Consciousness Among the Dock-workers of Dar es Salaam 1929-50," in Richard Sandbrook and Robin Cohen, eds., *The Development of an African Working Class: Studies in Class Formation and Action*, Pp. 49-72. Toronto: University of Toronto Press.

Interview #1. 1978. Raibai. Interview, October 1. Informant requested that her name never appear in any publication.

Itote, W. 1974. *Mau Mau General*. Nairobi: East African Publishing House.

____. 1979. *Mau Mau in Action*. Nairobi: Transafrica.

Jackson, Frederick (Sir). 1969. *Early Days in East Africa*. London: Dawsons of Pall Mall.

Jackson, Kennell A. 1972. An Ethnohistorical Study of the Oral Traditions of the Akamba of Kenya. Ph.D. dissertation, University of California, Los Angeles.

Jeffreys, M.D.W. 1976. "The Nyawa Society of Ibibio Women." *African Studies* 15: 15-28.

Johnson, Cheryl J. 1978. Nigerian Women and British Colonialism: The Yoruba Example with Selected Biographies. Ph.D. dissertation, Northwestern University.

Kaberry, Phyllis N. 1952. *Women of the Grassfields: A Study of the Economic Position of Women in Bamenda, British Cameroons*. London: H.M.S.O.

Kaggia, Bildad. 1975. *Roots of Freedom 1921-1963: An Autobiography*. Nairobi: East African Publishing House.

Kamau, Martha Gathoni wa. 1978. Kamburu. Interview, October 20.

Kamau, Nyina wa. 1978. Kamburu. Interview, October 29.

Kamunchulah, J.T. 1975. "The Meru Participation in Mau Mau." *Kenya Historical Review* 3 (2): 193-216.

Kanogo, Tabitha. 1977. "Rift Valley Squatters and Mau Mau," *Kenya Historical Review, 5 (1977)* :243-253.

____. 1987. *Squatters and the Roots of Mau Mau*. Columbus: Ohio University Press.

Karanja, Wanjiru wa. 1979. Githunguri. Interview, May 16.

Karing'a Tabitha Wanjiru. 1979. Ruiru. Interview, May 13.

Kariuki, Jesiah Mwangi. 1975. *Mau Mau Detainee: The Account by a Kenya African of his Experiences in Detention Camps 1953-1960*. London: Oxford University Press.

Kenya Colony and Protectorate. 1912-1959. Kiambu District Annual Reports.

____. 1916-1959. Kiambu District Political Record Book.

____. 1920-1959. Kiambu District Handing Over Reports.

____. 1925-1959. Native Affairs Department Annual Reports.

____. 1925-1952. Labour Department Annual Reports.

____. 1942-1947. Central Province Military Intelligence Report.

____. 1953. Kenya Prisons Annual Report. Nairobi: Government Printer.

____. 1953. *Report on the General Adminstration of Prisons and Detention Camps in Kenya,* by G.H. Heaton. Nairobi: Government Printer.

____. 1956. *Report on the General Adminstration of Prisons and Detention Camps in Kenya,* by G.H. Heaton. Nairobi: Government Printer.

____. 1954. Report on the Treatment of Offenders for the Year 1953. Nairobi: Government Printer.

____. 1954, 1955. African Affairs Department/Central Province. Nairobi: Government Printer.

____. 1954-1959. Community Development Annual Report. Nairobi: Government Printer.

____. 1955. Legislative Debates. October 18.

____. 1955. Report on the Treatment of Offenders, Kenya Prinsons for the Year 1954. Nairobi: Government Printer.

____. 1956. Treatment of Offenders Annual Report 1955. Nairobi: Government Printer.

____. 1957. Treatment of Offenders Annual Report 1956. Nairobi: Government Printer.

____. 1958. Treatment of Offenders Annual Report 1957. Nairobi: Government Printer.

____. 1959. Treatment of Offenders Annual Report 1958. Nairobi: Government Printer.

Kenya Land Commission Report, Evidence and Memoranda. 1946. Col. 91. Vol I. 1934. Orde-Brown, Granville, St.J. *Labour Conditions in East Africa.* Colonial Paper No. 193.

Kenya National Archives. 1908-1912. Political Record Book. Kiambu District. KBU/76.

____. 1912. Political Record Book. Kiambu District. KBU/ 109/Part II (K).

____. 1929. Native Affairs Department. Nairobi: Government Printer.

____. 1953. Political Record Book. Kiambu District. KBU/44.

____. 1953. Native Affairs Department. Nairobi: Government Printer.

____. 1959. Records of Proceedings and Evidence into the Deaths of Eleven Mau Mau Detainees at Hola Camp in Kenya. Nairobi: Government Printer.

Kenyatta, Jomo. 1937. "Kikuyu Religion, Ancestor Worship and Sacrificial Practices." *Africa* 10 (July): 308-328.

____. 1944. *Kenya: Land of Conflict.* Manchester: Panaf Service.

____. 1953 [1965]. *Facing Mount Kenya, The Tribal Life of the Gikuyu.* New York: Random House, Inc.

Kershaw, Greet. 1972. The Land is the People: A Study of Kikuyu Social Organization in Historical Perspective. Ph.D. dissertation, University of Chicago.

Kieran, J.A. 1969. "The Origins of Commercial Arabica Coffee Production in East Africa." *African Historical Studies* 2: 51-67.

Kilson, Martin. 1955. "Land and the Kikuyu: A Study of the Relationship Between Land and Kikuyu Political Movements." *Journal of Negro History* 40 (April): 103-153.

Kinyatti, Maina wa. 1977. "Mau Mau: The Peak of African Nationalism in Kenya." *Kenya Historical Review* 5: 287-311.

____. 1980. *Thunder from the Mountains: Mau Mau Patriotic Songs.* London: Zed Press.

Kipkorir, B.E. 1977. "Mau Mau and the Politics of Transfer of Power in Kenya, 1957-1960." *Kenya Historical Review* 5: 313-328.

Kitching, Gavin. 1980. *Class and Economic Change in Kenya: The Making of an African Petite Bourgeoisie 1905-1970.* New Haven and London: Yale University Press.

Kiyanjui, Kabiru. 1979. The Political Economy of Educational Inequality: A Study of the Roots of Educational Inequality in Colonial and Post-Colonial Kenya. Ed.D. dissertation, Harvard University.

Koplin, Roberta. 1968. Educational and National Integration in Ghana and Kenya. Ph.D. dissertation, University of Oregon.

Kore, Nduta wa. 1979. Tingang'a Interview. January 13; Kiambaa. Interview. April 21.

Kwame, Daaku Y. 1971. "Trade and Trading Patterns of the Akan in the Seventeenth and Eighteenth Centuries," in Claude Meillassoux, ed., *The Development of Indigenous Trade and Markets in West Africa,* Pp. 168-181. London: Oxford University Press.

Lambert, H.E. 1950. *The System of Land Tenure in the Kikuyu Land Unit.* Capetown: School of African Studies.

____. 1956. *Kikuyu Social and Political Institutions.* London: Oxford Press for the International African Institute.

Lancaster, C.S. 1976. "Women, Horticulture and Society in Sub-Saharan Africa." *American Anthropologist* 78: 539-564.

Lawrence, William L. 1968. "Masai and Kikuyu: An Historical Analysis." *Journal of African History* 9: 571-584.

Leakey, L.S.B. 1952. *Mau Mau and the Kikuyu.* London: Methuen & Company.

____. 1954. *Defeating Mau Mau.* London: Methuen & Company.

____. 1977. *The Southern Kikuyu Before 1903.* 3 Vols. London: Academic Press.

Lefaucheaux, Marie Helen. 1962. "The Contribution of Women to the Economic and Social Development of African Countries." *International Labour Review* 80: 15-30.

Leith-Ross, Sylvia. 1939 [1965]. *African Women: A Study of the Ibo of Nigeria.* New York: F.A. Praeger.

Leo, Christopher. 1984. *Land and Class in Kenya.* Toronto: University of Toronto Press.

Levine, Robert A. 1962. "Wealth and Power in Gusiiland, " in Paul Bohannon and G. Dalton, eds., *Markets in Africa,* Pp. 520-536. Evanston: Northwestern University Press.

Leys, Norman (Sir). 1924. *Kenya.* London: Hogarth Press.

Little, Kenneth. 1973. *African Women in Towns: An Aspect of Africa's Social Revolution.* London: Cambridge University Press.

Lonsdale, John. 1968. "Some Origins of Nationalism in East Africa." *Journal of African History* 9: 119-146.

Lonsdale, John and Bruce Berman. 1979. "Coping with the Contradictions: the Development of the Colonial State in Kenya, 1895-1914." *Journal of African History* 20: 487-505.

Low, D.A. 1965. "British East Africa: The Establishment of British Rule, 1895-1912," in Vincent Harlow, E.M. Chilver and Alison Smith, eds., *History of East Africa,* Vol II, Pp. 1-57. Oxford: Oxford University Press.

Lugard, Frederick (Lord). 1893. *Rise of Our East African Empire.* 2 Vols. Edinburgh: W. Blackwood.

MacPhee, A.M. 1968. *Kenya.* New York: F.A. Praeger.

McCall, Daniel. 1962. "The Korifidua Market.," in Paul Bohannon and G. Dalton, eds., *Markets in Africa,* Pp. 667-697. Evanston: Northwestern University Press.

Maina, Paul. 1977. *Six Mau Mau Generals.* Nairobi: Gazelle Books.

Maitha, J.K. 1974. *Coffee in the Kenyan Economy: An Economic Analysis.* Nairobi: East African Literature Bureau.

Maitha, Milka wa. 1979. Kitambaya. Interview, May 11.

Majdalany, F. 1963. *State of Emergency. The Full Story of Mau Mau.* Boston: Houghton Mifflin Company.

Man, Myth and Magic: Enclyclopedia of the Supernatural. 1970-1972. 7 vols. S.v. "Kikuyu," by James Wellard. London: Purnell for BPC Publishing.

Manners, Robert. 1962. "Land Use, Labor and the Growth Market Economy in Kipsigis Country," in Paul Bohannon and G. Dalton, eds., *Markets in Africa,* Pp. 493-515. Evanston: Northwestern University Press.

Mathu, Mohamed. 1974. *The Urban Guerilla: the Story of Mohamed Mathu.* D. Barnett, ed. Richmond, British Columbia: LSM Information Center.

Mboya, Tom. 1963. *Freedom and After.* Boston: Little Brown.

Meillassoux, Claude. 1971. *The Development of Indigenous Trade and Markets in West Africa.* London: Oxford University Press.

Middleton, John and Greet Kershaw. 1954. *The Central Tribes of the North-Eastern Bantu: the Kikuyu including Embu, Meru, Mbere, Chuka, Mwimbi, Tharaka, and the Kamba of Kenya.* London: International African Institute.

Millar, James. 1969/70. "A Reformulation of A.V. Chayanov's Theory of the Peasant Economy." *Economic and Cultural Change* 18: 219-229.

Miller, Joseph. 1970. "Cokwe Trade and Conquest in the Nineteenth Century," in Richard Gray and David Birmingham, eds., *Pre-Colonial African Trade: Essays on Trade in Central and Eastern Africa before 1900,* Pp. 175-201. London: Oxford University Press.

Miller, Norman. 1984. *Kenya: The Quest for Prosperity.* Boulder, Colorodo: Westview Press.

Mimi, Phyllis Wanjiko (Margo) wa. 1978. Tingang'a. Interview, December 20.

Miracle, Marvin. 1962. "African Markets and Trade in the Copperbelt," in Paul Bohannon and G. Dalton, eds., *Markets in Africa,* Pp. 698-738. Evanston: Northwestern University Press.

Mugo, E.N. 1982. *Kikuyu People: A Brief Outline of their Customs and Traditions.* Nairobi: Kenya Literature Bureau.

Mukaro-Ng`anga, D. 1978. *Thirty Years Before Mau Mau: A Study in Rural Resistance and Political Organization in Murang'a District, 1920-1952.* Nairobi: Institute of African Studies, Paper No. 104.

Mumbi, (no other name given) . Ndumberi. 1978. Interview, November 22.

Mumbi, Tabitha. 1979. Thika. Interview, May 24.

Munene, Fibi. 1977. "Women in Africa: The Kenya Perspective." *Africa Report* 22 (January/February): 18-20.

Mungai, Evelyn and Joy Awori. 1983. *Kenya Women Reflections.* Nairobi: Lear Publishing Co.

Mungeam, Gordon Hudson. 1966. *British Rule in Kenya, 1895-1912.* Oxford: Clarendon Press.

____. 1970. "Masai and Kikuyu Response to the Establishment of British Administration in East Africa Protectorate." *Journal of African History* 11: 127-143.

____. 1978. *Kenya Historical Documents, 1884-1923.* Nairobi: East African Publishing House,.

Munro, J. Forbes. 1975. *Colonial Rule and the Kamba.* Oxford: Clarendon Press.

Murdock, George P. 1959. *Africa, Its Peoples and Their Culture History.* New York: McGraw-Hill.

Muriithi, Kiboi. 1971. *War in the Forest.* Nairobi: East African Publishing House.

Murikwa, Julius Kabure. 1981. A Study of the Kikuyu Culture and the Communication of the Gospel. M.A. Thesis, Fuller Theological Seminary School of World Missions.

Muriuki, Godfrey. 1971. "Background to Politics and Nationalism in Central Kenya: The Traditional Social and Political Systems of Kenya Peoples." *Hadith* 4: 1-17.

____. 1974. *A History of the Kikuyu 1500 to 1900.* Nairobi: Oxford University Press

____. 1975. "The Kikuyu in the Pre-colonial Period," in B.A. Ogot, ed., *Kenya Before 1900*, Pp. 106-138. Nairobi: East African Publishing House.

Murray, Jocelyn Margaret. 1974. The Kikuyu Female Circumcision Controversy with Special Reference to the Church Missionary Society's `Sphere of Influence'. Ph.D. dissertation, Simon Fraser University.

Murray-Brown, Jeremy. 1972. *Kenyatta*. London: Allen and Unwin.

Muthoni, Hannah. 1979. Ruiru. Interview, May 18.

Mutiso, Gideon. 1975. *Kenya: Politics, Policy and Society.* Nairobi: East African Literature Bureau.

Mwangi, Naomi Wagira. 1978. Ndumberi. Interview, October 4.

National Atlas of Kenya. 3rd ed. 1970. Nairobi: Survey of Kenya.

Ndumbu, Abel. 1985. *Out of My Rib: A View of Women in Development.* Nairobi: Development Horizons.

Newsinger, John. 1981. "Revolt and Repression in Kenya: The "Mau Mau" Rebellion, 1952-1960." *Science and Society* 45 (2): 159-185.

Ngina, Milka. 1979. Kiambu Town. Interview, May 11.

Njeri, Magdalen. 1978. Kiambu Town. Interview, December 19.

Njeri, Maria. 1979. Ndumberi. Interview, May 15.

Njeri, Maria. 1979. Thika. Interview, May 24.

Njoki, Lilian. 1979. Kitambaya. Interview, May 11.

Njoki, Veronica 1979. Githunguri. Interview, May 20.

Njururi, N. 1966. *Agikuyu Folktales*. London: Oxford University Press.

Nthamburi, Zablon John. 1981. A History of the Methodist Church in Kenya, 1862-1967. Ph.D. dissertation, School of Theology at Claremont.

Nyambura, Gladis 1978. Kiambu Town. Interview, October 9.

Oboo, Christine. 1980. *African Women: Their Struggle for Economic Independence.* London: Zed Press.

Ogot, Bethwell A. 1977. "Politics, Culture and Music in Central Kenya: A Study of Mau Mau Hymns, 1951-1956." *Kenya Historical Review* 5: 275-286.

____., ed. 1972. *Politics and Nationalism in Colonial Kenya.* Nairobi: East African Publishing House.

____., ed. 1975. *Hadith 5: Economic and Social History of East Africa.* Nairobi: East African Publishing House.

____., ed. 1975. *Kenya Before 1900*. Nairobi: East African Publishing House.

Okonjo, Kamene. 1976. "The Dual-Sex Political System in Operation: Ibo Women and Community Politics in Midwestern Nigeria," in Nancy Hafkin and Edna Bay, eds., *Women in Africa*, Pp. 45-58. Stanford: Stanford University Press.

Oliver, Roland. 1952. *The Missionary Factor in East Africa.* London: Longmans and Green.

Omosule, M. 1974. "Kiama kia Muingi: Kikuyu Reaction to Land Consolidation Policy in Kenya" *Transafrican Journal of History* 4: 114-134.

Orde-Brown, Granville St. J. 1925. *The Vanishing Tribes of Kenya*. London: Seeley Service & Co.

____. 1933 [1967]. *The African Laborer.* London: Frank Cass.

Pala, Achola. 1974. *The Role of African Women Rural Development: Research Priorities.* Discussion Paper No. 203. Nairobi: Institute for Development Studies.

Pankhurst, R.K.P. 1954. *Kenya: The History of Two Nations.* London: Independent Publishing Company.

Patai, Raphael, ed. 1967. *Women in the Modern World.* New York: The Free Press.

Paulme, Denise. 1963. *Women of Tropical Africa.* London: Routledge and Paul.

Paulme-Schaeffner, Denise. 1948. "The Social Condition of Women in Two West African Societies." *Man* 48: 44.

Peace News. 1956, November 16. London.

Peace News. 1957, February 1. London.

Pedraza, J.G.W. 1956. "Land Consolidation in the Kikuyu Areas of Kenya." *Journal of African Administration* 8 (April): 27-36.

Perham, Margery. 1960. "The Psychology of African Nationalism." *Optima* 10 (1960): 27-36.

Perlman, M.L. 1966. "The Changing Status and Role of Women in Toro (Western Uganda)." *Cahiers D'Etudes Africaines* 6: 564-591.

Phillips, P.G. 1957. "The Metabolic Cost of Common West African Agricultural Activities." *Journal of Tropical Medicine* 57: 12-20.

Presley, Cora. 1986. The Transformation of Kikuyu Women and Their Nationalism. Ph.D. dissertation. Stanford University.

____. 1986. "Labor Protest Among Kikuyu Women, 1912-1947," in Claire Robertson and Iris Berger, eds., *Women, Race and Class in Africa,* Pp, 255-273. New York: Holmes and Meier Press.

____. 1986. "Women in the Mau Mau Rebellion," in Gary Okihiro, ed., *In Resistance: Studies in African, Afro-American and Caribbean Resistance,* Pp. 53-70. Amherst: University of Massachusetts Press.

Prins, Adriaan H.J. 1953. *East African Age-class Systems: An Inquiry Into the Social Order of Galla, Kipsigis and Kikuyu.* Groningen: J.B. Wolters.

Ranger, Terrence O. 1968. "Connections Between 'Primary' Resistance Movements and Modern Mass Nationalism in East and Central Africa: Part I." *Journal of African History* 9: 437-454.

____. 1968. "Connections Between `Primary Resistance' Movements and Modern Mass Nationalism in East and Central Africa: II." *Journal of African History* 9: 631-642.

____ and I.N. Kimanbo. 1972. *The Historical Study of African Religion.* London: Heinemann Educational Books, Ltd.

Rhodes, Willard. 1962. "Music as an Agent of Political Expression." *African Studies Bulletin* 5 (May): 14-22.

Richards, Charles and James Place. 1967. *East African Explorers.* Nairobi: Oxford University Press.

Rogers, Peter. 1979. "The British and the Kikuyu, 1890-1905: A Reassessment." *Journal of African History* 20: 255-269.

Rosaldo, Michelle Zimbalist and Louise Lamphere, eds. 1974. *Women, Culture and Society.* Stanford: Stanford University Press.

Rosberg, Carl. 1956. *The Struggle for Power in Kenya.* Boston: Boston University Press.

____ and John Nottingham. 1966 [1970]. *The Myth of "Mau Mau": Nationalism in Kenya.* New York: Meridian Books, The World Publishing Company.

Rosenstiel, Annette. 1953. "An Anthropological Approach to the Mau Mau Movement." *Political Science Quarterly* 67 (September): 419-432.

Ross, W. McGregor. 1927 [1968]. *Kenya From Within: A Short Political History.* London: Allen and Unwin.

Rotberg, Robert I. 1962. "The Rise of African Nationalism." *World Politics* 15 (October): 75-90.

____. 1963. "The Origins of Nationalist Discontent in East and Central Africa." *Journal of Negro History* 48 (April): 130-141.

____. 1966. "African Nationalism: Concept or Confusion." *Journal of Modern African Studies* 4: 33-46.

Routledge, W.S. and Katherine Routledge. 1910. *With A Prehistoric People: The Akikuyu of British East Africa.* London: Edward Arnold.

Sandbrook, Richard and Robin Cohen, eds. 1975. *The Development of an African Working Class: Studies in Class Formation and Action.* Toronto: University of Toronto Press.

Schapera, I. 1956. *Government and Politics in Tribal Societies.* London: Watts.

Seidenberg, Dana A. 1979. The Asians and Uhuru; The Roots of a Minority Community in Kenya Politics. Ph.D. dissertation, Syracuse University.

Shannon, M.I. 1954. "Women's Place in Kikuyu Society: Impact of Modern Ideas of Tribal Life--A Long-term Plan for Female Education." *Africa World* (September): 7-10.

Singh, Marhkam. 1969. *History of Kenya Trade Union Movement to 1952.* Nairobi: East African Publishing House.

Sluiter, Greet. 1957. *Confidential Report on Migrant Labour and Connected Matters in Four Villages in the Kiambu Reserve of Kenya.* Nairobi: Department of Social Service, Training and Research of the Christian Council of Kenya.

Smith, E.W. (Reverend). 1924. *The Christian Missions in Africa.* London: The International Missionary Council.

Sorrenson, M.P.K., 1962. Land Policy, Legislation and Settlement in the East African Protectorate. Ph.D. dissertation, Oxford University.

____. 1965. "Land Policy in Kenya: 1895-1945," in Vincent Harlow, E.M. Chilver and Alison Smith, eds., *History of East Africa,* Vol. II, Pp. 672-689. Oxford: Oxford University Press.

____. 1967. *Land Reform in the Kikuyu Country.* London: Oxford University Press.

____. 1968. *Origins of European Settlement in Kenya.* Nairobi: East African Literature Bureau, 1968.

Spencer, Dunstan. 1976. *African Women in Agricultural Development: A Case Study in Sierra Leone.* East Lansing: Michigan State University.

Spencer, I.R.G. 1975. The Development of Production and Trade in the Reserve Areas of Kenya, 1895-1929. Ph.D. dissertation, Simon Fraser University.

____. 1978. Economic Development of Kenya, 1895-1929: A Reconsideration. University of Nairobi Staff Seminar Paper No. 6 1978/1979, November.

____. 1980. "Settler Dominance, Agricultural Production and the Second World War in Kenya." *Journal of African History* 21: 487-514.

Spencer, John. 1974. "The Kikuyu Central Association and the Genesis of Kenya African Union." *Kenya Historical Review* 2 (1): 67-79.

____. 1977. "Kau and Mau Mau: Some Connections." *Kenya Historical Review* 5: 201-224.

____. 1983. *James Beauttah-Freedom Fighter*. Nairobi: Stellascope Publishing.

____. 1985. *The Kenya African Union*. London: KPI Limited.

Stichter, Sharon. 1975. "The Formation of a Working Class in Kenya," in Richard Sandbrook and Robin Cohen, eds., *The Development of an African Working Class: Studies in Class Formation and Action*, Pp. 21-48. Toronto: University of Toronto Press.

____. 1975. "Workers, Trade Unions, and the Mau Mau Rebellion." *Canadian Journal of African Studies* 9 (2) : 259-275.

____. 1978. "Trade Unionism in Kenya, 1947-1952: The Militant Phase," in Peter Gutkind, Robin Cohen and Jean Copans, eds., *African Labor History*, Pp. 155-174. Beverly Hills/London: Sage Publications, 1978.

____. 1982. *Migrant Labour in Kenya: Capitalism and African Response, 1895-1975*. Harlow: Longman

Strange, Bertha F. 1963. "Kenya Women in Agriculture." *Women Today* 6: 7-9.

Swainson, Nicola. 1980. *The Development of Corporate Capitalism in Kenya, 1918-1977*. London: Heinemann.

Swartz, Caroline. 1979. Human Capital, Labor Force Participation, and the Extended Family in Urban Kenya. Ph.D. dissertation, Yale University.

Tamarkin, M. 1976. "Mau Mau in Nakuru" *Journal of African History* 17 (1) : 119-134.

____. 1978. "Loyalists in Nakuru During the Mau Mau Revolt and its Aftermath." *Asian and African Studies* 12 (2): 247-261.

Temu, A.J. 1972. *British Protestant Missions*. London: Longman Group.

Thadani, Veena. 1976. The Forgotten Factor in Social Change: The Case of Women in Nairobi, Kenya. Ph.D. dissertation, Bryn Mawr College.

Thiong'o Ngugi wa (James Ngugi). 1964. *Weep Not Child*. Nairobi: Heinemann.

____. 1967. *A Grain of Wheat*. London: Heinemann.

____. 1971. *Detained: A Writers' Prison Diary*. Nairobi: Heinemann.

____. 1976. *The Trial of Dedan Kimathi*. London: Heinemann.

Throup, David W. 1987. *Economic & Social Origins of Mau Mau*. London: James Currey.

Thuku, Harry. 1970. *An Autobiography*. Nairobi: Oxford University Press.

Thuku, Tabitha [Mrs. Harry]. 1978. Muthiko. Interview, December 19.

Tignor, Robert. 1971. "Colonial Chiefs in Chiefless Societies." *Journal of Modern African Studies* 9: 339-359.

____. 1972. "The Maasai Warriors: Pattern Maintenance and Violence in Colonial Kenya" *Journal of African History* 13: 271-290.

____. 1976. *The Colonial Transformation of Kenya: The Kamba, Kikuyu and Maasai from 1900-1939*. Princeton: Princeton University Press.

Times. 1956. London.

Tribune. 1956, November 16. London.

Toulson, Thomas. 1976. Europeans and the Kikuyu to 1910: A Study of Resistance, Collaboration and Conquest. M.A. Thesis, University of British Columbia.

Uchendu, Patrick K. 1981. The Changing Cultural Role of Ibo Women in Nigeria. Ph.D. dissertation, New York University.

United Nations. 1961. *The World Coffee Economy* (FAO: Rome).

____. 1963. Economic Commission for Africa. *The Position of Women in Kenya* by Julius Carlebach (E/CN.14/URB/9), 16 July.

Urdang, Stephanie. 1979. *Fighting Two Colonialisms: Women in Guinea Bissau.* New York: Monthly Review Press.

Van Zwanenberg, Roger. 1975. *Colonial Capitalism and Labor in Kenya, 1919-1939.* Nairobi: East African Literature Bureau.

____. 1975. *An Economic History of Kenya and Uganda, 1900-1970.* London: MacMillan Press.

Vansina, Jan. 1962. "Long-distance Trade Routes in Central Africa." *Journal of African History* 2: 375-390.

Viva. 1978. "The Silence over Female Circumcision in Kenya." (August): 6-15, 72-3.

Wa-Githurmo, Mwangi. 1974. Land and Nationalism in East Africa: the Impact of Land Expropriation and Land Grievances upon the Rise and Development of Nationalist Movements in Kenya, 1884-1939. Ph.D. dissertation, New York University.

Wachanga, H.K. 1975. *The Swords of Kirinyaga: The Fight for Land and Freedom.* Robert Whittier, ed. Nairobi: East African Literature Bureau.

Wagarama, Wambui. 1979. Kabete. Interview, April 29.

Wainana, Wagara. 1979. Kitambaya. Interview, April 29.

Wajiru, Catherine. 1979. Kitambaya. Interview, May 11.

Wambaki, Priscilla. 1979. Ngenda. Interview, May 16.

Wambaki, Priscilla. 1979. Juja. Interview, May 23.

Wambui, (no other name given). 1978. Kiambu Town. Interview, October 3.

Wambui, Phyllis. 1978. Raibai. Interview, October 10.

Wambui, Sara. 1978. Kamburu. Interview, October 20.

Wambui, Sarah. 1978. Kamburu. Interview, October 20.

Wambui, Tabitha. 1978. Kiambu Town. Interview, October 3.

Wandia, Hannah. 1979. Thika. Interview, May 24.

Wanga, Cecelia. 1978. Raibai. Interview, December 12.

Wangeche, Hannah. 1979. Ruiru. Interview, May 15.

Wangui, Christine. 1979. Githunguri. Interview, May 16.

Wanjiko, Elizabeth. 1978. Tingang'a. Interview, December 29.

Wanjiko, Phyllis (Margo) wa Mimi. 1978. Tingang'a. Interview, December 20.

Wanjiko, Mary. 1978. Kiambu Town. Interview, November 22.

Wanjiru, (no other name given). 1979. Kiambu Town. Interview, January 12.

Wanjiru, Catherine. 1979. Kitambaya. Interview, May 11.

Ward, Kevin. 1975. "Evangelism or Education? Mission Priorities and Educational Policy in the African Inland Mission, 1900-1950." *Kenya Historical Review* 3: 243-260.

Warimu, Elizabeth. 1978. Ndumberi. Interview, October 18.

Wariruiu, (no other name given). Githunguri. 1979. Interview, January 12.

Waruchu, Martha. 1978. Kamburu. Interview, October 22.

Waruiru, Christopher. 1971. Female Initiation Controversy at C.S.M. Tumutumu, 1912-1937. B.A. Thesis, Nairobi University.

Watene, Kenneth. 1974. *Dedan Kimathi*. Nairobi: Transafrica,.

Welbourn, F.B. 1961. *East African Rebels: A Study of Some Independent Churches.* London: S.C.M. Press.

____. 1965. *East African Christian*. London: Oxford University Press.

Weller, Henry Owen. 1931. *Kenya Without Prejudice: A Balanced Critical Review of the Country and its People*. London: East Africa.

____. 1942. *A Short History of Kenya Colony*. Nairobi: CMS Bookshop.

White, Elaine F. 1978. Creole Women Traders in Sierra Leone: Economic and Social History, 1792-1945. Ph.D. dissertation, Boston University.

White, Luise. 1980. "Women's Domestic Labor in Colonial Kenya: Prostitution in Nairobi, 1909-1950." Working Paper No. 30, African Studies Center, Boston University.

Wilks, Ivor. 1962. "A Medieval Trade-route from the Niger to the Gulf of Guinea." *Journal of African History* 3: 337-341.

Wilson, C. 1953. *Before the White Man in Kenya*. London: McCorquodale.

Wilson, Monica. 1955. "Land and the Kikuyu: A Study of the Relationship Between Land and Kikuyu Political Movements." *Journal of Negro History* 40 (April): 103-153.

Wipper, Audrey. 1971. "The Politics of Sex: Some Strategies Employed by the Kenyan Power Elite to Handle a Normative-Existential Discrepancy." *African Studies Review* 14: 463-482.

____. 1972. "The Roles of African Women: Past, Present and Future." *Canadian Journal of African Studies* 6: 143-146.

Wolff, Richard D. 1974. *The Economics of Colonialism: Britain and Kenya 1870-1930*. New Haven: Yale University Press.

Wodis, J. 1960. *Africa the Roots of Revolt*. London: Lawrence and Wishart.

Women of Kenya: Review and Evaluation of Progress. 1985. Nairobi: Kenya Literature Bureau.

Wrigley, C.C. 1965. "Kenya: The Patterns of Economic Life, 1902-1945," in Vincent Harlow, E.M. Chilver and Alison Smith, eds., *History of East Africa*, Vol II, Pp. 209-264. Oxford: Oxford University Press.

Index

030423-100-6-50W